The Domestic Politics of
International Relations

The Domestic Politics of International Relations
Cases from Australia, New Zealand and Oceania

RODERIC ALLEY
Associate Professor of Politics
Victoria University of Wellington, New Zealand

LONDON AND NEW YORK

First published 2000 by Ashgate Publishing

Reissued 2018 by Routledge
2 Park Square, Milton Park, Abingdon, Oxon OX14 4RN
711 Third Avenue, New York, NY 10017, USA

Routledge is an imprint of the Taylor & Francis Group, an informa business

Copyright © Roderic Alley 2000

All rights reserved. No part of this book may be reprinted or reproduced or utilised in any form or by any electronic, mechanical, or other means, now known or hereafter invented, including photocopying and recording, or in any information storage or retrieval system, without permission in writing from the publishers.

Notice:
Product or corporate names may be trademarks or registered trademarks, and are used only for identification and explanation without intent to infringe.

Publisher's Note
The publisher has gone to great lengths to ensure the quality of this reprint but points out that some imperfections in the original copies may be apparent.

Disclaimer
The publisher has made every effort to trace copyright holders and welcomes correspondence from those they have been unable to contact.

A Library of Congress record exists under LC control number: 00132589

ISBN 13: 978-1-138-72968-1 (hbk)
ISBN 13: 978-1-138-72966-7 (pbk)
ISBN 13: 978-1-315-18973-4 (ebk)

Contents

List of Tables, Boxes and Maps vi
Acknowledgements viii
List of Abbreviations x

1 Introduction 1

2 New Zealand and the World Court Project 23

3 Australia and Climate Change 52

4 The Bougainville Conflict 85

5 Decolonisation 116

6 Indigenous Rights 150

7 Public Management in the South Pacific 183

8 Environmental Prescription in the South Pacific 219

9 Conclusions 249

Select Bibliography 259
Index 263

List of Tables

2.1	New Zealand Public Opinion and Nuclear-armed Ship Visits	31
3.1	Carbon Dioxide Emissions 1996: Australia Compared	62
5.1	Dependent Status in Oceania and Greater Melanesia	119
6.1	Australia, New Zealand, Fiji: Indigenous Populations and Land Tenure	154
6.2	Human Rights Conventions: Australia, New Zealand and Fiji	170
7.1	The South Pacific Forum	193
7.2	Pacific Island Countries: Selected Indicators	194
7.3	PIC Economic Indicators: 1990 and 1995	196
7.4	The South Pacific: Regional and Intergovernmental Affiliations	199
7.5	Oceania: Net ODA Receipts and Selected Indicators	204
7.6	Selected PIC Government Delivery Indicators: 1985-95	210
8.1	South Pacific Environmental Conventions: Accessions and Ratifications	225
8.2	South Pacific Forum Accessions and Ratifications to Global Environmental Conventions	228

Boxes

2.1	World Court Advisory Opinion on the Legal Status of Nuclear Weapons: Summary of the 'Dispositif'	35
4.1	Bougainville: The Key Entities	92

Maps

1.1	The Pacific Islands	16
4.1	Bougainville	89
5.1	New Caledonia	120
5.2	East Timor	124
5.3	West Papua	128

Acknowledgements

This study is the culmination of several years teaching and information gathering on international and comparative political developments affecting Australia, New Zealand and the Pacific Islands. The variety of cases presented derives from that experience. Comments received from readers of these chapters in draft form is gratefully acknowledged, subject to the author assuming sole responsibility for what is published.

A considerable debt of gratitude is owed to the many New Zealand non-governmental representatives involved in nuclear disarmament. Over several years, they helped provide the background of information and understanding needed for what the first chapter has to tell regarding the World Court Project. I am deeply indebted to Kate Dewes for many valuable comments on New Zealand's role on the World Court Project; her doctoral thesis, appropriately footnoted in the relevant chapter, stands as the seminal source on the subject. I am grateful to Robert Green for his comments on the same chapter, and also the shared insights and published contributions regarding the World Court Project of the late Erich Geiringer, Ian Prior, Alyn Ware and George Salmond. Central to all New Zealand efforts over the World Court Project stood the remarkable Harold Evans, a figure that inspired and sustained this project within his native New Zealand and abroad. His many observations on the World Court Project proved invaluable.

Dr Martin Manning of the New Zealand National Institute of Water and Atmospheric Research offered valuable insights to the chapter on Australia and Climate Change.

Dr John Henderson of the Department of Political Science at the University of Canterbury, New Zealand, assisted with an evaluation of the chapter on Bougainville.

Kate McMillan of the School of Political Science and International Relations, Victoria University of Wellington, furnished helpful criticism for the chapter dealing with Indigenous Rights.

Professor Barrie Macdonald found time from his senior management responsibilities at Massey University to furnish valued comments on public sector developments in the Pacific.

Officials at the New Zealand Ministry of Foreign Affairs and Trade kindly offered comments on the chapter dealing with environmental questions in the Pacific.

Fiona McDonald is thanked for assistance with textual preparation, as are Roger Steele and Philip Garside of Central Media Ltd, Wellington.

The author has benefited from the many meetings, seminars and conferences that he has attended under the New Zealand Institute of International Affairs. All subjects covered here have been before the Institute's proceedings in some form or other during the last decade.

The author acknowledges the opportunity to develop ideas germane to this study though publication in the Australian Defence Studies Centre Working Paper series.

Materials access is acknowledged to the Australian National University National Centre for Development Studies (map of New Caledonia); Jane Eckelman: Manoa Mapworks, Hawai'i (map of Pacific Islands); the United Nations Department of Information Cartographic Section (maps of Bougainville and East Timor). Although we encountered data deficiencies in gathering Pacific island statistics, Library staff at Victoria University of Wellington were consistently helpful.

I am enormously indebted to wife Elizabeth for much encouragement, incisive editorial advice, and patience beyond reason for my numerous evenings and weekends 'back at the office'. My extended family, colleagues, and friends are all warmly thanked for their encouragement and support.

List of Abbreviations

ABARE	Australian Bureau for Agriculture and Resource Economics
ACP	African Caribbean Pacific group
ADB	Asian Development Bank
ANZUS	Australia New Zealand United States security treaty
AOSIS	Alliance of Small Island States
APCET	Asia-Pacific Coalition on East Timor
APEC	Asia Pacific Economic Co-operation
ASEAN	Association of Southeast Asian Nations
ATSIC	Aboriginal and Torres Strait Islander Commission
BCL	Bougainville Copper Ltd
BIG	Bougainville Interim Government
BRA	Bougainville Revolutionary Army
BTG	Bougainville Transitional Government
CBD	Convention on Biological Diversity
CDM	Clean Development Mechanism
CNMI	Commonwealth of the North Mariana Islands
EEZ	Exclusive Economic Zone
ERDC	Energy Research and Development Corporation
ESCAP	Economic and Social Commission of Asia and the Pacific
EU	European Union
FAO	Food and Agricultural Organisation
FCCC	Framework Convention on Climate Change
FEMM	South Pacific Forum Economic Ministers Meeting
FFA	Forum Fisheries Agency
FLNKS	Front for the Liberation of the Kanak People
FSM	Federated States of Micronesia
G77	'Group of 77'
GCSDSIS	Global Conference on the Sustainable Development of Small Island States
GDP	Gross Domestic Product
GEF	Global Environmental Facility

GST	Goods and Services Tax
IALANA	International Association of Lawyers Against Nuclear Arms
ICCPR	International Covenant on Civil and Political Rights
ICERD	International Convention on Elimination of all Forms of Racial Discrimination
ICESR	International Covenant on Economic, Social and Cultural Rights
ICJ	International Court of Justice
IEA	International Energy Agency
ILO	International Labour Organisation
IMF	International Monetary Fund
IPB	International Peace Bureau
IPCC	Intergovernmental Panel on Climate Change
IPPNW	International Physicians for the Prevention of Nuclear War
MSG	Melanesian Spearhead Group
NAC	National Aboriginal Conference
NACC	National Aboriginal Consultative Committee
NAM	Non-Aligned Movement
NEMS	National Environmental Management Strategies
NGO	Non-governmental Organisation
NPT	Nuclear Non-Proliferation Treaty
OECD	Organisation for Economic Co-operation and Development
OPM	Operasi Papua Merdeka
PICs	Pacific Island Countries
PLA	Panguna Landowners' Association
PMG	Peace Monitoring Group
PNG	Papua New Guinea
PNGDF	Papua New Guinea Defence Forces
SIDS	Small Island Developing States
SPC	South Pacific Community
SPOCC	South Pacific Organisations Co-ordinating Committee
SPREP	South Pacific Regional Environment Programme
SOPAC	South Pacific Applied Geoscience Commission
TMG	Truce Monitoring Group
UN	United Nations
UNCED	United Nations Conference on Environment and Development

UNCLOS	United Nations Convention on the Law of the Sea
UNDP	United Nations Development Programme
UNEP	United Nations Environment Programme
UNPO	Unrepresented Nations Peoples' Organisation
WCP	World Court Project
WHO	World Health Organisation
WTO	World Trade Organisation
WWF	World Wide Fund for Nature

1 Introduction: International Relations and Domestic Politics

International relations and domestic politics interact in ways that help explain each other. That observation is not new, but its implications have expanded enormously and will continue doing so. We live in a world where the consequences of what occurs within the very strongest, yet also most abject of societies, can readily assume global ramifications. Sometimes the juxtapositions are acute: Americans dying in Somalia's lethal quarrels, shaped domestic United States opinion that turned the Clinton Administration away from supporting international intervention against Rwanda's 1994 genocide. In 1999 however, President Clinton decided international public opinion had tightened sufficiently against the Indonesian military's conduct in East Timor to warrant supporting a United Nations-backed 'coalition of the willing' to help halt the carnage. Under duress, the Indonesian government 'consented' to 'invite' such a force.

Among the factors explaining why the Clinton Administration's 1999 response differed from that five years previously, domestic/international interactivity deserves consideration. This extends beyond individual instances where domestic and international factors may interact, but the totality of that interactivity. As in the difference between a globe and a map, similar objects appear differently according to representation requirements. Events do not change by crossing borders or moving between the different 'worlds' of domestic politics and international relations. That transition may alter the way happenings are construed, explained, ignored, exaggerated, or manipulated, however. Such interpretations may inform policies that justify conduct previously found unacceptable. Intervention into former Yugoslavia avoided previously in Rwanda, meant life as a Kosavar Albanian in 1999 was safer than trying to survive as a Tutsi five years earlier. That difference is explained by more than domestic political considerations in say Britain or the United States, but they nevertheless remained significant.

External conduct justified as 'a necessary interest' may persist for a period, but ignores mounting domestic resentment to its cost. The Vietnam War's toll within the United States still haunts the State Department. Subsequent warnings to those conducting Washington's foreign relations emerged about safeguarding domestic interests – even to a point of exaggeration. Although conjectural, it is likely that had President Clinton acted to save Rwandan lives in 1994, he would have won re-election to the White House two years later. Much depends, therefore, upon how the interplay of domestic and international politics is 'read', by whom, and for what ends. In October 1999, British Prime Minister Blair, French President Chirac, and German Chancellor Schroeder wrote a joint letter to the New York Times, unsuccessfully appealing to the United States Senate not to block ratification of the Comprehensive Test Ban Treaty. Assuredly President Clinton, favouring ratification, and Republican Senate Foreign Relations Committee Chairman Helms who remained vehemently opposed read that appeal very differently.

What considerations, then, shape the investigation of domestic/international interactivity? We are concerned with not only the interaction of domestic and international developments, but the nature of that interactivity. How identifiable is that dynamic? Does its behaviour furnish valid generalisations? Given the range of potential determinants, what identifiable pointers exist?

First, we are concerned about activity that is *organised and purposeful*. It results in identifiable forms of public change. A dynamic *is* involved performing functions that may comprise institutional development, normative adjustment, and attitudinal change. A domestic/international interactivity approach may embrace multiple domestic actors: legislatures, courts, lobbies, information brokers, or a wide array of bureaucratic interests negotiating policy convergence with external counterparts for rule-governed or standard setting conduct. An empirical investigation of cases, as provided here, assists us appreciate how domestic and international factors interact and to what effect. This represents a useful basis for comparison and theory formation.

A second focus of the interactivity under investigation concerns the location of *responsibility*. The domestic governance, environmental stewardship, and internal political accountability of states may all affect their external conduct. Never distant is whether power-holders are ultimately bound by the consent of those they govern. That interrogation encourages reassessment of self-determination, autonomy, and sovereignty principles. Those who speak for states they claim to represent internationally, cannot perform that function divorced from the societies within which they live. But that 'society', as General Pinochet has found, extends well beyond conventional territorial borders. Accountability denied at home is being exerted from abroad.

Interactive processes linking domestic and international factors encourage other comparisons. They include the effects upon foreign relations of democratisation, human rights, civil-military relations, and the role of judicial institutions in upholding and promoting principles of rule-governed domestic order. Focus upon domestic/international interactivity helps expose external representation functions performed by contemporary governments.

A prescriptive challenge lies in comprehending why governments enter commitments abroad, but then fail to implement them at home. Here, a third task is determining how domestic/international interactivity effects particular forms of *response*. The response path may comprise a progression flowing beyond agenda setting into the negotiation of rules and agreements, their ratification, and eventual implementation. After agreeing to implement measures negotiated abroad, governments regularly encounter local implementation barriers. Attempting to enlist internal support may even galvanise local interests, anxious to obstruct an initiative deemed threatening because of its offshore origins.

This underlines the difficulties that governments face when conceiving, organising, or promoting something termed the 'national interest'. An intensity of domestic/international interactivity offers scope to redefine, alter, or reconfigure that interest. It does so by placing governments under pressure to respond to transnational agendas. They may resist that pressure, as has China over human rights. However, failure to make *any* accommodation incurs costs.

Although not always the culprit for what its critics may claim, globalisation is a ready target for domestic suspicion. Pressures for international competitiveness, deregulation and privatisation, can leave the domestic state structure not a protector from, but local facilitator to the forces and demands of the global economy (Cox, 1999: 12). This difficulty is often acute for governmental handling of international economic relations – for example, trade liberalisation and tariff reduction negotiations. Domestic opposition by material interests is one form of response, but there are many others.

An example is the use of domestic/international channels less in defence of sectional demands than in the promotion of international campaigns. Notwithstanding national, language, or cultural differences, domestic interests interact with counterparts abroad to gain information, further local support, and promote ideas in the formulation of transnational public strategies. Regardless of agenda, local groups inform international audiences about conditions that they deem unsatisfactory in their own and other countries. Subjecting governments to adverse international publicity is viewed as legitimate political leverage – although some companies confronting Greenpeace have thought otherwise.

Governments everywhere are uncertain about which developments may engage publics, at what level, and with how much intensity. Statehood is seemingly about control within physical limits, 'yet the citizens who reside within a state territory may feel multiple forms of allegiance which not only transcend cartography but shift in response to events both internal and external' (Bishai, 1998: 92).

In domestic political environments that are authoritarian or worse, a sudden telescoping of domestic and international events may jolt them towards fundamental policy redirection or, more drastically, outright regime collapse. As in Hamlet, their 'troubles come not as single spies, but in battalions'. Sometimes the linkages concerned are only dimly perceived, much less responded to – as when Southeast Asia's drought, debt, and devaluations helped oust Indonesia's Suharto regime in 1998. Less dramatic combinations of domestic and international events may offer warning signals allowing regimes scope to adjust in anticipation.

Given the potential range of imponderable 'rogue factors' that may shape domestic/international interactivity, what analytical challenges emerge? Between them, Comparative Politics and International Relations offer valued tools, although their collaborative utilisation remains inadequate. This is evident through the delayed investigation of ethnicity's international dimensions. Nevertheless, 'most scholars in comparative politics, together with a good many in international relations do recognise that the long separation of international relations from domestic political relations has been totally artificial' (Strange, 1996: 69). Keohane sees a need for 'better theories of domestic politics ... so that the gap between the external and the internal environments can be bridged in a systematic way, rather than by simply adding catalogues of exogenously determined foreign policy facts to theoretically more rigorous (international) structural models' (Keohane, 1989: 60). Yet because each country is unique, there is the risk that empirical detail and national distinctiveness may deter generalisations beyond a single case (Frieden, 1997: vii). Distinguishing between sovereign, plural, and the normative dimensions of the domestic/international dynamic is a beginning. They relate to foundation intellectual streams in the study of international relations that deserve attention. Next, cases surveyed by this study are introduced. Comments on comparative criteria employed conclude this Introduction.

The Sovereignty Paradox

As a philosophy of international relations, realism and its adherents view domestic factors as essentially irrelevant to the struggle for power, influence, and status identified as persisting features of external state conduct. Realism is pessimistic about reforming an international system, whose dominant influences ensure rules remain instrumental to discretionary application according to state interest. Reform does not reduce propensities for cheating, or preoccupation with relative gains. Necessarily, this diminishes the scope for national institutions to further international co-operation and evolve shared cross-border interests. Barriers demarcating foreign from domestic affairs persist; they are those imposed by priorities of survival in a potentially anarchic world. Article 2 (7) of the United Nations Charter is an example of a principle grounded in the belief that the domestic/international boundary is an essential component within a state-based international order.[1]

Under this approach, state discretion is extensive. Here the domestic/international nexus affords state operatives latitude to rationalise extra-legal conduct in the name of 'security'. Governments insist security imperatives exonerate the executive from compliance with laws applicable to the citizenry at large over wiretapping, trespass, breaking and entering, or search without warrant. Justifications are grounded in presumed linkages between internal and external threat. Conditions of 'emergency' are prolonged, and state agents operate with impunity from prosecution. International means of accountability, due process, or sanction only gradually emerge for the most egregious of violations.

Even in less drastic circumstances, executive dominance in the conduct of foreign relations, is widely evident. Utilising privileges of secrecy and exclusiveness, officials claim that as pragmatists and technicians, they are 'above' the daily hurly-burly of domestic politics and partisan strife. In sum, the realist perspective helps those willing to afford little weight to citizen efficacy or the intra-societal networking increasingly evident in much international non-governmental activity.

However, this should not belittle the importance of the domestic dimension in some foreign policy case studies drawn from orthodox, state-based appraisals.

Hanrieder (1967) saw external and internal dimensions linking in ways that help to inform judgements about feasible conduct in foreign relations. Feasibility is best evaluated by posing domestically inspired goals against external constraints. A sound understanding of the domestic environment is essential to gauge consensus over foreign policy means and ends. This understanding contributes to a store of prudence and judgement, derived from lessons of observed state conduct. Similarly Wallace (1971), believed domestic support, and the management of domestic interests, constituted a first call for those charting foreign relations. However 'the degree to which foreign policy has remained a separate area, or has become part of the domestic political process, is ... a matter of some uncertainty' (Wallace, 1971: 40).

Carlsnaes (1981) evaluated foreign relations conduct and domestic democratic processes. For that link to function, requirements included a critically reflective public; a corps of sufficiently informed politicians able to avoid domination by experts or professional bureaucrats; and an arena of public debate not beholden to any particular set of interests. Goldman (1988) investigated domestic forces for their role in stabilising the conduct of external relations. This occurred through institutionalisation, and the extent to which a government is committed to pursue a particular policy by using domestic supports. Issue salience was interpreted as a capacity to affect coalition outcomes following domestic political struggles. Externally, foreign relations are stabilised by treaties, agreements, customs, and norms whose violation is not cost-free (Goldman, 1988: 30).

These contributions reflect thought about domestic dimensions as components of statecraft. More recently, however, globalisation's surge has breached the internal/external demarcation at many points. Forces included the impact of international diasporas, large-scale migrant and refugee flows, transnational media networks, the flood of small weapons to non-state operatives in an unregulated arms market, and expanding global support for human rights. The frequency, complexity, and obduracy of protracted internal wars, embroiling neighbouring regions, and engendering controversy over intervention, is further testimony to the inextricability of domestic and external forces.[2] So are growing security apprehensions about non-military threats exploiting the 'grey zones' between domestic and international controls – crime, narcotics, trafficking in humanity, and money laundering. Should peace reconstruction move beyond declarations of intent, then implementation requires co-ordination between domestic and international institutions, humanitarian agencies, and funding providers.

Another line-breaker has occurred as international system change and state collapse have helped inflame state/nation dichotomies. Some believe there is 'historical tension between state sovereignty, which stresses the link between sovereign authority and a defined territory, and national sovereignty, which emphasises a link between sovereign authority and a defined population' (Barkin and Cronin, 1994: 108). Because both types fundamentally differ in the basis of their originating legitimisation, they necessarily affect inter-state relations in different ways. Walker (1993: 169-172) has viewed sovereignty as both a defining characteristic and a problem to overcome. This includes questions about whether it is exercised legitimately within states, of governments openly coercing people and denying them their rights, and of state weakness within an increasingly interdependent global capitalist economy. Thus across many fields of social endeavour and political activity, sovereign demarcations may seemingly count for little.

Nevertheless, ample evidence indicating boundary erosion between domestic and international concerns does not prevent promotion of interests asserting their retention. If anything, erosion has intensified, not diminished the psychological and political importance of borders – a reality to which refugees might readily attest. Adherence to boundaries of some sort is a social and psychological need that the current configuration of states may or may not protect. This leaves the contemporary modern state under pressure from sub-state actors as it simultaneously seeks the advantages of global competition (Mittelman, 1996: 7-8).

Friction at the domestic/international interface is exacerbated by emergent norms favouring intervention in the face of egregious human rights violations, mass slaughter, unrelieved conflict, or the dislocations of physical disasters and famines. These prescriptive principles have strengthened, notwithstanding dictates of sovereign prerogative and customary norms asserting minimal rules of co-existence and non-interference in the domestic affairs of states. Former United Nations (UN) Secretary General Boutros-Ghali's widely noted 1992 report to the UN Security Council, *An Agenda for Peace*, claimed: 'the time of absolute and exclusive sovereignty, however, has passed: its theory was never matched by reality ... Globalism and nationalism need not be viewed as opposing trends, doomed to spur each other on to extremes of reaction ... respect for democratic principles at all levels of social existence is critical, within states and within the community of states'.[3] A little later, the Secretary General reiterated a need to rethink sovereignty by recognising 'that it may take more than one form and perform more than one function. This perception could help solve problems both within and among states'.[4] There is now growing acceptance that governments can no longer claim that the way they treat their citizens is purely an internal matter (Beetham, 1995: 4). The final emergence of the International Criminal Court in 1998 epitomised this trend.

The Pluralist Synthesis

The liberal tradition in international relations accords the domestic dimension greater significance than does realism. The plural, liberal order acknowledges the role of prudence in safeguarding state interest within a mercantilist and threat prone world. Equally, though, it recognises that governments not only can, but must operate within a regulatory world, refusal to do so incurring material costs. Shared interests between states, particularly on economic matters, are rational, reciprocal, and self-rewarding. Influence is less about the credibility of threats than the capacity to alter the rules of the game (Everts, 1985). Through an array of domestic mechanisms, multiple actors perform bargaining, persuasive, and information sharing functions. This alters and expands agendas through institutionalised, cross-border policy formulation, and implementation processes. State functions diversify, may disaggregate, but certainly persist. Indeed, effective state performance requires 'a commitment both to the preservation and fostering of domestic and transnational society and to the capacity of state institutions to interact with actors in that society' (Slaughter, 1994: 412).

These observations risk appearing commonplace, since interdependence in its various guises through the functional project is hardly new. However technologically driven globalising processes have magnified its intensity and unpredictability. A remarkable mobility of assets has helped integrate markets and financial systems. Key decisions affecting large numbers – employment, future income security, life-style, or news media control – are subject to international decision. While locating responsibility for these pervasive influences may prove elusive, the corporate social allegiance of those who gain from them is less ambiguous. A weakening of sovereignty exposes vulnerabilities, but creates possibilities. Those possibilities have been exploited by civic organizations forming trans-boundary linkages through information technology. This facilitates a move 'from traditional hierarchies to more flexible networks and alliances' (Edwards et al, 1999: 119). This is part of the so-called 'globalisation from below', a reaction against 'choiceless democracy' that, given the frustrations of domestic electoral outcomes to deliver results, turns to transnational solidarities to achieve rights objectives (Falk, 1997: 337).

In some fields, the analytical task of tracing domestic/international interactivity may appear relatively uncluttered. Should a domestic agricultural lobby succeed in having protections included within its government's bargaining repertoire at an international trade round, then the lines of influence, process, and outcome are often discernible. When a government disappoints its interests by returning empty handed, after facing the concentrated opposition of trading partners, domestic responses are not difficult to identify. But responses are harder to judge once we move beyond issues like agricultural subsidies and trade rounds, to the non-material realm of ethical and moral imperatives, or of interests based on national or ethnic identity. Here, demands 'need not be conceived in terms of territorially defined, fixed and mutually exclusive enclaves of legitimate dominion' (Ruggie, 1993: 151).

However tracing influence is less obscure where institutional systems operate. This emerges from this study's chapters that deal with decolonisation and indigenous rights questions. Interrogation of domestic/international interactions helps locate institutions where identity and political community are unhindered by territoriality. As mentioned, literature dealing with ethnicity and plural society questions has lacked a discernible international dimension.

They include issues of language, family and kinship, local economy, religious activities, socialisation, associational activities and communal concerns. These forms are based on webs of social solidarity that shape and share ethical principles though forms of inclusion that are non-physical, or what has been termed 'non-territorial functional space' (Ruggie, 1993: 165).

A different question concerns operative reciprocity and complementarity between domestic and international institutions in the implementation of standards, targets, and monitoring functions. What a government may do, and the control that it exercises over its policies, are affected by the 'state's embeddedness in international structures of governance' (Risse-Kappen, 1995: 29). Once in place, international norms can assist domestic coalitions advocating compliance (Risse-Kappen, 1995: 31).

Discussing environmental policy issues, Raustiala (1997: 483) identifies what he terms 'regulatory politics' (where) 'variations in core domestic institutions critically shape the anticipated impact of regime rules and hence the domestic politics of international cooperation'. Common external commitments affect domestic institutions through what is termed anticipated 'refraction' (Raustiala 1997: 489). These are expectations about international impacts shaping domestic institutions, related political incentives, costs and benefits. Although official opaqueness may persist, it is under challenge since for most international trade, economic, and environmental negotiation, it is unnecessary. On numerous issues, non-governmental actors are as well, if not better, informed than governments on some issues at stake since relevant information is often within the public domain.

Whether focusing upon a governmental or public level, the pluralist formulation recognises a constant infusion of domestic and international interactivity, although that particular dynamic is inadequately generalised beyond individual cases. Some broad ranging characterisations offer insights about how global influences and local interests interact, but their applicability is problematic. From a developing country perspective, attempts to relate international determinants to domestic economic and social conditions have offered a *mélange* of dependency and world system approaches. This analysis is relational: dynamics of domination and dependence, established historically through colonialism and trade, reinforce class divisions within a loosely characterised 'periphery'.

More recently, Rosenau (1998) has envisaged change operating through gradations that start with citizens acquiring skills needed to perceive and then follow their interests. At another level, collectivities and authority structures reshape as they encounter legitimacy criteria of performance delivery. Globally, a multi-centric world sees a non-governmental sphere contesting and co-operating with sovereign interests, through engagements that stake out particular domains within an emergent order. All such processes assume borders are secondary and contribute to their increasing irrelevance.

Remaining with the pluralist theme, and looking to the role of domestic public opinion in foreign relations, Risse-Kappen (1991) devoted attention to the intervening role performed by institutional structures and coalition forming processes. Hagan (1994) considered domestic impacts upon regimes charting new external directions, finding central the role of supports, legitimacy and cohesion.

Treatments evaluating the interaction of international economic relations and domestic politics are extensive. Katzenstein (1978) assessed foreign economic policies of industrialised states in relation to domestic coalitions of business, state and policy interest. He saw a central purpose of external economic policy as rendering domestic policies compatible with the international political economy. Rogowski (1989) investigated international trade effects on domestic political cleavages shaped by class and urban/rural differences. Frieden (1991) evaluated global financial integration impacts upon domestic economic distribution, comparing advantages between tradable and non-tradable sectors in relation to exchange rate and monetary policy.

Putnam (1988) furnished a significant exposition about how domestic politics interacts with foreign relations through international negotiating processes. A two-level game is entailed: at one plane, domestic groups pressure their governments to favour policies they prefer, politicians reciprocating by building workable coalitions among these interests. At an international level, governments in negotiation seek to satisfy their domestic coalitions, but constrain potentially adverse foreign impacts. Effective conduct necessitates keeping external and domestic considerations sufficiently compatible to allow the entire process to move beyond negotiation to ratification. Neither game can go ignored while countries remain interdependent yet sovereign. Necessarily this process stretches 'rational' utility seeking conduct, since a government at one plane may commit in ways at odds with preferences in the other (Strange, 1996: 68). At any rate, Putnam's methodology further weakened the notion that in the international arena states perform as unitary actors.[5]

From still another perspective, projections about how sovereignty, market, and civil society forces might interact have seen claims that the state is increasingly an uneasy site of contest. Hence ' a deepening contradiction will occur between emerging processes of decentralisation and democratisation within and between societies, and the intensified centralisation and bureaucratisation of economic and political life. The state will tend to be a vehicle for the internationalisation of domestic conflict and localisation of international conflict' (Camilleri and Falk, 1992: 254). These observations confirm the view that globalisation underlines the need to ensure and maintain strong domestic public institutions.

The Normative Challenge

Between broad range characterisations and singular treatments, are constitutive questions about identity, appropriate sovereignty, normative conduct in international relations, and appropriate accountability. Aligned with constructivism, this approach envisages international relations as socially constituted. As interactive experiences occur, they may reorient interests, values and shared expectations. Non-material elements, like expected norms of appropriate and legitimate conduct, are part of the international system as much as material objects. The generation of norms facilitates new opportunities for voice. Thus with women's rights on the international agenda, rape as a war crime is better positioned to enter the policy discourse. Interests are created and evolve through participation in formulations of collective meaning. Rules and institutions perform significant *constitutive* functions in shaping conduct. Interpreting what exists in the international arena depends upon how it is understood – a good example being altered, post Cold War perceptions of Russia, notwithstanding its continuing nuclear weapons capability (Arend, 1998: 136).

The concern is less that of determining causal explanations between factors interacting on either side of the sovereign border. Rather, it is about entering a family of knowledge where such linkages exist, may interact, and are discernible. An improved understanding of these linkages helps uncover possibilities that better inform substantive questions at issue. Interests and identities are malleable; understanding necessitates historical understanding of their origins and progressions. A constructivist approach views the interactivity discussed here as adding fluidity to the social, non-material, and ethical environment that surrounds diplomatic activity and its outcomes. Legal systems contribute towards shared understanding about how co-operation might proceed, acts of participation helping to broaden and define interests (Finnemore, 1996). Rule-conscious discourse solidifies norms that influence conduct.

In some respects, the constructivist message is hardly new. In 1915, Arthur Ponsonby claimed that 'the acceptance of a responsibility is the essential preliminary for the proper capacity to discharge it. As with individuals, so with the people, unsuspected talents are brought to light when new duties are undertaken'.[6] As a public figure greatly concerned about the unaccountable conduct of the executive in foreign relations, Ponsonby's objectives have approached realisation through remedies designed to curb the so-called 'democratic deficit'. This arises where a national parliament, ostensibly accountable to the people, lacks a formal constitutional role in the process of international law making. These concerns have sharpened as international law has expanded its reach beyond inter-state questions to affect the everyday lives of individuals. Major changes in trade patterns, financial systems, the environment, and many other areas of international concern have meant an increasing amount of law derives from international processes. The 'increasing internationalisation of law has had a ripple effect throughout domestic law, both legislation and the common law' (Law Commission, 1997: 22).

The domestic/international dynamic has helped heighten demands to expand the applicability of accountability principles. Conditions in other countries driving people into exile, the plight of minorities, and individual histories of discrimination have galvanised external demands for information about, and accountability regarding the domestic conduct of foreign governments. Expanded non-governmental activity in human rights has furnished the means and the motivation to politicise domestic conditions for international purposes. The proliferation and specialisation of non-governmental organisations, and a related exploitation of electronic communications has exposed previously hidden aspects of domestic conduct to international scrutiny.

This has engendered a widely recognised counter-reaction. Hence 'internal and external pressures for democratisation, ... support for self-determination, and the elevation of human rights as a key global issue have heightened fears of increased intervention in the domestic affairs of sovereign states' (Soesastro, 1993: 372). Yet even the act of insistence that 'domestic problems' are not the business of outsiders assists in their internationalisation. Human rights discourse has assisted, through domestic and international interactions, to focus international attention upon responsibility for state conduct. That focus may invite diplomatic vexation regarding cultural sensitivity and unwarranted external intervention in domestic affairs.

Domestic normative principles and the democratic process may combine to afford more propitious prospects for peace than achieved through diplomatic accommodation or international security assurances. Doyle contends that democratic representation, an ideological commitment to human rights, and transnational interdependence, provide explanations as to the peace prone tendencies of democratic states. (Doyle, 1995: 180-4). Absence of such attributes offers a reason why non-democratic states tend towards war proneness. Conflicts arise between democratic states, but shared norms and institutional constraints mean democracies rarely escalate them to a point where they threaten force against each other. A benefit of democracy is that differences get managed, well before they turn violent (Doyle, 1986: 1151).

The constructivist configuration looks to domestic/international interactions producing outcomes that interests may not have expected but, in retrospect, do not surprise in the light of what eventuates. The probability that things may not emerge as anyone intended, a predictable unpredictability, encourages eclecticism. However 'it is one thing to argue that material factors and the external environment do not determine a state's behaviour and to point to the importance of regulative and constitutive norms, shared understandings, and common practices; it is quite another to say how norms are formed, how identities are shaped, and how interests become defined as they do' (Jervis, 1998: 974). Where it can, this study attempts to add lead to the constructivism pencil.

When compared, each of these paradigms offers something to the study of domestic/international interactivity. Few realists would claim that ethnic upheaval or internally inspired insurrection is just episodic for its impact upon relations between states. Pluralism's variegated offerings stem from a liberal tradition about restraints on power. Domestic/international interactivity generates unresolved contest about whether such restraint is liberty or license. Regardless of persuasion, free traders, trade unionists, or environmentalists find the domestic/international nexus an indispensable mechanism when promoting their values. Constructivism helps explain the potency of

Introduction 15

transformational possibilities. That is accompanied by a constant fusion of domestic and international preoccupations.

Chapter Scope of this Study

Moving from this wide-ranging discussion about some of the ideas that inform domestic/international interactivity, what does this study offer? The geographical focus is relatively selective: cases drawn from Australia, New Zealand and the Pacific islands. These locations differ sharply in their ethnography, history and international relations. The study is not state-focused and has selected issues of continuing resonance within these locations. All settings incorporate a plurality of domestic social and institutional formations. These vary according to capacity and interest in forming and sustaining external linkages. Where these linkages occur, internal constraints of a national or cultural nature may persist. To cite a specific example, non-governmental national coalitions advancing women's rights throughout the South Pacific, indicate a reluctance to alienate church support over reproductive rights issues.

Previous treatments of ethnicity and divided societies have often neglected the international dimensions. Widely deliberated questions of language, family and kinship, communal concerns, the local economy, socialisation, or religious and associational activities have neglected international referents. Structural adjustment programme impacts on ethnicity is another example of such neglect.

An opening chapter on New Zealand moves beyond its well publicised dispute with the United States over nuclear powered or armed ship visits, and considers continuing local pressure for comprehensive nuclear disarmament. The focus is the World Court Project, which led to the International Court of Justice delivering in July 1996 an advisory opinion on the legal status regarding the use, or threat of use, of nuclear weapons. The domestic/international dynamic entailed non-governmental activity among publics, before governments, and at the United Nations and World Health Assembly. Although assisted by discrete developments, such as the 1995 resumption of French nuclear weapons testing, the World Court Project was heavily self-reliant for impetus. It was normatively based, and acted from beliefs that effective nuclear disarmament required a democratisation of international rule formation.

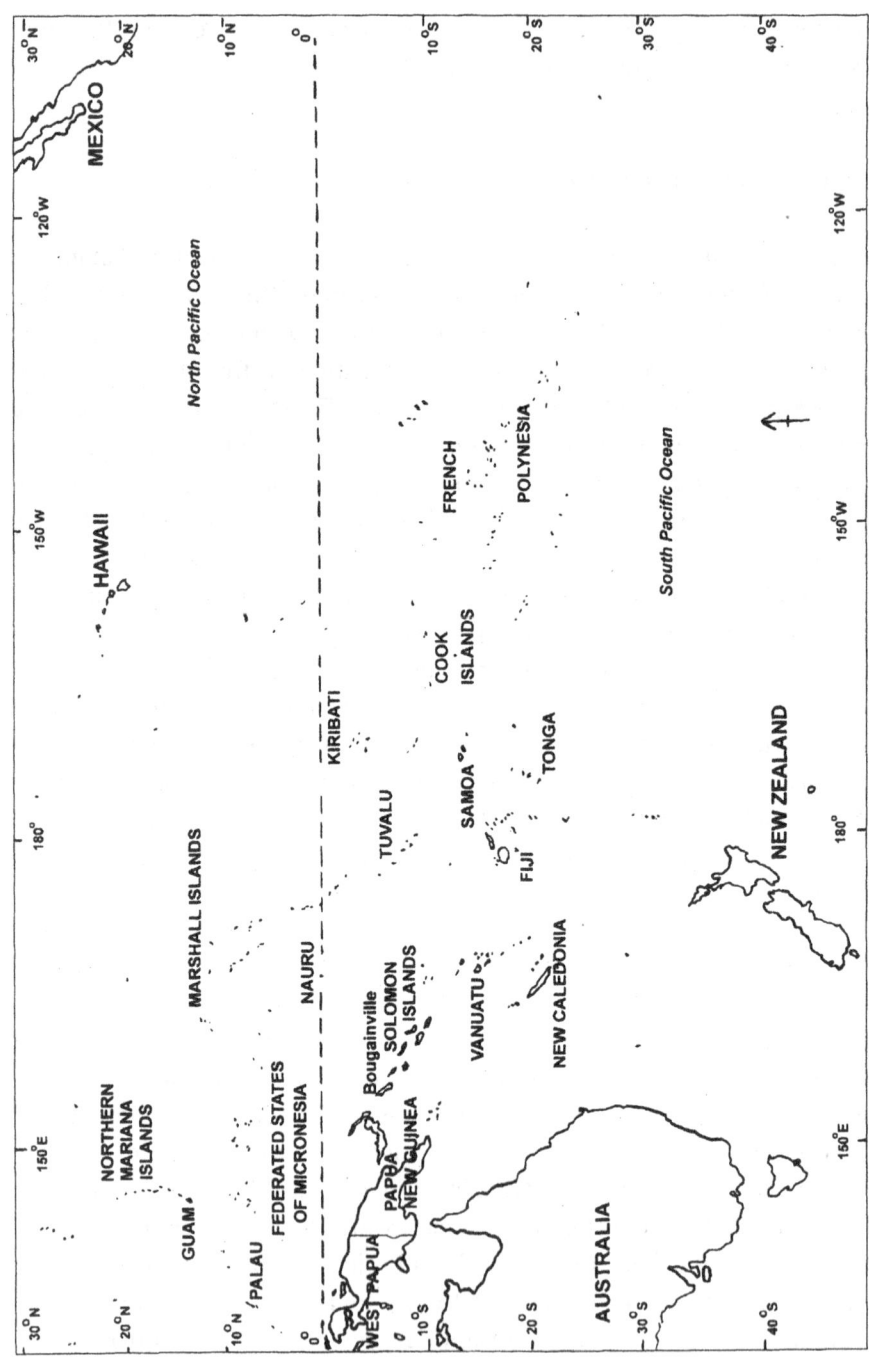

Map 1.1 The Pacific Islands

The following case considers Australia's controversial policy towards climate change. At the December 1997 Kyoto conference of parties to the Framework Convention on Climate Change, Australia gained concessions permitting future increases in the emissions of greenhouse gases. An effective de facto coalition of industry, federal, and state interests, backed by selected scientific evidence, helped project a robust national position. Domestic interests interpreted developing country and European Union positions as exonerating Australia's stance. International negotiations and their outcomes, Canberra decided, were relevant to the extent that they maintained and furthered national goals.

To Australia's immediate north-east, is located the troubled island of Bougainville (see map at page 89). Bougainville's conflict and attempts to settle it are addressed. In this instance, domestic and international interactions provoked, prolonged, but also helped precipitate moves towards settlement. Analytically, the experience confirmed the necessity, but inadequacy, of a conceptual inventory comprising such stock in trade as 'sovereignty', 'self determination', 'ethnicity', and 'state integrity'. Bougainville's peace process assisted towards a refurbishment of that inventory. The slow process of settlement, it is argued, was assisted by attempts to prevent its running aground over differences of future status. Muted, but not silenced, were polarisations regarding Bougainville's future status whether within Papua New Guinea, or as an independent entity.

The following two chapters deal with decolonisation and indigenous rights. They also deliberate sovereignty – whether under conditions of attenuated constitutional change (New Caledonia); high profile internationalisation (East Timor); and previously subjugated, but reawakening demands for self determination (West Irian). These cases reveal how contemporary state creation has proven something of a lottery. Attempts within these territories to gain the external leverage needed to hasten decolonisation, took their chances amidst a random progression of events. They included major external reorientations and regime upheavals within the colonising or external occupier.

Indigenous rights demands in Australia, New Zealand, and Fiji have assumed international dimensions. Relevant concerns include national compliance with emerging international norms; distortion of indigenous agendas abroad; and whether states learn from each other's indigenous restitution, compensation, and claim settlement experiences. Indigenous rights demands illustrate the politics of asserted identity. They also arouse dispute about whether consent legitimises governments via the ballot box, once 'the nature of "relevant community" is contested' (Held, 1997: 261-62). Sovereign principles distinguishing citizens within from those without, face challenge by loyalties transcending borders built from shared grievances of dispossession. The politics of restitution entails coming to terms with the past. Internationalising domestic histories adds pressure to governments to negotiate agreements with indigenous peoples more favourable than those reached without such exposure.

The remaining two chapters adopt an explicit Pacific island focus, dealing with public sector change and environmental management respectively. Both exhibit domestic/international linkages of significance. They raise questions about the kinds of public values guiding these countries into the new millennium. Environmental management and resource exploitation throughout Oceania entail an international relations that involves society, state, multinational corporate, and trade interactions (Kabutaulaka, 1998: 149). External economic interests find local counterparts among Pacific national economic and political élites, able and willing to derive power and privilege from foreign investment. These connections are explored for their implications to material covered in both final chapters.

Approach

Although not consistently applied for all chapters, the following schema asks how:
- Particular *preferences and interests* utilise the scope offered by domestic/international linkages to pursue their objectives. In doing so, how might such objectives change?
- Where interests relate to *affiliations of identity*, questions arise as to how they are sustained by supports straddling domestic and external locations.
- *Normative, rule formation* activities can expand, yet also stabilise expectations about the orderly management of change. However, this can highlight discontinuities of rule compliance as between domestic and international levels.
- International relations are regulated by *institutions* that perform prescriptive roles for problem-solving. The establishment of standard norms, rules and

procedures brings reciprocity and stability to international and domestic public conduct alike. Representation and accountability requirements may place externally introduced norms at odds with domestically derived values, institutions, and cultural practices. Human rights is an example, and debate about the relevance of 'good government' another.
- Overall, what kinds of *transformations* are evident through the increasingly diverse and complex domestic and external interactions evident throughout this study? How much effective emancipation has occurred?

These headings are not discrete. Transformations generate ideas that influence the development of institutions that, in turn, shape interests. Enough is contained in each of the following chapters to illuminate and test headings immediately identified. A challenge before this study lies in gaining the advantages offered by incorporating domestic and international determinants, but retaining manageability of subject material. To readers unfamiliar with the part of the world that informs these cases, it is a setting of considerable diversity. As diverse are issues traversed, extending from deliberations about the legality of nuclear weapons before the World Court, to problems of waste disposal in the Pacific Islands. The author's approach is eclectic and his interests are catholic. Although that breadth carries some disadvantages, the analysis offers sufficient to inform serious study of international and domestic political interactivity in Australia, New Zealand and the Pacific Islands.

Notes

1 This precludes the United Nations from intervening in matters 'which are essentially within the domestic jurisdiction of any state' but without prejudice to application of UN Charter Chapter Seven enforcement actions.
2 David Carment and Partrick James, 'Ethnic Conflict at the International Level', in David Carment and Partrick James (eds), *Peace in the Midst of Wars: Preventing and Managing International Ethnic Conflicts*, Columbia: University of South Carolina Press, 1998, p. 6.
3 Secretary General's Report to the Security Council, 1992, *An Agenda for Peace-Preventive Diplomacy, Peacemaking and Peace-Keeping*, New York: UN, paras 17, 19.
4 Boutros-Ghali, Boutros, 'Empowering the UN', *Foreign Affairs*, 71, (Winter), 1992-93, p. 98-99.
5 For subsequent applications of Putnam's methodology, see Peter F. Trumbore, 'Public Opinion as a Domestic Constraint in International Negotiations: Two-Level Games in the Anglo-Irish Peace Process', *International Studies Quarterly*, 42, 1998, pp. 545-65.

6 Arthur Ponsonby, *Democracy and Diplomacy: A Plan for Popular Control of Foreign Policy*, London: Methuen, 1915, p. 110.

References

Arend, Anthony Clark (1998), 'Do Legal Rules Matter? International Law and International Politics', *Virginia Journal of International Law*, 38, 2, pp. 107-53.

Barkin, Samuel and Cronin, Bruce (1994), 'The State and the Nation: Changing Norms and the Rules of Sovereignty in International Relations', *International Organization*, 48, 1, pp.107-30.

Beetham, David (1995), 'Introduction: Human Rights in the Study of Politics', *Political Studies*, XLIII, (special issue), pp. 1-9.

Bishai, Linda (1998), 'Altered States: Secession and the Problems of Political Theory', in Percy B. Lehning (ed), *Theories of Secession*, London: Routledge, pp. 92-110.

Camilleri, Joseph and Falk, Jim (1992), *The End of Sovereignty? The Politics of a Shrinking and Fragmenting World*, Aldershot: Edward Elgar.

Carlsnaes, Walter (1981), 'Foreign Policy and the Democratic Process', *Scandinavian Political Studies*, 4, 2, pp. 81-108.

Cox, Robert W. (1999), 'Civil Society at the turn of the millennium: prospects for an alternative world order', *Review of International Studies*, 25, pp. 3-28.

Dinnen, Sinclair (1998), 'In Weakness and Strength- State, Society and Order in Papua New Guinea', in Peter Dauvergne (ed), *Weak and Strong States and Asia-Pacific Societies*, Canberra: ANU, pp. 38-59.

Doyle, Michael (1986), 'Liberalism and World Politics', *American Political Science Review*, 80, 3, pp.1151-69.

Doyle, Michael (1995), 'On the Democratic Peace', *International Security*, 19, 4, pp. 180-4.

Edwards, M. et al., (1999), 'NGOs in a global future: marrying local delivery to worldwide leverage', *Public Administration and Development*, 9, 2, pp. 117-36.

Everts, P. P. (1985), *Controversies at Home: Domestic Factors in the Foreign Policy of the Netherlands*, Dordrecht: Martinus Nijhoff.

Falk, Richard (1994), 'The United Nations and the Rule of Law', Transnational Law and Contemporary Problems, 4, 2, pp. 611-42.

Falk, Richard (1997), 'State of Siege: Will Globalization Win Out?', *International Affairs*, 73, 1, pp. 123-36.

Falk, Richard (1997), 'The Nuclear Weapons Advisory Opinion and the New Jurisprudence of Global Civil Society', *Transnational Law and Contemporary Problems*, 7, 2, pp. 333-52.

Finnemore, Martha (1996), *National Interests in International Society*, Ithaca: Cornell University Press.

Frank, A. G. (1969), *Capitalism and Underdevelopment in Latin America*, New York: Monthly Review Press.

Frieden, Jeffrey A. (1991), 'Invested interests: the politics of national economic policies in a world of global finance', *International Organization*, 45, 4, pp. 426-451.

Frieden, Jeffrey A. (1997), 'Foreword', in David Skidmore (ed), *Contested Social Orders and International Politics*, Nashville: Vanderbilt University Press.

Goldman, Kjell (1988), *Change and Stability in Foreign Policy. The Problems and Possibilities of Detente*, Princeton: Princeton University Press.

Hagan, Joe (1994), 'Domestic Political Regime Change and Foreign Policy Restructuring: A Framework for Comparative Analysis', in J. Rosati et al., *Foreign Policy Restructuring*, Columbia: University South Carolina Press, pp. 138-63.

Hanrieder, Wolfram (1967), *West German Foreign Policy 1949-63*, Stanford: Stanford University Press.

Held, David (1997), 'Democracy and Globalization', *Global Governance*, 3, 3, pp. 251-67.

Jervis, Robert (1998), 'Realism in the Study of World Politics', *International Organization*, 52, 4, pp. 971-91.

Kabutaulaka, T. (1998), 'Deforestation and Politics in the Solomon Islands', in Peter Larmour (ed), *Governance and Reform in the South Pacific*, Policy Paper No. 23, Canberra: National Centre for Development Studies/RSPAS, ANU, pp. 21-53.

Katzenstein, Peter (1978), *Between Power and Plenty: Foreign Economic Policies of Advanced Industrial States*, Madison: University of Wisconsin Press.

Keohane, Robert O. (ed) (1989), *International Institutions and State Power. Essays in International Relations Theory*, Boulder: Westview Press.

Koskenniemi, Martti (1995), 'International Law in a Post-Realist Era', *The Australian Yearbook of International Law*, 16, pp. 1-19.

Law Commission (1997), *The Treaty Making Process and the Reform of Parliament*, Report 45, Wellington: Law Commission.

McCarthy, John D. (1996), 'Constraints and opportunities in adopting, adapting and inventing', in Doug McAdam, John D. McCarthy, and Mayer N. Zald (eds), *Comparative Perspectives on Social Movements*, Cambridge: Cambridge University Press, pp. 141-51.

Mann, Michael (1996), 'Authoritarian and Liberal Militarism: A Contribution from Comparative and Historical Sociology', in Steve Smith, Ken Booth and Marysia Zalewski (eds), *International Theory: Positivism and Beyond*, Cambridge: Cambridge University Press, pp. 221-39.

Mayall, James (ed) (1996), *The New Interventionism 1991-94. United Nations Experience in Cambodia, former Yugoslavia and Somalia*, Cambridge: Cambridge University Press.

Mittelman, James H. (ed) (1996), *Globalization: Critical Reflections*, Boulder: Lynne Reinner.

Mittelman, James H. (1997), 'Rethinking innovation in International studies: global transformation at the turn of the millennium', in Stephen Gill and James H. Mittelman (eds), *Innovation and Transformation in International Studies*, Cambridge: Cambridge University Press, pp. 248-63.

Moravcsik, Andrew (1995), 'Explaining Human Rights Regimes: Liberal Theory and Western Europe', *European Journal of International Relations*, 1, 2, 1995, pp. 157-89.

Ponsonby, Arthur (1915), *Democracy and Diplomacy*, London: Methuen.

Putnam, Robert D. (1988), 'Diplomacy and Domestic Politics: the Logic of Two-Level Games', *International Organization*, 42, 3, pp. 427-60.

Raustiala, Kal (1997), 'Domestic Institutions and International Regulatory Co-operation: Comparative Responses to the Convention on Biological Diversity', *World Politics*, 49, 4, pp. 482-509.

Rayner, Steve (1991), 'A Cultural Perspective on the Structure and Implementation of Global Environmental Agreements', *Evaluation Review*, 15, 1, pp. 75-102.

Risse-Kappen, Thomas (1991), 'Public Opinion, Domestic Structure, and Foreign Policy in Liberal Democracies', *World Politics*, 43, 4, pp. 479-512.

Risse-Kappen, Thomas (1995), 'Introduction', in Thomas Risse-Kappen (ed), *Bringing transnational relations back in: non-state actors, domestic structures and international institutions*, Cambridge: Cambridge University Press, pp. 3-33.

Rogowski, Ronald (1989), *Commerce and Coalitions: How Trade Affects Domestic Political Alignments*, Princeton: Princeton University Press.

Rosenau, James (1998), 'The United Nations in a Turbulent World', in Albert J. Paolini et al., *Between Sovereignty and Global Governance: The United Nations, the State and Civil Society*, London: Macmillan, pp. 252-73.

Ruggie, John Gerard (1993), 'Territoriality and Beyond: Problematising Modernity in International Relations', *International Organization*, 47, 1, pp. 139-74.

Slaughter, Anne-Marie (1994), 'The Liberal Agenda for Peace: International Relations Theory and the Future of the United Nations', *Transnational Law and Contemporary Problems*, 4, 2, pp. 377-420.

Soesastro, H. (1993), 'Implications of the Post-Cold War Politico-Security Environment in the Pacific Economy', in C. Fred Bergsten and Marcus Noland (eds), *Pacific Dynamism and the International Economic System*, Washington DC: Institute for International Economics, pp. 365-88.

Strange, Susan (1996), *The Retreat of the State: The Diffusion of Power in the World Economy*, Cambridge: Cambridge University Press.

Walker, R. B. J. (1993), *Inside/Outside: International Relations as Political Theory*, Cambridge: Cambridge University Press.

Wallace, William (1971), *Foreign Policy and the Political Process*, London: Macmillan.

Wendt, Alexander (1992), 'Anarchy is What States Make of It: the Social Construction of Power Politics', *International Organization*, 46, (Spring), pp. 391-425.

Wendt, Alexander (1998), 'On Constitution and Causation in International Relations', *Review of International Studies*, 24, pp. 101-117.

2 New Zealand and the World Court Project

Introduction: A Conference in New York

At a major conference held in New York during 1995, the Nuclear Non-Proliferation Treaty (NPT) gained extension for an indefinite period. To those observing the chemistry of non-governmental/official interactions, the conference proved instructive. While international deliberations convened by the United Nations (UN) often permit regular, mutually advantageous interchange between non-governmental organisation (NGO) activists and officials, this occasion was different. A concerted attempt to block and divert non-governmental access to officials was mounted. According to observers, the NGOs were 'banished to the rafters of the General Assembly Hall'.[1]

Nuclear weapons state officials encouraged this distancing. They were concerned about non-governmental campaigning for the total elimination of nuclear weapons.[2] They accurately suspected that pressure from this quarter had influenced a 1994 United Nations General Assembly resolution endorsing an approach to the International Court of Justice (ICJ). This requested an advisory opinion from the ICJ as to whether the threat or use of nuclear weapons is permitted under any circumstances in international law.[3]

To nuclear weapons states, this initiative threatened to obstruct indefinite NPT extension. Indeed, when a previous General Assembly resolution was blocked a year earlier, an observer noted 'the United States, Britain and France were roused into a frenzy of transcontinental lobbying to stop the initiative before it reached the General Assembly'.[4]

The key concern was to prevent the NPT's indefinite extension being tied to fulfilment of relevant treaty Article VI provisions. This obligates all signatories to pursue good faith negotiations to end the arms race through complete and general disarmament, necessarily including nuclear weapons. Contention over implementation of this particular article is longstanding, having haunted previous NPT review conferences. Those opposing indefinite extension, believed that this outcome would allow nuclear weapons states indefinite opportunities to postpone fulfilment of their Article VI obligations. After 1995, some went further in claiming that 'once the NPT was indefinitely extended, the non-nuclear states lost whatever leverage they had in forcing the nuclear weapons states to live up to their end of the deal' (Blackaby, 1997).

By procedural dexterity, the 1995 NPT Conference reached a 'consensus' supporting indefinite treaty extension. 'Strengthened' review procedures of the NPT were agreed, and pending the completion of a comprehensive test ban treaty, the nuclear weapons states undertook to 'exercise the utmost restraint'. The cynicism of that commitment stood revealed as China promptly resumed nuclear weapons testing followed in short order by France. This triggered intense international protest, inflamed by perceptions that, having secured indefinite NPT extension, then it was 'business as usual' for the nuclear weapons states.[5] Claims that the Chinese and the French advanced their testing programmes for completion prior to the long delayed Comprehensive Test Ban Treaty (finalised in 1996), did nothing to allay widespread condemnation.

Nuclear Disarmament

These events relate to this case analysis of domestic/international interactivity. The focus is on the way that New Zealand disarmament groups pursued international strategies through a project designed to promote the abolition of nuclear weapons.[6] Central to that endeavour was the World Court Project (WCP), seeking to have the ICJ deliver an advisory opinion about the legal status of nuclear weapons. This initiative was part of a strategy for the total elimination of nuclear weapons under an appropriately verified, enforced international Convention.

The 1995 NPT Review Conference occurred at a significant moment. Emerging with sharper clarity was a contrast between either acquiescing in the indefinite retention of nuclear weapons, or moving decisively towards their abolition. Since the Cold War's demise, sufficient time had elapsed to gauge whether the nuclear weapons states were committed to comprehensive nuclear disarmament, as distinct from reducing so-called 'overkill' capacity by retiring redundant nuclear weapons systems. Doctrines of nuclear deterrence sustained during the Cold War, now faced more searching military, moral, and political challenges. Critics argued that these doctrines offered little to abate worsening internal conflict, non-military threats, or upheavals caused by economic destabilisation, ethnic particularity, and regime decay. To the claim that nuclear deterrence was never designed to abate such threats, came responses asking just what were its functions?

Revelations about genocide in Cambodia (1975-78), and Rwanda (1994), galvanised moves to institute international tribunals to try war crimes. This sharpened inquiry about the legal culpability for *any* indiscriminate, wholesale destruction of humanity, necessarily including that by nuclear weapons. This recalled a 1949 report to the United States Atomic Energy Commission on the then proposed 'superbomb' or thermonuclear weapon that had claimed 'such a weapon goes far beyond any military objective and enters the range of very great natural catastrophes. By its very nature it cannot be confined to a military objective, but becomes a weapon which in practical effect is almost one of genocide'.[7] These sentiments were subsequently echoed through UN General Assembly Resolution 1653 (XVI) of 1961, declaring the use of nuclear weapons a crime against mankind and civilisation.[8]

By the mid-1990s, the divide separating nuclear 'haves' from nuclear 'have-nots' was as prominent as ever. The WCP initiative added grist to this mill, nuclear weapons states attacking it as misplaced and non-governmental disarmament lobbies seeking developing country support for nuclear weapons abolition. Unless abolition proceeded, further nuclear weapons proliferation was inevitable. An inherent instability and impracticality lay in the maintenance of power hierarchies based on egregious 'have, have-not' distinctions.[9] The route to nuclear non-proliferation lay through commitment to total nuclear disarmament. Articulating this view, 1995 Nobel Peace Laureate Joseph Rotblat claimed when winning this award that 'if the militarily most powerful - and least threatened – states need nuclear weapons for their security, how can one deny such security to countries that are truly insecure? The present nuclear policy is a recipe for proliferation. It is a policy for disaster'.[10]

By contrast, nuclear weapons states sought to restrict nuclear weapons proliferation by treaty and arms control processes that left doctrines of deterrence undisturbed. Nuclear weapons retention was required to deter proliferators of weapons of 'mass destruction', a post-Cold War categorisation embracing chemical, biological and nuclear devices. These threats made the abolition quest appear utopian, even quixotic. For the United States: 'Nuclear deterrence has played a vital role in maintaining our common security and defending the United

States and its allies over the past 50 years. Nuclear deterrence continues to make an essential contribution to preserving peace, security, and stability'.[11]

Calls for abolition challenged doctrines of nuclear deterrence at source, built trans-border social linkages, and acted from beliefs that the global impact of nuclear weapons rendered governments possessing them accountable before the bar of international citizenry. Nuclear disarmament entailed nothing less than complete dismantling of these devices. Abrogating the status and justifications for nuclear deterrence was an essential step towards achieving that goal. To abolitionists, nuclear deterrence was more vulnerable than ever - increasingly an emperor without clothes.[12] The views described stood in uncompromising polarisation. That divide adds background to the WCP initiative, and the domestic/international linkages that sustained its promotion.

Origins of the World Court Project

Formally inaugurated in 1992 to pursue the specific objective of going to the ICJ, the WCP coalesced a variety of non-governmental organisations. The three official co-sponsors included the International Peace Bureau (IPB), the International Association of Lawyers Against Nuclear Arms (IALANA), and the International Physicians for the Prevention of Nuclear War (IPPNW). Antecedents included the 1985 London Nuclear Warfare Tribunal that concluded current nuclear deployments violated basic rules of international law, justifying recourse to the ICJ as a means of remedy. In 1986, former Irish Foreign Minister, human rights jurist, and 1974 Nobel Peace Prize recipient Sean MacBride organised a global petition. This declared nuclear weapons illegal, called for their prohibition, and gained signatures from over eleven thousand lawyers and judges worldwide.[13] Critical for its promotion was Harold Evans, a retired New Zealand magistrate. Single-minded and articulate, he remained the central, originating figure for the WCP project within New Zealand as well as abroad. He was a mentor to many, but in particular two New Zealand peace workers, Kate Dewes and Alyn Ware, both playing pivotal domestic and international roles in the WCP.

In 1989, the IALANA's Hague Declaration asserted that the use, or threat of use of nuclear weapons, was a war crime, a crime against humanity, and a gross violation of other norms of international customary and treaty law (Dewes, 1998: 405-06). These developments coincided with the UN Declaration for the Decade of International Law that encouraged greater use of the ICJ.

When distinguished academic international lawyer Richard Falk spoke at the WCP launch in Geneva in May 1992, he warned that even a favourable ICJ advisory opinion would face limitations through its lack of binding authority. Nevertheless, it could prove a significant step in de-legitimising nuclear weaponry and facilitating a treaty regime embracing the prohibition, and then complete dismantling of nuclear arsenals.[14] Falk enumerated principles from the laws of war that Nicholas Grief had collated as memoranda. They included claims that nuclear weapons warranted prohibition because their use occasioned unnecessary human suffering; failed to discriminate between civil and military targets; resulted in disproportionate damage; released poisons and toxic substances causing genetic damage; sustained long term environmental damage; violated the rights of neutral countries; produced genocidal impacts; and violated the 1945 Nuremberg Principles that had been reaffirmed by the International Law Commission's 1950 statement that wanton destruction of cities, towns, or villages, or devastation not justified by military necessity was a war crime (Grief, 1992: 5-16).

Coinciding with findings from 'nuclear winter' impact investigations, the IPPNW warned that a total medical services breakdown would follow the aftermath of a nuclear conflagration. International humanitarian law outlawing indiscriminate attack, mass killings, and the use of terror against civilian populations in war was publicised as well.[15] In combination, these warnings from professional medical and legal sources conveyed credibility.

For public purposes, the WCP's central feature lay in its conscious attempt to link local, citizen-based initiatives to internationally instituted legal processes. Kate Dewes, and United Kingdom national Robert Green were central figures on the International Steering Committee of the project. Dewes and Green (1995), stress MacBride's seminal role in conceptualising and furthering that linkage. When he attended the Teheran UN Human Rights Conference in 1968, MacBride saw draft formulations on humanitarian law yielding possibilities via the Martens clause. First mentioned in the 1899 Hague Convention concerning Laws and Customs of War on Land, this held that: 'populations and belligerents remain under the protection and empire of the principles of international law, as they result from the usages established between civilised nations, from the laws of humanity and the requirements of the public conscience'.[16] The clause was subsequently restated in some binding instruments of international law.

British legal scholar and anti-nuclear activist Keith Mothersson's 1992 guide to the World Court Project, endorsed invocation of the Martens clause through individually signed declarations of public conscience.[17] It also affirmed the desire of individuals to live in a world free from the threat of nuclear destruction; opposed the use of nuclear weapons as an unspeakable atrocity and violation of international law; sought international relations based on peace and justice, not the threat and use of force; and supported an approach to the ICJ for an advisory opinion on the legal status of nuclear weapons (Mothersson, 1992).

From 1991, the WCP initiative gathered support, many New Zealanders joining citizens from other countries in signing individual declarations. They believed it was effective to directly petition lawful authority through channels uncluttered, 'interpreted', or delayed by state officials. By 1996, there were nearly four million signatures delivered to the UN and the ICJ. Approximately 32,000 came from New Zealand with backing from some 90 civic, local authority, religious, educational, environmental, peace and professional groups (Dewes, 1998: 408-13). Organisations with long standing involvement in humanitarian law supported the WCP initiative.[18] This process acted on assumptions that nuclear weaponry was subject to international rules and norms, attitudes evolved from New Zealand's experiences of confronting nuclear weapons testing in the Pacific.

New Zealand: From Nuclear Ally to Nuclear Free Activist?

During the Cold War, New Zealand governments cultivated their country's reputation as a reliable western ally. That role grew more difficult as the United States placed heavier emphasis on extended nuclear deterrence. This did not restrict New Zealand's support for a comprehensive test ban which strengthened after the 1963 Partial Test Ban Treaty outlawed atmospheric testing of nuclear weapons. France ignored this treaty by continuing atmospheric testing in French Polynesia. In retaliation, New Zealand and Australia instituted contentious proceedings at the ICJ against France in 1973 and 1974. New Zealand's claim concerned violation of 'the rights of all members of the international community' to be free from nuclear tests which gave rise to radioactive fallout and the right to be preserved from 'unjustified artificial radioactive contamination of the terrestrial, maritime and aerial environment'.[19]

The ICJ decided in 1974 that, insofar as New Zealand's complaint was concerned, a unilateral declaration from France indicating an end to its atmospheric nuclear testing absolved the Court from reaching a decision - a narrow finding not beyond dispute (Keith, 1996 a: 21). In a dissenting opinion, Judge de Castro, citing the *Trail Smelter* case (prohibition by neighbouring countries of noxious fumes), believed the applicant was entitled to ask the Court to uphold its claim for France to end the deposit of radioactive fallout on its territory.[20]

After ceasing atmospheric testing in 1974, France moved its programme underground where it continued intermittently until 1996. When France broke a moratorium by resuming testing in 1995, New Zealand unsuccessfully requested the ICJ to revisit the case that it had originally filed in 1973. This option was possible, because previously the ICJ had not ruled conclusively as to whether it possessed the jurisdiction making the case admissible. Although New Zealand's initiative failed, it highlighted the role of the ICJ, and confirmed beliefs that New Zealand had unfinished business with France over nuclear testing.

French/New Zealand differences aside, the longer nuclear weapons testing continued in the Pacific, the greater the strain that it placed on the tripartite Australia-New Zealand-United States (ANZUS) military cooperation arrangement. If this was one side of a triangle, the others being nuclear testing and nuclear deterrence, then the ANZUS component appeared the most vulnerable to immediate challenge. To a growing body of New Zealand opinion, these three components could not coexist. In response, the United States reiterated the indivisibility of ANZUS security, entry of nuclear-armed ships into New Zealand ports and harbours a *sine qua non* for effective military cooperation. Differences over the issue came to a head when the Lange-led Labour government instituted a nuclear ship visit ban early in 1985.

Details of New Zealand's dispute with the United States over nuclear weaponry have been fully described elsewhere (McMillan, 1987; Bercovitch, 1988; Pugh, 1989; Clements, 1988; Lange, 1990). Suffice to note that once in place, the ship visit ban not only resisted American and British pressure for repeal, but solidified sufficiently to jeopardise the electoral prospects of any party threatening its reversal. In addition, international developments consolidated New Zealand's anti-nuclear policy as a relaxation of Cold War rigidities facilitated long delayed movement on arms reductions. Thawing Soviet/US relations witnessed the abortive, but still significant, Reagan-Gorbachev 1986 Reykjavik Summit. To the horror of British Prime Minister Thatcher, this openly canvassed the possibility of comprehensive superpower nuclear disarmament. The 1987 Intermediate Range Nuclear Force Treaty pledging disarmament of these systems followed. It contained comprehensive intrusive verification requirements that rendered even more anomalous American adherence to 'neither confirm nor deny' doctrines regarding the location of US nuclear weaponry. New Zealand's anti-nuclear policy, it seemed, was moving with, not against, the tide of international disarmament.

Fortuitous developments shaped New Zealand public opinion. They included the 1985 bombing of the Greenpeace vessel *Rainbow Warrior* by French agents in Auckland harbour, and the 1986 Chernobyl nuclear plant disaster within the former Soviet Union (Alley and Ravenhill, 1996: 176). Both events reinforced the Lange government's claims that, notwithstanding sharp differences with Washington's neither confirm nor deny policy, the quarrel was less with the United States than nuclearism generally. Hostility to the nuclear generic engaged wider community support, husbanding environmental concerns, gender equality demands, and aspirations for stronger independence in foreign relations. Prime Minister Lange (1984-89) believed New Zealand's foreign policy could not move in isolation from the domestic policy of his government. 'If New Zealand's foreign policy has taken a new direction, it is because New Zealand as a whole has taken a new direction, and pursues new interests' (cited Levine, 1988: 82).

The anti-nuclear policy even assumed a certain totemistic quality – a credo of New Zealand's national identity and independence projected abroad. This increased following enactment of 1987 legislation that effectively banned the entry of nuclear-powered or nuclear-armed ships from New Zealand ports. The passage of that statute resulted in the United States formally 'suspending' its security cooperation commitments towards New Zealand under the ANZUS treaty. Washington chose this terminology in the belief that a future, non-Labour government might repeal the 1987 legislation.

The enactment of the legislation, strongly urged by backbenchers Jim Anderton and future Prime Minister Helen Clark, enabled Lange to rally the Labour Party behind him in an ongoing contest that he staged with his officials over the anti-nuclear issue. American retaliation against New Zealand's anti-nuclear ban included suspension of training, intelligence, and higher level diplomatic and political contacts. However, these actions strengthened support for the Lange government's position.

Table 2.1 New Zealand Public Opinion and Nuclear-armed Ship Visits

Do you agree that New Zealand should allow American ships equipped with nuclear weapons into New Zealand ports?

Date	Agree %	Disagree %	Other %	Sample	Area
1978	61.5	31.5	6.9	537	National
1982	49.0	41.0	8.0	142	Auckland
1983	46.1	40.2	13.7	1000	National
1984	30.4	57.4	12.3	2000	National
1984	23.1	72.4	4.5	303	Auckland
1985	29.0	56.0	15.0	533	National
1985	30.0	59.0	11.0	2000	National

Source: Campbell 1987.

A receding Cold War also helped erode the notion of a 'supreme alliance interest' justifying secrecy, possible total use of force, and deterrence doctrines needed to face down adversaries. These changes gave the National Party sufficient leeway to announce that it would not repeal the 1987 legislation. This shift occurred before its commanding victory at the 1990 General Election. Although provoking the front-bench resignation of opposition spokesperson McKinnon, (soon the Foreign Minister), this policy change neutralised Labour claims that it monopolised the high ground on nuclear disarmament.

Although local opposition to nuclear weaponry had acquired centre ground respectability by the 1990s, the incoming National government was reluctant to endorse calls for nuclear weapons' abolition. It accorded higher priority to securing a comprehensive test ban treaty, a measure opposed by Washington pending changes to laboratory techniques permitting continued nuclear weapons development without testing. Once the comprehensive test ban emerged to join treaties outlawing chemical and biological weapons, nuclear weapons stood isolated as the major obstacle to a complete ban on all weapons of mass destruction.

New Zealand and the World Court Project

Under New Zealand's 1987 anti-nuclear legislation, a statutory Public Advisory Committee on Arms Control and Disarmament was established. From its inception, the Committee was in regular communication with a retired Christchurch magistrate, Harold Evans. He sought official New Zealand sponsorship of a UN General Assembly resolution requesting an ICJ advisory opinion on the nuclear weapons legality question. In November 1988, the Advisory Committee brought together former Ombudsman, Sir Guy Powles, former Australian Liberal member of Parliament, Edward St. John QC, and Harold Evans. Official response to the Committee's recommendation to proceed with the Evans initiative was guarded. It was hedged by concerns that the United States and its NATO allies would respond negatively to any outcome criminalising their stated policy of possible first use of nuclear weapons (Boanas-Dewes, 1993: 85-86). Officials also believed it possible the Court might decline justiciability on the grounds that there was no point of international law requiring its determination.

Claiming resource constraints, the government left the proposal in abeyance. Evans continued to circulate a series of detailed 'Open Letters' addressed to governments and interested organizations, specifying arguments supporting an approach to the ICJ.[21] Often responses were negative, for example Australian Prime Minister Hawke expressed doubts that the course of action Evans suggested constituted a practical step.[22]

Although his single-mindedness alienated some, Evans and his supporters confronted the public with the principle of nuclear weapons state accountability before the processes and customs of international humanitarian law. Neither widely known, nor much heeded abroad during the initial stages of his campaign, Evans maintained contact with interested individuals abroad including Richard Falk (Dewes, 1998: 133). New Zealand activists were impressed by Falk's philosophical approach stressing the independence of peace movement activities from existing political parties and state institutions, including beliefs about altering relations of power by process rather than capture. Falk recommended active utilisation of normative democracy, including an emphasis on human rights, non-violence, transparency, and effective modes of participation and accountability. He encouraged New Zealand activists to persist at local levels, involve women, and reject national self-deprecation by projecting anti-nuclear activities abroad (Dewes, 1998:

112-13). In other words, the so-called 'Kiwi disease' of anti-nuclearism was eminently suitable for export.

Prior to the 1993 New Zealand General Election, Prime Minister Bolger and Opposition Leader Moore agreed during a televised exchange that they supported the World Court Project.[23] New Zealand activism on the World Court Project was also congruent with Pacific concerns including environmental health and safety in French Polynesia, delayed decolonisation in New Caledonia, and Palau's attempts to retain a nuclear free status in the face of continued American pressure to reverse that position. After continued lobbying by local WCP activists, the New Zealand government by late-1994 had decided to make a submission to the World Court.[24] Resumed French nuclear testing in 1995 smacked of calculated national aggrandisement, not security imperatives. It moved the New Zealand government closer towards opposition to doctrines of nuclear deterrence. By the late 1990s, New Zealand was closer to endorsing nuclear weapons abolition, a position not shared by Australia.

Nuclear Weapons and the World Court

The ICJ was seized with the issue of nuclear weapons through deliberations that have raised substantive issues at international law. These matters have proven controversial, complex, and politically charged. Unhelpful has been the undeveloped state of relevant international law, some seeing the Permanent Court of International Justice's 1927 Lotus case outcome and its benediction of undiluted sovereign prerogative, casting a dating but still substantial presence in an interdependent world. Yet as the previously mentioned Martens Clause indicates, international law is not limited to positive law: things not expressly forbidden by treaties are not necessarily permitted. Either way, a vacuum has been evident, a delay in moving 'the impermissibility of the existence of nuclear weapons in a civilised world from the twilight zone of dimly perceived morality into the daylight of legal certainty' (Weiss et. al. 1994: 716). When reaching decisions on such contentious questions, it was not surprising ICJ judges had scope to evince hospitality towards the views of their nominating governments.

The 1992 World Health Assembly considered, but did not authorise a World Health Organisation (WHO) approach to the ICJ for an advisory opinion on the legal status of nuclear weapons. During the preceding decade, the WHO commissioned studies where Joseph Rotblat's contribution proved seminal. These indicated that nuclear disarmament was the only effective means of ensuring maintenance of public health systems facing devastation in a nuclear conflict. This position was sustained consistently: namely that prevention is the only medical repose to the threat of nuclear war. After active lobbying by New Zealand-based WCP supporters, including former Director General of Health, Dr George Salmond, Dr Erich Geiringer, and others, the 1993 World Health Assembly approved a resolution supported by several Pacific Island states, adopted by secret ballot, and asking: *In view of the health and environmental effects, would the use of nuclear weapons by a State in war or other armed conflict be a breach of its obligations under international law including the WHO constitution?*[25] The message behind the request was direct and simple: nuclear war, as the ultimate health disaster, rendered the notion of health care meaningless, genetically contaminating the planet for untold generations.

On the initiative of Zimbabwe, the 1993 UN General Assembly addressed the nuclear weapons legality issue. After concerted pressure from nuclear weapons states and NATO countries, the NAM caucus withdrew support, ostensibly from grounds that it could complicate progress towards a Comprehensive Test Ban Treaty.[26] Anti-nuclear activists regarded this retreat a setback, but not a defeat. After regrouping at a Cairo meeting in mid-1994, the NAM states re-introduced the resolution which passed that year's UN General Assembly assisted by intense lobbying by key WCP figures, particularly Ware (Dewes and Green, 1999: 66-68). Citing UN Charter Article 96, this requested the ICJ for an advisory opinion, namely: *Is the threat or use of nuclear weapons in any circumstance permitted under international law?*

This initiative gained support from Pacific Island states and New Zealand, the latter parting company with other western governments choosing to either vote against, or abstain on the resolution. Aligning Pacific Island neighbours was important to New Zealand. It did not wish to jeopardise the substantial commitment of political and diplomatic effort invested in building regional cooperation. Nuclear weapons state response to the preparation and passage of this resolution was hostile.[27] In the event, the ICJ agreed to hear the UN General Assembly request, but declined the WHO resolution that was eventually forwarded following foot dragging by its Secretariat. This was

Box 2.1 World Court Advisory Opinion on the Legal Status of Nuclear Weapons: Summary of the 'Dispositif'

In its main advisory opinion, the Court in a final section termed the 'Dispositif' stated the following:

(i) By thirteen votes to one, decides to comply with the request for an advisory opinion.
(ii) Replies to the question put by the General Assembly:
A. Unanimously, that there is in neither customary nor conventional law any specific authorisation of the threat or use of nuclear weapons;
B. By eleven votes to three, that there is in neither customary nor conventional law any comprehensive and universal prohibition of the threat or use of nuclear weapons;
C. Unanimously, a threat or use of force by means of nuclear weapons that is contrary to Article 2, paragraph 4, of the United Nations Charter and that fails to meet all the requirements of Article 51, is unlawful;*
D. Unanimously, A threat or use of nuclear weapons should also be compatible with the requirements of international law in armed conflict particularly those of the principles and rules of international humanitarian law, as well as with specific obligations under treaties and other undertakings which expressly deal with nuclear weapons;
E. By seven votes to seven, (by the president's casting vote), it follows from the above mentioned requirements that the threat or use of nuclear weapons would generally be contrary to the rules of international law applicable in armed conflict, and in particular the principles and rules of international humanitarian law.
However, in view of the current state of international law, and of the elements of fact at its disposal, the Court cannot conclude definitively whether the threat or use of nuclear weapons would be lawful or unlawful in an extreme circumstance of self-defence, in which the very survival of a State would be at stake;
F. Unanimously, there exists an obligation to pursue in good faith and bring to a conclusion negotiations leading to nuclear disarmament in all its aspects under strict and effective international control.

Source: Green (1998: 38).

Note: * Article 2 (4) of the UN Charter precludes the use of force, or the threat of force in the conduct of international relations, Charter Article 51 not excluding its use for the purposes of self defence.

ironic since, from a legal perspective, the WHO formulation was the more appropriately worded, a point strongly underlined in Judge Weeramantry's dissent to the delivered opinion.

After eight months of substantive deliberation, the ICJ found *inter alia* that '... a threat or use of nuclear weapons would generally be contrary to the rules of international law applicable in armed conflict, and in particular the principles and rules of humanitarian law'. Numerous legal commentaries on this outcome soon followed.[28] Suffice to note that the Court's just cited use of the word 'generally' aroused strong, albeit sharply differing dissents by its judges.

In his dissenting opinion, Judge Weeramantry attempted to put nuclear weaponry in perspective. He claimed that the general principles of law recognised by civilised nations remains law 'even though indiscriminate slaughter *through the nuclear weapon*, irreversible damage to future generations *through the nuclear weapon*, environmental devastation *through the nuclear weapon*, and irreparable damage to neutral states *through the nuclear weapon* are not expressly prohibited in international treaties. If the italicised words are deleted from the previous sentence, no one could deny that the acts mentioned therein are prohibited by international law. It seems specious to argue that the principle of prohibition is defeated by the absence of particularization of the weapon'.[29]

Transformational Conduct

How did domestic New Zealand pressures for nuclear disarmament translate as an international dynamic? Some view social action at its most potent when conditions of heterogeneity and interdependence offer stronger incentives for collective action than where homogeneity and discipline is more evident. It may also occur where opportunities widen, policy-making élites divide, and public realignments occur (Tarrow, 1994: 150). Others see domestic social initiatives interacting at international levels via inter-subjective understandings - beliefs that shape qualitatively different kinds of response to problems previously monopolised through governmental determination of interests. This extends beyond alternative agenda setting, to incorporate social interactions facilitating persuasion, learning, and the knowledge sharing that shapes and determines interests.

How does this level of generality translate to the WCP initiative? Both approaches relate to the New Zealand experience. To take Tarrow first, characteristics of domestic peace movement activity in New Zealand – heterogeneity and decentralisation – encouraged social skills suited to the uncertainties of international non-governmental disarmament lobbying. These skills were resourcefulness, flexibility, and continued attention to information access. Opportunities to translate domestic pressure for nuclear disarmament into concerted international action widened as the Cold War retreated. Continued nuclear testing now stood exposed to growing isolation. McKinnon's Opposition front bench resignation apart, New Zealand's policy élites were less divided than cautious. The depth of global reaction against resumed French testing, however, gave the impetus needed to push beyond habituated deference to nuclear deterrence. This was backed by the New Zealand public's steadily deepening opposition to engagement with nuclear weaponry.

Second, the promotion of nuclear abolition as a health issue served to highlight humanitarian law principles regarding the need to avoid unnecessary civil suffering in military conflict. Perceptions about the nature and locus of accountability also shifted. Rather than seeing New Zealand summoned by the United States to explain aberrant alliance conduct, the focus shifted towards nuclear weapons states. The onus now lay with them to explain continued possession of weapons of mass destruction. Their inadequate progress over nuclear disarmament opened opportunities for non-governmental activism. With enhanced public support for the ICJ initiative, New Zealand was less fixated by either United States pressure or anti-American sentiment. Through public calls for nuclear weapons state accountability, citizen efficacy deepened in capacity. This was paralleled by human rights and gender equality demands, and the linkages formed through transnational networks and project-based international institutional activity (Dewes and Green, 1999: 76-78).

The WCP as Transformational Conduct

Sikkink (1993: 415) has described an 'international issue network' as comprising 'a set of organizations bound by shared values and by dense exchanges of information, working internationally on an issue'. The WCP conformed to that characterisation in certain respects but not others. To a core group of New Zealand activists, closely involved throughout the WCP, a substantial international information exchange was conducted for lobbying and promotional purposes. This fed from, and sustained complementary domestic activities. Much New Zealand anti-nuclear activity was decentralised and small scale, some of it originating with the creation of local authority 'nuclear free zones' designed to build public support and legitimise the symbolic impact of anti-nuclear positions. This conformed to a distinctive 'do it yourself' pragmatism of New Zealand public organisational activity, solidified opposition to nuclear ship visits, and embodied symbols and aspirations of independence, nationhood, gender equality, and social emancipation (Alley, 1987: 1999). WCP activities included public meetings, conferral with local international legal experts of standing, church-related activities, declaration of conscience pledging, and continual lobbying of officials and parliamentarians (Dewes, 1998: 364-67).

In some instances, the determination of New Zealand activists such as Harold Evans and Erich Geiringer to push the project clashed with those favouring gradualism. Differences emerged over objectives: tactically, New Zealand WCP activists asserted national values of immediate, pragmatic problem-solving by dealing with each objective as it arose. This included gaining IPPNW endorsement of the initiative; an abortive foray at the World Health Assembly in 1992 (but success a year later); and a similar pattern repeated at the UN General Assembly in 1993 and 1994 respectively. Gaining these footholds as each proved attainable meant constantly evolving priorities. The transnational social network was utilised to shape and disseminate relevant strategies.

By contrast, a philosophy of social linkage envisaged the WCP project as part of slower moving, but comprehensive change process utilising legal and political processes. Falk believed a 'principled network' could emerge from current conditions where 'the foundations for a greatly enhanced system of global governance lie dormant, but these latent possibilities are unlikely to be activated by leading governments unless they are prodded by mobilised and focused social forces associated with transnational democratic initiatives including possibility of recourse to the International Court of Justice for advisory opinions on issues of contested legality' (Falk, 1994: 639). Keith Mothersson, envisaged the initiative playing a part in developing a global civil society where 'every society, club, union, guild, municipality, party, small business, cooperative, kinship network, ethnic group, artistic project, band, team, religious community, round table, fraternity, sisterhood ... can be seen as one node of a global ecological system' (Mothersson, 1992: 135).

Differences concerned were those of relative emphasis - between utilising social networks for what they offered instrumentally, or seeing such activity performing highly valued, slower moving institutional and agenda transformations. This view conceded that to shift national voting positions at the UN in support of the World Court Project, diplomats needed persuading. However, this risked dignifying the means by which sovereign interest compromises have pushed effective disarmament to the periphery. No less committed to transformative objectives, the pragmatists saw no alternative to taking this risk. The defining issue was whether a sufficient consensus could form for nuclear weapons abolition. Unless it did, the entire question risked remaining hostage to sovereign preference and the glacial incrementalism of negotiated arms control processes.

This contrast of perspectives did not leave key objectives at odds. A consensus existed for prohibiting, de-legitimising, and abolishing nuclear weapons through prescriptive clarification mandated by an international Convention. Retrospective evaluations looking to the movement to abolish slavery were shared. That had mobilised domestic pressure through a campaign designed to isolate the bigotry, ignorance, and moral bankruptcy underpinning the international slave trade. Importantly it fastened upon the use of collective pressure to 'unlearn' a practice which, while never fully abolished, was consigned to the level of unacceptable conduct among civilised nations. Slavery henceforth was, *prima facie*, disreputable. Although to this day far from eradication, slavery has nevertheless earned universal abhorrence for its practitioners.[30] This was the attitudinal shift sought by the WCP nuclear abolitionists. Like anti-slavery in Britain, they looked to middle class support, active role of women, involvement of religious bodies, access to the news media, and use of petitioning.

The WCP as a 'Politics of Project'

Few advocating the effective elimination of nuclear weapons saw the challenge in those terms alone. Aspirations for peace and security can prove irreconcilable through failure to address abiding problems of denied social equity and commitments to justice. This was noted by a seasoned veteran of disarmament attempts under the League of Nations, Salvador de Madariaga. He believed those wanting to disarm had to get at the cause of armaments which was fear of conflict, itself a problem that has become poisonous. And what is a problem? 'It is a question that has been neglected ... an everyday matter that needs our attention. If therefore we want to avoid wars, it is very little use in waiting to tackle our ordinary humdrum matters until they are unattended, neglected or poisoned, so that they have become conflicts' (de Madariaga, 1973: 283). These dilemmas are less acute where governments are subject to the norms of constitutional accountability at home, peaceful settlement abroad, and rule-governed behaviour regarding recourse to force in either setting.

While local peace action for nuclear disarmament evolved through international orientations, de Madariaga's emphasis on local problem-solving as antidote to conflict, war and arms racing was never remote. Civil rights, gender, poverty, health, and environmental concerns persistently saw their objectives running parallel to those of nuclear disarmament. This is sought by reshaping national agendas via information sharing, accountability of power-holders, and project-based strategies. A 'politics of project' may enliven social interactions that activate dormant or neglected preferences, pointing towards future directions for dismantling nuclear weapons. To the oft-repeated claim that 'nuclear weapons cannot be disinvented', came the response querying where such devices stood without supporting doctrines of nuclear deterrence? If particular conditions justified the need for such doctrines, then what was needed to alter those conditions?

Giving one answer, Falk believed that: 'For the anti-nuclear movement to succeed, it desperately needs "a politics", that is, a clear understanding of what must be changed and how to do it. This understanding must also include an alternative idea of security ... it will not succeed unless it combines a negation of nuclearism with the persuasive creation of new ways to protect the independence and territorial integrity of the states that make up world society' (Falk, 1982: 133).

Looking ahead, those building on the 1996 ICJ outcome to develop a nuclear weapons elimination Convention have emphasised societal condemnation of nuclear weapons, and the codification of the customary norm against all weapons of mass destruction. A Convention's impact 'will therefore be deeper and more far reaching than the treaty language itself. Such a treaty would reflect a broader social and political movement away from reliance on weapons of mass destruction and military solutions to conflicts, and would incorporate the desires and responsibilities of global civil society for a less militarised world'.[31]

Norm Creation and Social Energy

To succeed, social movements attempt to accumulate mounting awareness and purposeful engagement. While electoral campaigning seeks to build, sustain, and capitalise upon the dynamic of a 'momentum' organised to peak as voters head to the polls, issue campaigning differs. Given the uncertainties and vicissitudes facing poorly resourced, disparate, and part-time teams of activists, succeeding in this task is often problematic. Even in New Zealand's generally benign public climate, building the WCP's 'momentum' at times appeared difficult. Locally the New Zealand government remained guarded, emphasising negotiated arms control outcomes such as the Chemical Weapons Convention and a Comprehensive Test Ban Treaty. The government also expressed concerns that the Court could rule to confer legality on the ownership, and hence possible use of nuclear weapons, a position advanced in the United Kingdom's submission before the ICJ.

Sustaining New Zealand's anti-nuclear movement was a body of experience tempered by previous national disputes over sport with apartheid South Africa, Maori land entitlements, gender equity claims, and environmental accountability. This paralleled a growing South Pacific regional consciousness, inflamed by continued French nuclear weapons testing. The social activism demanding effective nuclear disarmament was motivated from concerns that, in less fortunate countries, such action was either derailed, diverted, or shunned by ensconced state security establishments and supporting corporate, technical, and diplomatic interests. It was against this background that New Zealand activists took up the challenge of initiating and then implementing the WCP strategy.

Domestic/international interactivity was epitomised by relationships New Zealand activists developed at the World Health Assembly and the UN General Assembly, although constraining considerations did intrude. Some were short-run, such as cost complaints by governments over adopting the initiative, or the WHO Director General's inordinate delay in conveying, as required, the request to the Court (Keith, 1996 b: 57). Some apparent setbacks were turned to advantage: lack of support by key governments during critical 1993-94 stages at the World Health and United Nations General Assembly meetings allowed regrouping. Although under-resourced, the Project's network was sufficiently attuned to detect growing public support linked to environmental, nuclear energy and nuclear waste shipment concerns (Dewes, 1998: chapters 9 and 11).

Despite post-Cold War international system changes briefly promising relaxed tensions and progress in disarmament, activists discerned how policy inertia and status considerations maintained their grip on nuclear weapons state conduct. This was confirmed by resumed Chinese and French nuclear testing in 1995, and as the United States nuclear weapons modernisation continued regardless of the Comprehensive Test Ban Treaty. As the WCP campaign progressed, its lobbying activities before the World Health and the UN General Assemblies generated increasingly visible opposition from nuclear weapons states (Dewes, 1998: 365-68). This consolidated support among WCP followers who viewed opposition as evidence of the campaign's growing salience, although it complicated support from governments concerned about nuclear weapons state retaliation. That concern was real: to a Swedish representative attending the UN General Assembly World Court referral question in 1993, 'I followed this debate closely, and saw the pressure from the nuclear powers to have the resolution withdrawn. This unacceptable coercion of the non-nuclear states shows that they are determined to retain their freedom to threaten the use of nuclear weapons'.[32] The New Zealand government was less exposed in supporting the World Court initiative once the NPT gained indefinite extension, the French resumed nuclear testing, and a Comprehensive Test Ban Treaty came within reach. Opposition to nuclear testing provided an irreducible platform which all shared. Anger at the resumption of French nuclear weapons testing 1995-96 distilled maintenance of deterrence as a core obstacle.

Overall, momentum was sustained and objectives achieved because New Zealand's WCP activities were directed by individuals with the experience and knowledge necessary to utilise domestic and international linkages via non-governmental networking.[33] They had a familiarity with the New Zealand policy environment, its parliamentary arena, and political party processes. Internationally they were at home in the corridors and assembly rooms of UN conferences arenas in Geneva and New York where Lawyers Committee on Nuclear Policy Executive Director, New Zealander Alyn Ware and Kate Dewes, developed working contacts with permanent delegation representatives and UN staff (Dewes, 1998: 365-68). Ware's organisation was instrumental in devising and promoting a model Nuclear Weapons Convention for the abolition of nuclear weapons. Related development following the ICJ ruling, now considered, assumed importance as continued institutionalisation of the WCP outcome.

Post-1996 Moves to Institutionalise Abolition

The Canberra Commission

In August 1996, the Canberra Commission on the Elimination of Nuclear Weapons reported its findings. Convened by the Keating-led Labour government, this 'had its origins in the convergence of both international and domestic considerations' (Hanson and Ungerer, 1999: 7). Deliberating were seventeen independent specialists drawn from diplomacy, strategic studies, legal, military, academic, and senior public life. Two had had intimate professional involvement with the United States military at the highest levels, General Lee Butler, former Commander in Chief of US Strategic Command, and former Secretary of Defence Robert McNamara.

The Commission held that the unique security benefits nuclear weapons states insist they maintain are discriminatory and cannot be sustained. Hence the 'possession of nuclear weapons by any states is a constant stimulus to other states to acquire them' (Canberra Commission Report: Opening statement). Furthermore, the Commission held that nuclear arsenals serve no military purpose, nuclear deterrence is suspect, possible terrorist use or risk of accidental discharge cannot go ignored, while the use of nuclear weapons is in critical violation of basic humanitarian law. Furthermore, nuclear weapons states needed to commit unequivocally to a nuclear weapons free world, and move to negotiate that outcome immediately. Recommended steps included taking nuclear weapons systems off alert; ending testing; ending deployment of non-strategic systems; removing warheads from delivery systems;

progressing Russian-US arms reduction; and instituting no-first use agreements against non-nuclear countries.

As to an elimination timetable, the Commission did not deny possible reactivation – or breakout – of a nuclear weapons programme. It backed enhanced methods of technical detection and verification, and emphasised the political costs of condemnation facing proliferation within a global regime of total prohibition. The incoming (March 1996) Howard administration accorded the Canberra Commission report a non-committal reception. Elsewhere its findings received serious attention and evaluation.

The New Agenda Coalition

In June 1998, New Zealand Foreign Minister McKinnon joined counterparts from Brazil, Egypt, Mexico, Ireland, Slovenia, South Africa, and Sweden to promote an eight nation Declaration on behalf of what was termed the New Agenda Coalition. A letter was submitted to the UN Secretary General that called on all nuclear weapons states to undertake general and complete disarmament.[34] Ireland and Sweden were instrumental in planning the New Agenda initiative. The statement endorsed existing nuclear arms control negotiating formulae for an international ban on the production of fissile materials, additional nuclear weapons free zones, completion of the Strategic Arms Limitation process, and full adherence to the NPT. Although planned before Indian and Pakistani nuclear testing, the initiative's launch immediately following those detonations gave it added impetus.

The total elimination of nuclear weapons was recommended, beginning with those states possessing the largest arsenals – effectively a call to begin retiring doctrines of nuclear deterrence. The Declaration endorsed the unanimously agreed component of the ICJ advisory opinion regarding nuclear disarmament. A second endorsement supported the Canberra Commission's finding that: 'the proposition that nuclear weapons can be retained in perpetuity and never used – accidentally or by decision – defies credibility. The only complete defence is the elimination of nuclear weapons and assurance that they will never be used again' (Green, 1998: 50). Although the Canberra Commission report was a seminal statement for the eight nations initiative, Australia was not invited to participate. This stemmed from concern that Australia would circulate its difficulties with the statement to other governments and undermine it from the outset. Such conduct was considered unremarkable from a state in formal militarily alignment to the United States.

The New Agenda Coalition's UN General Assembly resolution, passed in 1998, requested nuclear weapons states to demonstrate an unequivocal commitment to the speedy and total elimination of their nuclear arsenals. Contrary to American, British, and French calls for them to oppose this resolution, most NATO countries recorded abstentions.[35]

The Middle Powers Initiative

In 1998 the Middle Powers Initiative was launched. This emerged from a grouping of NGOs drawing upon the experiences of the World Court Project. Initiated by former Canadian Disarmament Ambassador Douglas Roche, this sought to encourage nuclear weapons states 'to the immediate practical steps and negotiations required for the elimination of nuclear weapons' (Green, 1998: 6). Most sponsoring organisations had previous involvement in the World Court Project, including the previously identified IPPNW, IPB and IALANA. The Middle Powers Initiative was grounded on principles of domestic non-governmental activity encouraging and persuading intergovernmental and diplomatic conduct towards an acceptance of nuclear weapons abolition objectives (Green, 1998: 8). Key figures developing the Middle Powers Initiative retain close New Zealand connections.

Relevant to the Initiative was experience gained through the so-called 1996 'Ottawa Process' where, faced with US-backed delay and emasculation by amendment, Canadian Foreign Minister Axworthy instigated processes that 'fast-tracked' a Convention totally banning landmines. This removed negotiations from the Geneva-based Conference on Disarmament, non-governmental organisations providing essential impetus. Non-governmental activists supporting the Middle Powers initiative saw in the 'Ottawa Process' a mechanism for emulation in nuclear disarmament (Green, 1998: 9).

South Asian Nuclear Testing

Developments described in this chapter help explain the unpopularity and disapprobation that greeted Indian and Pakistani nuclear weapons testing in 1998. This evinced a torrent of international condemnation, including a statement signed by 47 governments before the Geneva Conference on

Disarmament insisting that the tests were totally 'irreconcilable with claims by both countries that they are committed to nuclear disarmament'.[36]

Yet for every condemnation uttered against India and Pakistan, came the riposte that continued weapons capability by existing nuclear weapons states lay at the core of the proliferation problem. Collectively, the tests further exposed unpalatable questions about the durability of existing arrangements designed to curb the spread of nuclear weapons. To Krieger, the 'message of India's tests is that we can have a world in which many countries have nuclear weapons or a world in which no countries have nuclear weapons, but we will not have a world in which only the five permanent members of the UN Security Council plus Israel retain nuclear weapons in perpetuity'.[37]

Conclusions

This case has indicated that while international social connections proved vital in executing the WCP initiative, the project's initial design and impetus remained domestically based. New Zealand support systems were resilient, resourceful, and decentralised. Without the confidence provided by established domestic networks of consultation, information, and access to local decisional sources, the quality of New Zealand's international input faced diminution. Limited funding of New Zealand anti-nuclear activities made nationwide co-operation essential in order to survive. Better endowed United States non-governmental bodies lacked that imperative; unused to co-operating nationally, they proved less effective internationally.

New Zealand objectives were legitimised by statute through the 1987 nuclear free legislation. This provided a normative basis to anti-nuclear activities projected abroad and recourse to the World Court. The legislation added credibility to attempts to facilitate contact between activists, parliamentarians, and officials in allied projects designed to ban nuclear testing, strengthen nuclear free zones, and encourage NPT Article VI implementation. The domestic/international linkage was manifest through New Zealand's involvement with regional South Pacific concerns. They included shared legacies of exposure to nuclear radiation, environmental impacts of previous nuclear weapons testing, active opposition to testing, and joint formulation of the 1985 South Pacific Nuclear Weapons Free Zone Treaty.

An expansion of international NGO activity shaped anti-nuclear conduct and priorities within New Zealand. Domestic/international interactions directly engaging environment, human rights, and disarmament placed established diplomatic processes in clearer perspective. Less conspicuous lobbies also supported the WCP, including the World Federalists (Dewes, 1998: 168-70). An approach that emphasised principles, value objectives, and norm-based criteria, put diplomatic modalities in perspective. To WCP activists, the Conference on Disarmament had allowed such modalities to dominate as ends in themselves.

As a campaign of social efficacy, the New Zealand WCP built from lobbying and promotion experiences accumulated during the years of protest against atomic testing and visiting nuclear warships. The government and its policy élites did not divide over approaching the ICJ, but retained sufficient contact with activists to allow active lobbying of officials. Domestic political realignment did not occur in New Zealand during the key 1992-95 phase, although it was anticipated as the country moved to a mixed member proportional system of election in 1996. This fostered deal making and coalition formation, adding scope for lobbying with politicians anxious not to offend potential segments of electoral support. While international dimensions furnished the location and *raison d'être* for the World Court Project, local factors drove the initiative.

In retrospect, the New Zealand's approach to the WCP comprised a continual interleafing of domestic and international activities. The original case filed by New Zealand before the ICJ in 1973 shaped domestic opinion, and heightened international news media attention to continued French nuclear testing. Official caution about moving to question nuclear deterrence eased from 1995. This was accompanied by growing attention to non-nuclear security concerns, including United Nations peacekeeping, growing attention to the immediate neighbourhood's security needs exemplified by the Bougainville conflict, and maritime resource management considerations. New Zealand's active civil society and open democracy, facilitated participation in major international policy developments via UN conference activities on human rights, the environment, and the advancement of women. As people thought more about the role, utility, and the potential costs of nuclear weapons in a post-Cold War environment, scope for domestic debate and institutions as a route to reform assumed sharper focus. This activity projected domestic experiences abroad, including a willingness to assume unhindered access to sources of information and decision.

Having the legal status of nuclear weapons directly addressed via the WCP entailed the effective exploitation of, and generation of interdependence between domestic social action and international legal and diplomatic processes (Dewes, 1998: chapter 13). That interdependence broadened through familiarisation with the diplomatic geography of disarmament. This entailed non-governmental activism, serving the apprenticeships of patience needed to acquire understanding about how to maximise lobbying and access opportunities before intergovernmental meetings. Governments also began appreciating that non-governmental groups possessed sources and insights of direct use to them (Alley, 1999: 314-15).

Finally, the WCP outcome revealed how NGOs can place international institutions like the World Court at the service of the world's people, not just their governments. Even a decade earlier, that notion might have appeared novel. New Zealand social activism was seminal in reaching this result, its strategic and conceptual capacity to link local aspirations with international processes and institutions critical.

Notes

1. Tariq Rauf and Joanne L. Charnetski, 'The 1995 Review and Extension Conference of the Non-Proliferation Treaty: How History was Made?' *Pacific Research*, Canberra: ANU, 8, 3, 1995, p. 21.
2. At the 1995 NPT Conference, the non-governmental 'Abolition 2000' network issued a statement calling for the timebound abolition of nuclear weapons under a Convention with provisions for effective verification and enforcement. Abolition 2000 Statement, New York, 25 April 1995.
3. UN General Assembly doc. A/C.1/49/L.36.
4. Mark Shapiro 'Mutiny on the Nuclear Bounty', *The Nation*, 27 December 1993, p. 799.
5. Comment of 1995 NPT Review Conference Chair, Jayantha Dhanapala, *UNIDIR Newsletter*, 37, 1997, p. 9.
6. Examples included the New Zealand Foundation for Peace Studies; the Lawyers for Nuclear Disarmament; United Nations Association; and the Women's International League for Peace and Freedom, Aotearoa (Dewes, 1998: 405).
7. Report of the General Advisory Committee to the United States Atomic Energy Commission, October 1949, Washington DC: Government Print.
8. Resolution 1653, UNGAOR,16th Session, UN.doc. A/5100, 1962.
9. The view of British nuclear physicist and 1995 Nobel Peace Laureate, Joseph Rotblat, as cited by Brahma Chellaney, *UNIDIR Newsletter*, 39, 1998, p. 17.
10. Cited by Alyn Ware, 'The Nuclear Bomb: A Weapon in Search of a Target', *New Zealand International Review*, XXI, 4, p. 24.

11 Press Statement, United States Department of State, Washington DC, 8 July 1996.
12 See for example Robert Green (2000).
13 Dewes (1998), sections 4.2; 4.8; p. 402; p. 408. This thesis can be accessed at the University of New England (NSW); and Canterbury, Victoria and Waikato universities in New Zealand.
14 Richard Falk, 'Nightmare Weapons in a New World Order', in *World Court Project: International Launch*, Geneva: IPB: p. 9.
15 On prohibition of indiscriminate attack, see Articles 51 and 52 of Additional Protocols to the 1949 Geneva Conventions; on prohibition of mass killings, Article 3 (1a) 1949 Geneva Conventions, and Article 75 of Additional Protocols to the 1949 Geneva Conventions; on prohibition on use of terror in conduct of war, Geneva Convention IV 1949, and Article 33 and Article 51 of the Additional Protocols to the 1949 Geneva Conventions.
16 The Martens clause is included in Article 1 (2) of Addition Protocol I (1977) to the Geneva Conventions of 12 August 1949.
17 Keith Mothersson, *From Hiroshima to The Hague: a Guide to the World Court Project*, International Peace Bureau, Geneva, 1992; Dewes (1998: 239-40; 408).
18 For example the International Commission of Jurists (New Zealand and Australia branches), International Association for Democratic Lawyers, International Institute for Humanitarian Law, and the World Federalist Movement (Dewes, 1998: 409).
19 *Nuclear Tests Case (New Zealand v. France)*, (Interim Measures) *ICJ Reports*, 1973, pp. 135-39.
20 *Nuclear Tests Case (New Zealand v. France), ICJ Judgement,* 20 December 1974.
21 The list of 'Open Letters' is cited in Dewes (1998), pp. 462-64.
22 Australian Senate (Hansard), 29 August 1988, p. 382.
23 *World Court Project Bulletin,* (Wellington), 3, 1993, p. 3.
24 Author interview with New Zealand Ministry of Foreign Affairs officials, 10 December 1994.
25 46th World Health Assembly, WHO, A46/B Conference paper No.4.
26 *The Annual Register: A Record of World Events 1994*, London: Longman, p. 433.
27 Maj-Britt Theorin, 'Can Use of Nuclear Weapons Ever be Legal?' *Parliamentarians for Global Action*, December 1993, p. 8. Ambassador Mason of Canada's comments 'that hysteria was not too strong a word' for the nuclear weapons state response are cited by Peter Weiss et al., 'Introduction' (Draft Memorial in support of the WHO Application to the ICJ), *Transnational Law and Contemporary Problems*, 4, 2, 1994, p. 710; Dewes (1998: chapter 11).
28 See Peter Weiss, 'The World Court tackles the fate of the earth: an introduction to the ICJ advisory opinion on the legality of the threat and use of nuclear weapons', *Transnational Law and Contemporary Problems*, 7, 2, 1997, pp. 313-32; Richard A. Falk, 'The Nuclear Weapons Advisory Opinion and the new jurisprudence of global civil society', ibid., pp. 331-52; Michael J. Matheson 'The opinions of the International Court of Justice on the threat or use of nuclear weapons', *American Journal of International Law*, 91, 1997, pp. 417-35; Dapko Arkande, 'Nuclear Weapons, unclear law? Deciphering the Nuclear Weapons advisory opinion for the International Court', *The British Yearbook of International Law*, 68, 1997, pp. 165-217.
29 ICJ Nuclear Weapons Advisory Opinion, dissenting opinion of Judge Weeramanty, at 45, sec. III (8), reprinted in *International Legal Materials*, 809 and 1343, 902, 1996.
30 See Green (1995: 79-80).
31 Merav Datan and Alyn Ware, *Security and Survival: The Case for a Nuclear Weapons Convention*, Cambridge, Mass.: IALANA/IPPNW/INES, 1999, pp. 1-9.
32 Maj-Britt Theorin, 'Can Use of Nuclear Weapons Ever be Legal?', op. cit., 1993, p. 8.

50 *The Domestic Politics of International Relations*

33 This received international recognition when the New Zealand WCP gained an Honourable Mention award of the UNESCO 1998 Prize for Peace Education.
34 UN General Assembly doc. A/53/138.
35 Among abstentions were Canada, Germany, Greece, Italy, Netherlands, Norway, Japan and Australia.
36 Statement of 47 Conference on Disarmament members and observers, delivered by New Zealand Ambassador Pearson to the Special Session of the Conference on Disarmament, Geneva, 2 June 1998.
37 Krieger, David (1998), 'India's Nuclear Testing is a Wake-up Call to the World', *Nuclear Age Peace Foundation*, (online, http:// www.wagingpeace@napf.org, 15 May).

References

Alley, Roderic (1987), 'ANZUS and the Nuclear Issue', in Jonathan Boston and Martin Holland (eds), *The Fourth Labour Government*, Oxford: Oxford Universtiy Press, pp. 198-213.

Alley, Roderic (1999), 'The Public Dimension', in Bruce Brown (ed), *New Zealand in World Affairs III 1972-90*, Wellington: VUW Press/NZIIA, pp. 295-317.

Alley, Roderic and Ravenhill, John 'Labour and Foreign Relations', in Francis Castles, Rolf Gerritsen and Jack Vowles (eds), *The Great Experiment. Labour Parties and Public Policy Transformation in Australia and New Zealand*, Auckland: Auckland University Press, pp. 170-91.

Bercovitch, Jacob (ed) (1988), *ANZUS in Crisis. Alliance Management in International Affairs*, Christchurch: University of Canterbury/Macmillan Press.

Blackaby, Frank (1997), 'Time for a peasants' revolt', *The Bulletin of the Atomic Scientists*, 53, 6, November/December, p. 4.

Boanas-Dewes, Katie (1993), 'Participatory Democracy in Peace and Security Decision Making: the Aotearoa/New Zealand Experience', *Interdisciplinary Peace Research*, 5, 2, pp. 80-108.

Campbell, David (1987), 'The Domestic Sources of New Zealand Security Policy in Comparative Perspective', Working Paper 16, Canberra: ANU Peace Research Centre.

Canberra Commission Report (1996), (online, http://www.dfat.gov.au/dfat/).

Clark, Roger and Sann, Madeleine (eds) (1996), *The Case Against the Bomb: Marshall Islands, Samoa, and the Solomon Islands before the International Court of Justice in Advisory Proceedings on the Legality of the Threat or Use of Nuclear Weapons*, Camden: Rutgers University School of Law.

Clements, Kevin (1988), *Back From the Brink: the Creation of a Nuclear Free New Zealand*, Wellington Allen and Unwin.

de Madariaga, Salvador (1973), *Morning Without Noon. Memoirs*, Farnborough: Saxon House.

Dewes, Catherine (1998), *The World Court Project. The Evolution and Impact of an Effective Citizens' Movement*, unpublished PhD Thesis, University of New England.

Dewes, Kate and Green, Robert (1995), 'The History of the World Court Project, *Pacifica Review*, 7, 2, pp. 17-37.

Dewes, Kate and Green, Robert (1996), 'The World Court Project: How a Citizen Network Can Influence the United Nations', *Social Alternatives*, 15, 3, pp. 35-37.

Dewes, Kate and Green, Robert (1999), 'The World Court Project: History and Consequences', *Canadian Foreign Policy*, 7, 1, pp. 61-83.

Falk, Richard (1982), 'Political Anatomy of Nuclearism', in Robert Jay Lifton and Richard Falk, *Indefensible Weapons: The Political and Psychological Case Against Nuclearism*, New York: Basic Books, pp. 128-265.
Falk, Richard (1994), 'The United Nations and the Rule of Law', *Transnational Law and Contemporary Problems*, 4, 2, pp. 611-42.
Graham, Kennedy (1989), *National Security Concepts of States. New Zealand*, New York: Taylor and Francis.
Green, Robert (1995), 'Nuclear Weapons: The Legality Issue', *Medicine and War*, 11, 3, pp. 79-88.
Green, Robert (1998), *Fast Track to Zero Nuclear Weapons: The Middle Powers Initiative*, Cambridge Mass.: Middle Powers Initiative.
Green, Robert (2000), *The Naked Nuclear Emperor. Debunking Nuclear Deterrence. A Primer for Safer Security Strategies*, Christchurch: Disarmament and Security Centre.
Grief, Nicholas (1992), *The World Court Project on Nuclear Weapons and International Law*, Northampton Mass.: Aletheia Press.
Hanson, Marianne and Ungerer, Carl (1999), 'The Canberra Commission: Paths Followed, Paths Ahead', *Australian Journal of International Affairs*, 53, 1, pp. 5-17.
International Physicians for the Prevention of Nuclear War (1995), *Abolition 2000: Handbook for a World Without Nuclear Weapons*, IPPNW, Cambridge: Mass.
Keith, Sir Kenneth (1996 a), 'The International Court of Justice and Nuclear Weapons', *New Zealand International Review*, XXI, 1, pp. 2-23.
Keith, Sir Kenneth (1996 b), 'The Advisory Jurisdiction of the International Court of Justice: Some Comparative Reflections', *Australian Yearbook of International Law*, 17, 1996, pp. 39-58.
Lange, David (1990), *Nuclear Free-The New Zealand Way*, Australia: Penguin Books.
Levine, Stephen (1988), 'Labour to Power: Commentaries on the Lange Government's First Term', *Political Science*, 40, 2, pp. 74-83.
McMillan, Stuart (1987), *Neither Confirm Nor Deny: The Nuclear Ships Dispute between New Zealand and the United States*, Wellington: Allen and Unwin/Port Nicholson Press.
Mitrany, David (1933), *The Progress of International Government*, London: Allen and Unwin.
Mothersson, Keith (1992), *From Hiroshima to the Hague*, Geneva: International Peace Bureau.
Pugh, Michael C. (1989), *The ANZUS Crisis, Nuclear Visiting and Deterrence*, Cambridge: Cambridge University Press.
Roche, Douglas (1997), *The Ultimate Evil*, Toronto: James Lorimer and Co.
Sikkink, Kathyryn (1995), 'Human rights, Principled-Issue Networks and Sovereignty in Latin America', *International Organization*, 47, 3, pp. 411-42.
Tarrow, Sidney (1994), *Power in Movement. Social Movements, Collective Action and Politics*, Cambridge: Cambridge University Press.
Weiss, Peter, et al., (1994), 'Introduction' (Draft Memorial in support of the WHO Application to the ICJ), *Transnational Law and Contemporary Problems*, 4, 2, pp. 709-16.
Weiss, Peter (1997), 'Symposium: Nuclear Weapons, the World Court and Global Security', *Transnational Law and Contemporary Problems: Journal of University of Iowa College of Law*, 7, 2.

3 Australia and Climate Change

Introduction

An accumulating body of scientific evidence indicates causal linkages between human (anthropogenic) impacts and global warming. Fossil fuel burning, agriculture, and deforestation are injecting carbon dioxide, nitrous oxide, methane, and other greenhouse gases more quickly into the atmosphere than natural processes can remove them. These gases heighten earth surface temperatures by letting in solar radiation, but blocking reflected infra-red radiation back into space, as does a horticulturist's greenhouse. Knowledge of the greenhouse gas effect is not new, Swedish scientist Arrhenius providing seminal findings in 1896.[1] Because of their longevity, the long-term impacts of these gases are substantial – even should their accumulation cease. 'Put simply, the climate problem will always be worse than it appears to be' (Repetto and Lash, 1997: 85). However the international politicisation of climate change, global warming, and greenhouse gas emissions is a relatively recent occurrence.

Current greenhouse gas emissions levels have increased substantially. A widely noted Intergovernmental Panel on Climate Change (IPCC) Working Group, reported in 1995 that climate models 'project an increase in global mean surface temperature of about 1–3.5° C by 2100, with associated sea level increase of about 15–95 cm' (IPCC, 1995: 3). Impacts included 'an increase in some regions in the incidence of high temperature events, floods, droughts, with resultant consequences for fires, pest outbreaks, and ecosystem composition, structure, and functioning, including primary productivity' (IPCC, 1995: 3). After doubling in three decades, global carbon emissions stabilised briefly during the early 1990s following the collapse of the Soviet Union, but increased later in the decade to a figure of approximately 6.5 billion tons per annum. Although the science debate is incomplete, sufficient evidence exists indicating current uncertainties are less about whether emissions levels generate adverse effects, than their extent, incidence, and location. Looking ahead, the IPCC has reviewed 256 scenarios for future greenhouse gas emissions. This found the lower quartile of those scenarios gave 40 per cent growth by 2050 and the upper quartile 140 per cent growth (Nakicenovic et al, 1998).

Nevertheless, governments continue to voice uncertainty about the reliability of trends indicating global warming. Evident is wider 'lack of understanding of the interactions of climate change, the environment and the global socio-economic system' (Hasselmann, 1997: 225). Deliberate avoidance also occurs since modifying greenhouse emission impacts directly affects material interests, particularly the 'engine' of modern economics, energy policy (Skærseth 1995: 158). This is evident in the United States; with less than 5 per cent of the world's population, it accounts for 23 per cent of global energy related carbon dioxide emissions.[2] Without substantial reductions by the United States, an unlikely immediate prospect, greenhouse gas emissions worldwide will not decline.

Regardless of national situation, there is growing recognition that climate change will exact increasingly negative domestic environmental impacts. This includes worsening droughts in some locations, but heavier sudden rainfall concentrations in others, sea level rise, saline penetration of soils, and unstable fluctuations between La Niña and El Niño weather systems. Not all impacts will prove negative however, as plants in many regions could grow more rapidly.

Given long term cumulative emission effects, abatement costs will increase the longer they are delayed. Hence the IPCC warned policy makers to consider uncertainties against information 'indicating that climate-induced environmental changes cannot be reversed quickly, if at all, due to the long time scales associated with the climate system' (IPCC, 1995: 4). Economic risks of delay justify immediate introduction of abatement measures into energy systems.

Although international regulatory mechanisms designed to influence domestic environmental activities have increased, they are modest relative to the problems faced. Greenhouse gas abatement measures embrace problems of countries wanting to let others carry the abatement burden; equity incorporation under differing income levels and growth needs; the relationship between policy action and scientific certainty; instrumentality issues including quotas, taxes and tradeable permits; technology application to alternative energy sources; related policy areas including population growth; and location of diplomatic responses within a context of historical North/South differences

(Cline, 1992: 323). Outcomes may also depend upon the distribution of relative gains and losses, nature and numbers of interests involved, available information about preferences, and opportunities available under prevailing international political conditions (Peterson, 1998: 415). In sum, we observe here a complex array of domestic/international interactivity.

Added complexities embroil the politics of climate change. They straddle technical and scientific concerns, demographic change, ecological responsibility, and establishment of workable transnational law and institutions. Pertinent constraints include weakness among intergovernmental structures, short-term goal seeking, political autonomy, and longstanding historical conflicts lurking within the international system's cultural, economic, and political heterogeneity (Hurrell, 1995: 152). Numerous barriers impede effective collective management and appropriate national implementation capacity. The science debate, and particularly its interpretation, complicates the formation of informed public opinion needed to support national abatement policies. Beyond that, the organising of transnational environmental regimes make domestic politics seem simple by comparison (Lipschutz, 1997: 97).

Such difficulty confirms realist beliefs as to the unreliability of international co-operation when confronted by the demands of state interest, contingency, and perceived relative national gains. Contemplation of a future beyond the next decade, let alone the next century, is not welcome ground for immediate policy deliberation. Those alive now are unenthusiastic about altering energy habits and lifestyles for the sake of those unborn. Although the precautionary principle and intergenerational equity have begun to register, their recognition as practised rules of customary international law is limited.

Numerous developing countries harbour suspicions towards international environmental regime formation. They see it linked to 'conditionality', and denounce attempts to attach environmental conditions to flows of trade, aid, investment, loans, or technology transfer. Whatever their validity, these claims illustrate how the politics of climate change – as an equity issue – penetrates international and domestic demands, constraints and interests.

Australia and the Framework Convention

By the 1970s, Australia faced increasingly volatile and unsettled conditions of international interdependence in energy. Unlike some fellow Organisation for Economic Cooperation and Development (OECD) members, Australia did not treat the 'oil shocks' of the 1970s as a 'wake-up call' to begin moving beyond traditional energy sources. A strongly consumer–oriented society, and an economy heavily wedded to a fossil fuels energy base, viewed calls for greenhouse gas reduction with apprehension.

This chapter traces Australia's policy towards greenhouse gases reductions up to, and since the key December 1997 Kyoto conference of parties to the United Nations Framework Convention on Climate Change (FCCC). From a posture as good international environmental citizen during the 1980s, Australia's approach towards global warming hardened perceptibly during the 1990s. This occurred as its governments encountered greater difficulty in squaring objectives endorsed internationally with industrial, agricultural, and energy policies pursued at home. These tensions are addressed by considering how the FCCC's evolution evoked particular Australian responses over the climate change question. With that ground traversed, we then ask what this case offers about the nature and effects of domestic/international political interactivity.

With the exception of some liquid petroleum requirements, Australia's energy resource base provides most of its needs. This allows relatively low cost production, facilitating energy intensive enterprises such as alumina refining and smelting. The electricity supply industry utilises coal for 80 per cent of its production. Australia is the world's largest coal exporter; with natural gas and uranium added, it is the third largest OECD energy exporter. The economy is also heavily dependent on the export of energy-intensive processed primary products.

Data supplied in 1995 under FCCC reporting provisions indicated 37 per cent of Australia's greenhouse gas emissions came from energy production; 23 per cent land use and forestry; 17 per cent agriculture; 11 per cent transport; and 6 per cent fuel fugitives. Land use and forestry data is not fully reliable due to information gaps (Gumley, 1997: 350).

National councils representing coal, aluminium production, agriculture, minerals, and energy extraction, enjoy regular access to the highest political levels in Australia. They constitute a platform of shared interests actively promoting a robust expansion of national economic growth and trade opportunities. This has predisposed the government to treat emissions cuts as subordinate to industry interests. The high export profile of coal and minerals industries augments their influence over climate change policy. When looking to Asia, Australian Energy Minister Parer claimed that 'an effective, long term strategy to mitigate climate change will need to take into account the important role of coal in the region's development'.³

From Rio to Berlin

In 1992, the United Nations Conference on Environment and Development (UNCED or 'Earth Summit') formulated the FCCC. This called for a 'stabilization of greenhouse gas concentrations in the atmosphere at a level that would prevent dangerous anthropogenic interference with the climate system' (Article 2). The term 'dangerous' was unspecified, a determination perhaps ultimately clarified by the future affordability of insurance premiums (Edmonds, 1998: 129). Under the FCCC, industrialised countries (Annex I parties) entered a non-binding pledge to voluntarily stabilise their 1990 greenhouse gas emissions levels by the year 2000.

Parties undertook to protect the climate system on a basis of equity through common, but differentiated responsibilities according to respective capacities. The FCCC approved the principle of greenhouse gas emissions reduction sharing, or 'joint implementation'. This meant investor countries could financially support reduction projects in recipient countries in exchange for emission credits. Specific emission reduction targets were not set for developing countries. Richer economies, it was claimed, bore historical responsibility for greenhouse gas accumulations, and accordingly incurred most obligation for their reduction. Inclusiveness and precautionary principles would embrace cost effectiveness, if under different national socio-economic circumstances.

When perusing this language, the fine hand of calculated diplomatic ambiguity is soon discernible. However, terminology designed to read differently in order to sell the FCCC politically, necessarily generated problems for implementation specifics. Prescribed means for removal of greenhouse gases, or 'sinks' (Article 4(2)), entailed 'possibly the most opaque treaty language ever drafted' (Sands, 1995: 277). Policy divisions within the United States delegation over priorities helped contribute to this equivocation. Senior White House advisors, in particular John Sununu, believed controlling emissions would prove costly to the United States economy (Harris, 1998). Sununu resisted moves to fund developing country transitions, and evinced scepticism towards scientific evidence that global warming was sufficiently serious to justify United States cost accommodations (Victor, 1995: 365). Although challenged by the United States Environmental Protection Agency, the strength of Sununu's internal position was noted with interest by Australian officials.

Influenced by the 1987 Brundtland Report, the FCCC attempted to square potentially conflictual principles of sustainable development, the precautionary principle, 'polluter pays', intergenerational equity, and broad-based participation. Fragility characterised compromises trying to reconcile public demands, diplomatic interest, cost effectiveness, ethical standards, as well as energy, industrial, and commercial systems in transition. Nevertheless, the FCCC institutionalised a system of complex policy engagement likely to continue well into the new century. Australia was an early signatory to the FCCC, which entered into force in March 1994. By mid-1999, it had gained 179 ratifications and accessions.

When the FCCC's First Conference of Parties (COP) met in Berlin in 1995, it was evident major industrialised states would not meet their voluntary greenhouse gas reduction targets by 2000. Indeed, an Australian Cabinet submission on domestic FCCC implementation indicated no more than minimal commitment to these reductions (Henderson, 1995: 238-39). The meeting agreed to a schedule (the so-called 'Berlin Mandate') aimed at producing a quantified, legally binding agreement on reductions, needed to guide post–2000 phased reductions of greenhouse gas emissions. This would comprise a Protocol to the FCCC strengthening Annex I party commitments through a conference subsequently convened at Kyoto in December 1997. At Berlin, Australia joined Japan, Canada, the United States and New Zealand in seeking reduction commitments from more advanced, industrialising developing countries such as China and India. This faced strong opposition from developing countries; rightly or wrongly they construed this as an attempt to exploit their existing divisions.[4]

In 1996, the goal of legally binding emission emissions limitations and reductions received confirmation at a second conference of parties in Geneva. Because oil producing countries over-played the veto potential inherent in consensus formulation procedures, the meeting simply took note of contrasting positions. Australia opposed this side-lining of the consensus principle. The European Union (EU), the United States, and most developing countries, indicated that they would push on to formulate a Protocol, regardless of any dissenting minority. Australian officials reiterated the differentiation principle, and the necessity for emission reduction targets that reflected individual country circumstances.

Approaching Kyoto, key group positions included:
- United States, supported by Canada, Japan and Australia, favouring an agreement that included legally binding targets for developed nations; maximum flexibility in achieving them; and participation by all countries in greenhouse gas reduction measures;
- China and the 'Group of 77' (G77) developing countries demanding industrialised country, Annex I parties agree to quantified, legally-binding objectives for emission limitation within specific time frames (e.g. 2005, 2010, and 2020);
- The EU recommending a uniform 15 per cent reduction from 1990 levels of three principal greenhouse gases by the year 2010;
- The Alliance of Small Island States (AOSIS), calling for legally binding measures upon industrialised countries, requiring a 20 per cent reduction of their 1990 greenhouse gas levels by the year 2005.[5] (AOSIS was then a 42–member consultative caucus, formed in 1990 to lobby on climate change and development issues, particularly as they affect small island countries).

Regarding remedies, the EU favoured a co-ordinated policy approach ahead of market mechanisms. The Americans supported market mechanisms such as energy taxes and international carbon trading, but insisted countries choose their own approaches. Developing countries resisted commitments to specific international measures, although they had raised national energy prices and cut local subsidies in some instances. A news media outlet characterised these positions as the EU wanting 'dramatic, immediate regulatory action for what it regards as a major threat. The United States prefers long-term market oriented responses to a problem it considers serious, though not immediately pressing. And most developing countries are happy enough to consider global warming a problem so long as it is not theirs'.[6]

Australia's 'Special Case'

Before the Kyoto conference and since, the differentiation principle has stayed central to Australia's official position over greenhouse gas reductions. In essence, this holds that to achieve cost efficiencies, each country should follow policies and measures tailored to meet national circumstances. Hence future agreements 'must provide that each country's particular circumstances, economic costs and available opportunities to limit emissions be taken into account in determining an equitable target for each participating state'.[7] This approach rejected across the board emission reduction targets as unfair and ineffectual.

To back its position before the Kyoto conference, the Australian government marshalled an array of findings, data, and selected expert opinion. A Foreign Affairs and Trade Report asserted that emissions stabilisation at 1990 levels would cost in excess of 90,000 jobs, and reduce an estimated $A12 billion from $A68 billion of planned energy investments.[8] Reduction costs would mean 'little or no global environmental benefit' on account of so-called 'carbon leakage' – that is, the international transfer of economic activities generating greenhouse gas emissions to developing countries granted effective exclusion from the proposed reduction regime.

The Foreign Affairs and Trade Report's findings were disputed, although not as vigorously as those of the Australian Bureau for Agriculture and Resource Economics (ABARE). That agency claimed a ten per cent emission cut would raise electricity charges and lower the standard of living. Under ABARE auspices, a complex model (MEGABARE/GIGABARE) generated findings that should 'business as usual' conditions prevail between 1995 and 2020, projected OECD emissions would grow at 0.85 per cent, compared to 3.38 percent in developing countries. Stabilisation of greenhouse concentrations would prove effective only if all countries participated in abatement strategies (ABARE, April 1997: 2-3). The Australian government backed this claim; it estimated that every person in Australia faced material losses if 1990 level greenhouse gas emissions should sustain ten per cent cuts by 2020.[9]

Differentiation Contested

Underpinning Australia's official case was an omnibus concept of 'net per capita welfare loss' between countries. This comprised inter-related criteria of gross domestic product (GDP) per capita growth; projected population growth; emissions intensity of GDP (the higher this factor, the lower the emissions calculation); emissions intensity of exports; and fossil fuel intensity of exports.

How did officialdom sustain these arguments and to what response? To focus that debate, salient aspects of the Australian government's position are followed by rejoinders from the Australian Conservation Foundation, a research centre supportive of strong greenhouse gas reduction measures.[10]

High GDP Growth. Because of its strong rate of growth, Australia should face less stringent emission reduction targets.

Response: Enhanced GDP would generate sufficient income and capacity to implement emission reduction. Australia could achieve so-called 'no regrets' cuts without difficulty.

High Population Growth. Countries with high population growth warranted less stringent targets; while the EU's population was likely to grow by only 1.7 per cent over the 1990-2020 period, Australia's would increase by 30 per cent.

Response: Australia's increased population would generate economic and other benefits; it was a legitimate charge against these accrued advantages that they generate the resources to fund emission reductions.

Emissions Intensity of GDP. Countries with high emissions intensity should be subject to less stringent emission reduction targets because of their more limited scope to take mitigating action.

Response: Countries with high emissions GDP intensity face low marginal abatement costs. These intensities partly reflect market imperfections carrying scope for 'no regrets' emission reduction potential in energy production, and controls on land clearance.

Emission Intensive Export Profile. The cost of limiting emissions in relevant export industries would dent Australia's international competitiveness. This would encourage job and plant relocation offshore to emission intensive sites where controls are non-existent.

Response: Although Australia's distinctive emission intensive export profile is a factor, this ignores a legacy of substantial federal and state subsidisation of fossil fuel industries and weak thermal efficiencies in brown coal locations. If Australia is serious about international competitiveness, then such subsidisation is dispensable.

Fossil Fuel Intensity. Because of its significant level of fossil fuel exports, Australia warranted less stringent emission targets.

Response: This has confused fossil fuel trade with emission reduction targets. Greenhouse concerns might lower demand and prices for fossil fuels, but this would not justify compensating exporters through less stringent emission targets. Doing so would result in fossil fuel importing countries reducing emissions as Australian exporters continued on a business as usual basis – a perverse outcome.

These exchanges failed to foster common ground. Partly this was because those expressing strongest opposition also recommended significant structural changes to Australian energy, industry, and consumption patterns. They looked to IPCC findings that indicated technically possible, economically feasible reductions in net greenhouse gas emissions through improved efficiencies in industry, transport, commercial and residential sectors; more efficient conversion of fossil fuels; and a slowing of deforestation.[11] Opponents also utilised a 1997 International Energy Agency (IEA) survey. This found Australia's low cost energy and low energy taxes 'makes investments in energy efficiency less profitable than in the average IEA country ... the results of energy audits, the absence of general mandatory standards for buildings and domestic appliances, and all the high costs of fuel consumption for passenger cars all indicate there is great improvement for improvements in the energy sector'.[12]

A broader division existed over whether to treat threat or opportunity as the greater priority in determining future national greenhouse emission cuts policy. Was the glass half empty or half full? From the government's perspective, the opportunity costs of unilateral abatement measures stood to increase through liberalised trade and investment arrangements presaged by the World Trade Organisation (WTO), and possibly Asia Pacific Economic Cooperation (APEC) innovations. Assuming compliance with abatement measures, domestic industry could lose competitiveness. By contrast, those opposing official policy saw an emission cuts regime offering opportunities to develop renewables technologies. These could help meet local needs as well as find markets abroad.

Table 3.1 Carbon Dioxide Emissions 1996: Australia Compared

	Total (mmt)	Per capita (mt)	Petroleum (mmt)	Coal (mmt)
USA	5301	20.0	621	521
China	3363	2.8	138	652
Russia	1579	10.7	102	125
Japan	1168	9.3	191	75
India	997	1.1	61	161
Germany	861	10.5	106	82
UK	557	9.5	66	38
Canada	409	13.7	63	32
South Korea	408	9.0	71	31
Italy	403	7.0	76	11
Ukraine	397	7.8	15	48
France	361	6.2	69	14
Poland	356	9.2	13	74
Mexico	348	3.8	66	5
Australia	**306**	**16.7**	**29**	**41**
South Africa	298	7.3	17	78
Brazil	273	1.7	62	8
Saudi Arabia	268	13.8	43	-
Iran	267	4.4	42	1
Indonesia	245	1.2	35	10
Spain	232	6.0	43	17

mmt: million metric tons   mt: metric tons

Sources: World Bank; US Department of Energy

Controversy occurred in debates over the data reliability, objectivity, assumptions, and methodology utilised in the ABARE/GIGABARE – sponsored model. It was animated by revelations that the model's research was 80 per cent funded by interests actively marketing fossil fuels including Broken Hill Proprietary, the Australian Coal Association, Exxon, Mobil Oil Australia, and Texaco. In response, the Australian Conservation Foundation filed a complaint with the Commonwealth Ombudsman who investigated the transparency of fossil fuel industry contributions to ABARE's applied research funding. The February 1998 Ombudsman's report criticised use of a $A50,000 entry tag for joining the ABARE research steering committee. This 'did not conform to the characteristics of a government steering committee dealing with an important – and controversial public policy matter' (Ombudsman ABARE Report, 1998: 4). Furthermore ABARE 'adopted a funding structure and administrative practices for its climate change research projects which failed to adequately protect ABARE as a public sector research agency from allegations of undue influence by vested interests' (Ombudsman ABARE Report, 1998: 3). The Ombudsman also noted that sponsors contributed funds so that ABARE's climate change models could develop quickly enough to inform government policy before the December 1997 Kyoto conference (Ombudsman ABARE Report, 1998: 18).

Elsewhere, predictions about the electricity sector's greenhouse gas emissions were disputed because they assumed a 60 per cent growth in coal fired power sources. ABARE claims that a ten per cent emission cut would raise electricity charges and lower the standard of living, faced challenge from local economists and the Australia Institute.[13] The model's perceived failure to account for potential energy efficiency improvements was noted in a June 1997 statement signed by 131 local professional economists. They urged the government to participate more positively with fellow OECD members through efforts to conclude agreed targets for greenhouse gas emission reductions. Further, 'the economic modelling studies on which the government is relying to assess the impacts of reducing Australia's greenhouse gas emissions overestimate the costs and underestimate the benefits of reducing emissions'.[14]

These episodes confirmed claims that, over large scale environmental problems, knowledge itself may prove a source of conflict, particularly when major interests face unresolved scientific uncertainties (Victor, 1995: 364). To some extent, the Australian experience with ABARE mirrored what was occurring internationally under the IPCC: namely, the way that strong contest over public issues can render factual objectivity the instrument of bargaining about values. In a contest of core material interests, arguments based on scientific evidence could not match government calls on public attention. Those claims insisted that greenhouse gas reductions meant putting the jobs and livelihoods of Australians at risk. Countering these claims was difficult for science professionals, more attuned to getting at the truth than the arts of public persuasion.

By presenting its position as promoting jobs, growth, and national economic well being, the government believed it enjoyed public backing. However, Greenpeace Australia polling surveys findings indicated majorities did not believe the country should increase greenhouse gas emissions if other developed countries made cuts. An AC Nielsen-McNair poll, sampling 1000 voters in November 1997, found 76 per cent of respondents disagreeing with the government's wanting to increase greenhouse gas emissions while other developed countries sustained cuts. Having greenhouse gas emission cuts made legally binding was supported by 71 per cent, while 67 per cent wanted the Australian government to take firmer action to reduce global warming. A separate survey of Australian company directors, conducted by accounting firm KPMG and the Australian Institute of Company Directors, found that 69 per cent of those polled favoured the establishment of greenhouse gas reduction targets for Australia, 70 per cent believing they should be legally binding (Greenpeace, 27 November 1997). Greenpeace International concluded that Australia's official position on emissions left them nowhere to go other than upwards.[15] Nor was it clear how government concern to provide 'breathing space' adjustment for mining industry transnationals, squared with demands made by these corporates for substantial reductions to the industry support, welfare, and tariff protection afforded to domestic Australian interests.

How effectively did the domestic interests opposing Australia's official position on greenhouse gas reductions utilise international linkages? When assessing domestic opposition to its climate change policy, the government believed environmental activism was losing its bite. After peaking in the early 1990s, this had conceded ground to competing public concerns over jobs, health, and republicanism. Yet although the tempo of environmental activism had reduced, general concern for environmental welfare remained intact (Pakulski, Tranter and Crook, 1998: 246). Australian environmental lobbies have found their influence capacity contingent upon numbers; political and bureaucratic leverage skills; and resources available through which to mobilise support, enhance networking, and utilise news media outlets (Stewart and Jones, 1997: 954). Over climate change, these determinants were no more than partially evident.

Greenpeace International publicised its disquiet over Australia's stance, particularly during the lead-up to the 1997 Kyoto conference. Other external connections were utilised, but international messages designed to shape Australian opinion was either scattered, reactive, or episodic. This was not surprising. In previous environmental campaigns, public purchase on the issue was helped by target specificity – acid rain for example, or the widening 'ozone hole' detected over Antarctica. In the latter instance, this was the 'smoking gun' that galvanised pressure needed to finalise the 1987 Montreal Protocol's objectives of phasing out use of chlorofluorocarbons. Compared to ozone depletion, greenhouse gas emission effects – although pervasive – were harder to isolate for accountability and remedy identification purposes.

Domestic Institutions

Australia's international position on greenhouse gas emission reductions harnessed domestic resistance to modification of existing local energy practices. Complex inter-governmental arrangements facilitate this resistance, with the administrative capacity needed to implement international agreements resting at state levels. While federal authorities set tax measures, and states provide infrastructure and determine some pricing policies (provided they are not excise measures), local authorities supervise building controls and waste management – activities with significant scope for greenhouse gas reduction. Implementation lags behind stated intent, a good example being the precautionary principle which commonwealth, state, and local governments have signed but only as a guiding non-binding accord.

Some states have privatised and expanded fossil fuel based energy and private transport systems. In its 1997 budget, the Victorian government reduced taxes on petrol (Gumley, 1997: 352). Co-ordination between levels of government sees lack of alignment between fiscal and functional responsibilities (Hendy 1996:115). This complicates the provision of a simplified structure offering incentives to curb excess energy use, and encourage renewable technologies.

Another difficulty is the variable use of price, fiscal, and investment mechanisms to encourage efficient energy use applications. Where information gaps exist about how best to increase energy efficiency, then market functions do not perform effectively (Walker 1996: 483). Experts have criticised the use of *Develop Australia Bonds* to invest in greenhouse *enhancing* infrastructures, such as additional electricity supply capacity at the expense of solar power renewable energy sources (Pears and Wilkenfeld: 1997). Previous policy has also left its legacies. When the world price of oil approached $A40 a barrel in the late 1970s, and as heavy debt exposure and excess capacity appeared a lesser evil, the Federal government helped states expand electricity generating capacity in expectation of a continuing minerals resources boom (Saddler 1996: 471).

Cutting emissions risks exacerbating state divisions between relatively more energy efficient locations in Queensland and Western Australia, and older, unrefurbished, relatively labour intensive facilities in Victoria and New South Wales. Should an open market for emission credits eventuate, the less efficient, labour intensive facilities face heavier adjustment burdens. Allowing older industries time to adjust ('grandfathering'), and either foregoing or downsizing new capital intensive and export-oriented investment projects risks export growth, even though preserving some jobs. Overall, regional economic differences within Australia's federal structure have constrained its support for international environmental agreements. To a local observer 'our country's environmental problems are huge and complex. They will not be adequately addressed if governments limp along in the bearpit of federalism as it is now played out' (Toyne, 1994: 190).

How have these issues played in the national political arena? Among the Howard Coalition's parliamentary opponents, the Australian Labour Party supported cross-border trading discounts on emissions. This would permit Australia's gaining credit for net greenhouse gas emission reductions, where local production was relatively more environmentally efficient than previously utilised offshore processes.[16] This was scarcely the stuff of strong opposition. When in office, Labour was never more than lukewarm about greenhouse gas reductions, unwilling to impose costs on either industry or consumers. The Australian Democrats, initially at least, believed substantial cuts to greenhouse gas emissions possible through application of rigorous efficiency standards to transport and industry, rendering a carbon tax unnecessary.[17] Most opposed to the official line, the Australian Greens supported ambitious AOSIS targets that sought industrialised country 1990 greenhouse gas levels cut 20 per cent by 2005.

Although environmental protest interests had access to advisory channels, this was insufficient to challenge official policy with its links to major industry interests and organised labour. The business, industry and federal bureaucratic nexus inherited from previous Hawke-Keating Labour administrations, was by now increasingly institutionalised (McEachern, 1993:182). In addition, the government enjoyed significant support from sections of the broadsheet print media. High profile International Editor of *The Australian*, Paul Kelly, emerged as a committed proponent of the government's cause. Following the December 1997 Kyoto conference he decried 'the complete refusal of so many people throughout the year to accept the integrity of Howard's up-front defence of Australia's national interest over greenhouse gas emissions'.[18]

Australia and the 1997 Kyoto Conference

In the run-up to the December 1997 Kyoto Conference of FCCC Parties, Australia's international position on greenhouse gas emission cuts became increasingly isolated. Canberra rejected a Japanese proposal that industrialised countries cut their 1990 levels by an average of 5 per cent by 2012. In fact, this proposal accepted the differentiation principle; it helped accommodate Australia's position suggesting that it need reduce by no more than 1.8 per cent from 1990 levels. In June 1997, United States Ambassador to Canberra, Genta Hawkins Holmes, warned the Howard government that it would need to compromise on greenhouse gas emissions. She criticised Australia's 'relatively inefficient use of hydrocarbon energy'.[19] Rejecting emission reduction proposals advanced by the United States, Japan, and the EU, Prime Minister Howard claimed 80 per cent of Australia's exports – petroleum products, basic metals, agriculture and chemicals – comprised energy and greenhouse intensive goods.[20] Australia's stance also faced attack from international conservation lobbies, provoked sharp exchanges with EU governments, and engendered hostility among island state colleagues in the South Pacific Forum.

Hostility to the EU 'bubble'

A particular target for Australian criticism was the so-called EU greenhouse gas reduction 'bubble' formula. Here, the EU proposed a uniform 15 per cent cut in greenhouse gas emissions from 1990 levels by 2020, for both itself and other industrial nations. However, actual targets for respective EU members differed widely, spanning a 40 per cent rise for Portugal to a 30 per cut for Luxembourg. For whatever reasons – closing former East Germany's inefficient smokestack industries, French nuclear power, or continuing fallout from the Thatcherite blitz on uneconomic British coal pits – key EU players had reduced greenhouse gas emissions. In parlance the Australians understood, these were runs on the board, an achievement that British Environment Minister Prescott believed the Australian government needed to appreciate when responding to Canberra's attacks on the EU position. Prescott used these results to warn Australia about the unacceptability of the exceptions it sought.[21]

To Australia and others however, the averaging process contained serious anomalies. Bigger reductions by some EU members, such as Germany and Belgium, allowed leeway for substantial increases by Portugal, Greece and Spain. Allowing such internal differences, but opposing Australia's stance on differentiation smacked of hypocrisy. In effect, the 'bubble' principle was carrying 'free-riders' among some EU members avoiding the international disapprobation now facing Australia. Canberra however did not rule out the 'bubble' principle's applying elsewhere, including emissions trading within Australia (Wilkenfeld, 1997: 15).

South Pacific Frictions

Within its immediate regional neighbourhood, Australia's greenhouse gas emissions policy provoked sharp exchanges. At the September 1997 South Pacific Forum heads of government meeting in the Cook Islands, Australia insisted that island state support for the AOSIS position, and for uniform targets was totally unacceptable. Either targets for greenhouse emissions should operate from a differentiated basis recognizing equity of national sacrifice, or they remain voluntary. Although criticism of Australia's position from Pacific Island countries was not new, having surfaced at the 1995 Berlin COP meeting, in this instance it was more barbed.[22] To palpable island state resentment, the 1997 Forum's position over greenhouse gas emission limits was diluted to accommodate Australia's interests. This called for the 'highest level of net reduction in global greenhouse gas emissions by means of a legally binding protocol or other legal instrument' (South Pacific Forum, 1997:12).

Tuvalu Prime Minister Paeniu regarded this outcome as 'just a win by John Howard against 15 nations. Being small, we depend on them so much, we had to give in to what they wanted. From Australia there was no compromise, it was just no, no, no'.[23] Paeniu insisted that island state dependence on Australian aid left little option other than acquiescence to Canberra's pressure. Cook Islands Prime Minister Henry indicated Forum members were unhappy with Australia, but had agreed to preserve the group's unity.[24] The confrontation had a sub-text, occurring shortly after unflattering observations about Pacific Island state policies and leaderships had appeared in leaked Australian government documents.[25] The President of Nauru, Kinza Clodumur, said he was not impressed when Howard 'openly scorns the critical nature of the situation in order to bow to the will of the fossil fuel industry in Australia'.[26]

Australia's pre-Kyoto Positioning

Immediately preceding the November 1997 Vancouver APEC Summit, Howard announced a five year A$180 million greenhouse plan. This would cut emissions growth by a third from levels forecast between 1990 and 2010. The government hoped to see this goal achieved by voluntary means, an approach that did not impress critics.[27] The package made no allocation for research into alternative energy. That followed the government's controversial May 1997 decision to retire the Energy Research and Development Corporation (ERDC), an entity promoting energy conservation and alternative technology research.

Scientific opinion in Australia voiced resentment over the cost-cutting that forced ERDC closure. This came from a government funding a new nuclear reactor research facility at Lucas Heights in suburban Sydney, and assisting a Queensland shale oil project considered environmentally and economically suspect. In the political arena, the Australian Democrats alleged ERDC abolition had occurred at the prompting of Resources and Energy Minister Senator Parer, a figure holding significant personal interests in coal mining.[28]

In local consultation prior to the Kyoto conference, the government effectively sidelined that component of Australia's internationally reputable climate change scientific community opposing its policy. Advice from Graeme Pearman went unheeded, then leading the country's largest programme of climate research at the Commonwealth Scientific and Industrial Research Organisation (Pockley, 1997: 323).

In a transparent pre-conference manoeuvre, Australia's earlier projections about a possible 28 per cent increase in greenhouse gas emissions, were 'reduced' to 18 per cent, although Canberra believed it unlikely the Kyoto conference would accept that level of increase. Howard admitted as much by refusing to confirm it as final, since doing so could surrender 'bargaining chips' and 'telegraph in advance our negotiating position' (Lunn, 1997). Australia however threatened to walk out of the Kyoto conference if its key objectives were not met.

As the Kyoto conference approached, the Howard government claimed Australia was being unfairly singled out for simply following national interests principles pursued by most states across other issues. One Nation Party propaganda, and resentment that strong Asian competitors like Singapore qualified as 'developing countries' on the climate change issue were added irritants.[29] A certain public alienation from international policy making processes was another factor. Although not alluding to climate change controversy, former Governor General Sir Ninian Stephen spoke of a decline in national sovereignty where 'policy affecting Australia's citizens is determined at levels altogether too remote, in international forums by people largely immune to the sorts of pressures that citizens can still exert over policy making by Australian governments if sufficiently determined and if their determination is shared by sufficient others'.[30]

The observation was relevant. High-profile conservation cases have featured as substantive challenges to the federal parliament's treaty implementation powers in areas of traditional state concern. Australia's participation in international environmental law-making has aroused more domestic controversy than any other aspects of international law (Tsamenyi, 1995: 171). High Court rulings, upholding relevant federal legislation as a valid exercise of the external affairs power, incurred local resentment.[31]

The Kyoto Conference and Outcome

After intense deliberations that almost collapsed over developing country objections to buying and selling pollution rights and their commitments to emission curbs, the Kyoto conference set legally binding targets for future reductions of greenhouse gas emissions.[32] Agreed national targets ranged from eight per cent for Switzerland, many Central and East European states and the EU; seven per cent for the United States; and six per cent for Japan and Canada. Some states, including Russia, made commitments to stabilise their emissions. Increases were permitted to Norway and Iceland of one and ten per cent respectively. Industrialised and former Eastern bloc states agreed to reduce their overall emissions of six greenhouse gases by at least 5 per cent between 2008 and 2012.

Cuts in the three most important gases – carbon dioxide, methane, and nitrous oxide – were measured against a 1990 base year; those for three long-lived industrial gases (hydrofluorocarbons, perfluorocarbons and sulphur hexafluoride) against either a 1990 or 1995 baseline. This mattered for Australia because targeting six key gases rather than three (as favoured by the EU), eased pressure for reduction of carbon dioxide, coal-related emissions.

Australia achieved an increase of eight per cent, well below the 18 per cent demanded, but doubtless an outcome Canberra gladly accepted given the terms involved. Significantly, Australia secured agreement to have carbon released from previous land clearance incorporated in the formula used to calculate Australia's 1990 greenhouse gas emissions baseline. Extracted through hard bargaining during the conference's concluding phases, this represented a major concession. Some estimates claimed land clearing accounted for as much as 24 per cent of Australia's 1990 greenhouse emissions. This added a big buffer cushioning Australia's estimated net fossil fuel emissions. Land clearance incorporation was thus an essential item for Canberra, loss of which would have seen it reject any final deal done at Kyoto. For one estimate, the inclusion of land clearing meant emissions per head in 1990 rose from about 21 tonnes per year to about 26 tonnes. This made Australia officially the world's highest greenhouse emitter per capita.[33]

The Kyoto Protocol also established emissions trading, 'joint implementation' between developed countries, and a 'clean development mechanism' to facilitate joint emission reduction projects between developed and developing countries through project-based emissions reduction technology transfer. Under the Protocol, countries gained the opportunity to claim credit for increases to carbon 'sinks', mostly forests.

Adoption of the legally binding emissions targets specified under the Protocol is contingent upon its ratification by at least 55 countries. This has to incorporate Annex I countries which accounted for 55 per cent of the 1990 carbon dioxide emissions of Annex I parties. By August 1999, the Kyoto Protocol had been signed by 84 states (including Australia) and received 14 accessions and ratifications, none of which included an Annex I party. Signatories included the United States, although American ratification remains a remote prospect after the Senate carried without dissent an October 1997 resolution indicating that, without 'meaningful' participation from developing countries, it would block any agreement submitted for ratification.

The Australian government was pleased with its Kyoto conference achievement, Prime Minister Howard welcoming it as a 'splendid result, particularly gratifying for Australia' (Taylor, 1997: 15). Threats made by Australia during 1997 that it would exit the FCCC if it did not get a Kyoto outcome that it could accept carried credibility. Senior Kyoto conference official Zammit-Cutajar believed it likely Australia would have rejected attempts to restrict its demands and that 'they would have walked away from it' (Taylor, 1997:15). This assumed a sufficient number of key actors wanted an agreement enough to have it stretched to encompass Australian demands. Chief EU negotiator Ritt Bjerregaard reproached Australia, saying that it had 'got away with it' at Kyoto, its position now 'a problem for the future' (Taylor, 1997: 15). These post-conference expostulations counted little to Canberra.

Australia's hopes that the Kyoto Protocol might commit third world countries – in particular China – towards additional emissions reductions were disappointed. Like Washington, Canberra believed that an agreement lacking full and effective developing country participation rendered it weak and inequitable. Yet the Australian government faced the difficulty of wanting criteria it sought for itself denied to others; increased GDP and population growth claims used to justify exemptions could also apply to developing countries. Canberra rejected this argument, claiming 'we see differentiation as an enticement for developing countries to eventually come on board'.[34]

Finally, the Kyoto Protocol legitimised flexibility by allowing emission abatement to occur in relatively low cost locations. This was approved through joint implementation, the clean development mechanism and emissions trading. However no agreement was reached as to the principles and guidelines needed to steer an emissions trading regime. Significantly, the Protocol included a condition (Article 17) that such trading remain *supplemental* to domestic emissions limitation and reduction commitments.

Post-Kyoto

The Sustainable Energy Industries Council of Australia called the Kyoto outcome a setback for sustainable local gas industries and their job creation capacity. Whatever the Government's 'commitment' to reduce emissions, the reality remained an increase over 1990 levels, achievable by land clearance alone, and without need to cut energy waste or encourage renewable energy sources.[35] The Council saw no evidence that the Government understood the potential contribution of renewable energy and energy efficiencies, whether to abatement or the Australian economy generally.

When American Secretary of State Albright visited Australia in July 1998, she claimed that 'in both our nations, we have those who insist that the scientific warnings are wrong; or that, even if they are right, we can't afford to take the steps required to slow the release of greenhouse gases. But the one thing we truly cannot afford to do is wait and see. For if the warnings are right, the cost of reversing climate change and cleaning up the damage will be infinitely greater than the cost of preventing it'.[36] This message carried little weight. Soon after, Senator Parer confirmed the contents of minutes leaked from an Australian and New Zealand Minerals and Energy Council meeting. They revealed that the Australian Cabinet had decided not to proceed with ratification of the Kyoto agreement until the United States did so. According to Senator Parer 'our position was very clear as was the US. They are not going to ratify it until the developing countries come in, and we are not going to ratify it until the Americans agree'.[37]

Greenpeace representatives excoriated this statement as a breach of faith with the Australian electorate, and one undermining Australia's credibility in continuing negotiations.[38] As of 1999, future support by Australia for the Kyoto protocol remained dependent on a 'wide-ranging treaty impact analysis' involving extensive domestic consultation. This was code for saying the Australians would play for time, a similar message conveyed via expectations that considerable delay would occur before the Protocol received the requisite ratifications bringing it into force.[39]

Greenpeace also took its contest with the Australian government into the South Pacific, claiming that failure to ratify the Kyoto agreement was the truest indication of Canberra's lack of support for its Pacific Islands neighbours. 'The Pacific doesn't need handouts from Australia. It needs real action, which means Australia signing the Kyoto Protocol as soon as possible, and setting in place concrete action to reduce its emissions'.[40] South Pacific disquiet over FCCC Annex I party policy has continued.[41]

At the November 1998 fourth conference session of parties, held in Buenos Aires, the United States failed to persuade developing countries to accept voluntary commitments for emissions reductions. China and India led this opposition. The resulting stand-off hardened existing differences between the United States and the EU. This included Washington's proposals to establish a system of trading in pollution allowances, and purchasing options allowing industrialised countries to shift a share of their required emissions reductions to poorer countries that pollute less. While the EU believed rich countries should make most cuts at home, the United States, backed by Australia, supported no restrictions to amounts available for credit through offshore purchasing of allowances. These contrasting emphases reflected unresolved differences: namely whether to give higher priority to combating global warming at source, or utilise carbon trading for burden sharing via the market.

In March 1998, the Howard government announced legislative changes designed to devolve responsibility for environmental standards to state governments. These plans faced attack as a dilution of environmental impact assessment procedures.[42] More controversial was the government's June 1999 introduction of a comprehensive Goods and Services Tax (GST). This reduced diesel fuel rebates and electricity for business purposes, but increased prices for non-renewable energy sources and gas. The GST package appeared to contravene the Kyoto Protocol's Article 2 endorsing enhanced energy efficiency in national economies by reduction or phase out of market imperfections, fiscal incentives, tax and duty exemptions, and subsidies in all greenhouse gas emitting sectors. Local environmentalists were dismayed that the Australian Democrats provided the support necessary for GST passage.

Explaining Australia's Position

The details traversed have indicated the nature of domestic Australian interests, international policy frameworks, and salient outcomes of the FCCC/Kyoto process. Throughout, various manifestations of domestic/international interactivity were evident. Viewed more closely, what did Australia's conduct on the climate change question suggest? Reduced to essentials, its case at Kyoto was based on three key points: national economic need, differentiation, and developing country inclusion within a future regime of emission controls. A failure to achieve the third objective did nothing to harm, and may have assisted in securing the preceding two goals. Either way, strain between domestic demands and international imperatives was evident. The nature and implications of that strain is explored by considering it under sub-headings of *equity, economic development*, and *balance of responsibility*.

Equity

The case is interesting for the way the Australian government marshalled domestic support against the inequities that it perceived within FCCC arrangements. Although initially supportive of its formulation, Australian interest in the FCCC waned as evidence mounted of developing country resistance towards joining emissions reduction arrangements. At the 1995 Berlin conference, Australia only grudgingly agreed that new commitments for developing countries not proceed. Heading a 1996-elected government having no originating stake in the FCCC, Howard viewed it with continued misgivings. He claimed that 'we should never have got aboard this particular truck in the first place at the Rio conference and those that put us aboard that truck didn't understand the national interest ... the economic implications are quite serious for Australia'.[43]

Differences identified between the EU (favouring a regulatory regime) and the United States (supporting economic instrumentalities) remained unsettled. An effective regulatory regime was no more in existence than were market forces in controlling greenhouse gas emissions. Those gaining most from harmful emissions impacts were not carrying global warming costs. Differences over the relative weighting accorded to regulatory or economic instruments, stayed secondary to economic growth and trade liberalisation objectives. Here Australia pursued interests of material importance.

The Australian position epitomised features of North/South equity differences. For most developing countries, a climate change regime could not ignore developmental problems. It needed to help pay for cuts to population growth, provide technologies curbing anthropogenic greenhouse gas emissions, and curb consumption patterns based upon exploitation of goods based on energy intensive production. Unless they encompassed these agendas, climate change rules risked promulgating restrictive rules hindering sustained economic growth and reasonable standards of living (Ramakrishna, 1996: 226). The Global Environmental Facility, established following the 1992 UNCED to assist developing country adjustment programmes, was considered inadequate.

Australia was 'disappointed' that the Kyoto outcome failed to agree over steps facilitating future commitments by developing countries. Moreover, these states had vetoed a provision allowing individual advanced developing countries an opportunity to negotiate voluntarily individual differentiated commitments. Australia was also sceptical towards developing countries that committed internationally to cuts, but whose domestic controls were either weak or non-existent.

With the FCCC increasingly perceived by Australia's political leadership as either weak, ambiguous, or invidious in its potential application, scope to develop relevant compliance seeking constituencies within the Australian bureaucracy were constrained. According to 1995 Environment Ambassador, Penny Wensley, 'bureaucrats and public servants in this era of economic rationalism feel compelled to find hard-headed economic reasons for justifying our actions. Unless at the end of the day we can point to some positive contribution towards resolving Australia's balance of trade deficit, our expenditure of time and resources is somehow suspect' (cited Henderson, 1995: 241). Canberra's institutional culture of national decision-making, as well as more obvious factors of economic and self interest, thus played a role.

Economic Development

Australia was prepared to support initiatives designed to strengthen a voluntary regime of emissions controls, but resisted legally binding cuts. The 'soft law' approach chosen for the FCCC in 1992, along with implementation loopholes on greenhouse gas emissions, opened the door to maximise national advantage. Once it was evident legally binding cuts would proceed under the 'Berlin mandate', then a strategy designed to minimise perceived costs to exports, economic growth, and the established energy industry was pursued with vigour. Australian concerns illustrated a Scandinavian finding that 'efforts to change patterns of production and consumption within states by means of international regulation require measures that are aimed at these primary activities. This activity penetrates more deeply and directly than does other foreign policy activity' (Hanf and Underdal, 1995: 2).

An economic agenda dominated Australia's approach to greenhouse gas reductions. In revealing language, Howard warned the Australian Chamber of Manufacturers prior immediately prior to Kyoto that 'there is a call that Australia's growing economy be burdened with a new, unrealistic and unfair speed limit on growth'.[44] At Kyoto, a senior Australian negotiator confided that the talks were conducted not from any sense of the greater environmental good, but as a quasi-trade protocol.[45] This reflected policy continuity; the Australian National Greenhouse Response Strategy of 1992, (released after the Rio UNCED Conference), setting out domestic policies to help stabilise greenhouse gas emissions, carried a substantial rider. It claimed targets were 'subject to Australia not implementing response measures that would have net adverse effects nationally or on Australia's trade competitiveness, in the absence of similar action by major greenhouse gas producing countries'.[46]

Domestic economic rationalisation, including Australian tax reform or removal of subsidies for enhanced energy efficiency, incurred no more than limited interest by other governments. Removal of market distortions, or application of 'polluter pays' principles within Australia, gained greater international amplification through non-governmental channels. While Australia committed resources of $A100 million per annum to 'sink' enhancement, this was less a greenhouse gas abatement programme than one of carbon offsets. Support to rural Australia through subsidies to land management activities was a higher priority than tackling emissions problems at points of origin. Although a source of growing emissions, motorised transport remained essentially unaffected. This is 'politically sensitive due to the high incidence of car ownership, large land area, low population densities, and socio-economic factors that combine to make car travel highly popular' (Gumley, 1997: 351).

To achieve emissions reductions at least cost, Australia endorsed the development of emission trading and joint implementation. It joined the so-called 'umbrella group' which includes Canada, the United States, Japan,

New Zealand, Russia and Ukraine to plan trading in emission rights and reduce compliance costs. By supporting the clean development mechanism, joint implementation, the national greenhouse strategy, and aid programmes designed to abate greenhouse gas emissions, Australia has sought to play a constructive role and not appear a 'free-rider' on global emissions reductions. Its conduct post-Kyoto confirmed claims that, over international environmental matters, governments are generally 'hostile to being identified as laggards and non-compliers' (Peterson, 1998: 424). Through ABARE auspices, the Australian government assisted release of information on emissions trading.[47] Unresolved questions include appropriate allocation of income from such exchanges, and whether they are determined according to historical emissions, population, equity needs, or political bargaining (Edmonds, 1998: 130).

Appropriate Responsibility

The climate change regime's effectiveness will depend upon how seriously the participating governments follow prescribed targets and timetables for a limitation of greenhouse gas emissions. This entails jurisdictional responsibilities of the state moving both upward and downward, enhancing political authority at global and local levels. Australia's federal government has indicated that it can warn and encourage, but not insist that the country's different tiers of government pursue appropriate greenhouse abatement strategies.

In its foreign economic relations, Australia faced difficulties in reconciling the special treatment it sought on greenhouse gas reductions, with an insistence that others make the domestic adjustments needed for the greater good of trade liberalisation. The increased GDP and population growth used by Australia to justify its exemption could as readily apply to developing countries. Canberra did not accept that view however, claiming 'we see differentiation as an enticement for developing countries to eventually come on board'.[48] The Australian government, like the United States, insisted that developing countries must be included in any agreements to reduce emissions given their high population, and possible economic growth.

Australia's case for differentiation ran the risk of appearing as exceptionalism and special treatment, and did not accord with developing country demands that industrialised countries take greatest responsibility for greenhouse gas reductions. Claims that Australia's total contribution to greenhouse gas production was negligible, any cuts of only marginal impact, sat uneasily with the high per capita rates involved. Australian lifestyle advantages, it seemed to developing countries, were not for compromise.

As indicated in the Introduction, some findings suggest that while compliance with non-binding international environmental agreements may be low, they can still exert considerable influence on state behaviour. Such influence is strengthened by review and monitoring of national conduct. Victor (1998: 241) has claimed the FCCC process should allocate as much attention to effective national review procedures, as trying to wring results from a contentiously negotiated binding regulatory protocol. National review allows for peer pressure; it is non-confrontational; the process is more expert than political; and visiting review teams can consult a wide spectrum of local interests. An Australian National Farmers' representative claimed declining rates of tree clearing indicate 'that raising awareness about these issues can in itself produce beneficial effects not always induced by regulation'.[49]

Conclusions

Australia pursued a single-minded, national interest approach when securing its goals at Kyoto. Domestic industrial and energy producing associations supported the Howard government's resistance to cuts to greenhouse gas emissions. These considerations outweighed competing foreign policy concerns. To Senator Robert Hill, Australian Minister for the Environment, 'We have come away from Kyoto firmly entrenched in the global effort to reduce greenhouse gas emissions Environment. Australia did not seek a free ride at Kyoto, just a fair go'.[50]

The substantial bonus gained by the Australians in getting land clearance included in base line calculations at Kyoto, could have cushioned a lower than final eight per cent increase. This could have alleviated some of the adverse publicity fielded about running a 'hardball', beggar thy neighbour international campaign. That consideration did not prevail through official beliefs that the domestic forces determining Australia's greenhouse gas emissions policy were themselves subject to global configurations of power and dependency. Put bluntly, it in effect told others to organise their own affairs before criticising Australia.

A less defensive posture would have revealed that, as a global actor in the fields of relevant climatic science and research, no-regrets technological applications, and development of education and training programmes promoting energy efficiency, Australia had ample to offer. This included information about non–fossil fuel source applications. The need for these services has strengthened with East Asia's economic recuperation. Providing such services could assist Australia's standing throughout Asia-Pacific.

Tactically, Australia's repeated public threats about leaving an agreement not meeting its interests smacked of brinkmanship. Key actors that included Japan, the United States, and EU members distanced themselves from Canberra's position, wondering why Australia did not conduct a less shrill, transparently hard-edged but more accommodating campaign. The 'good global citizen' record, accumulated by Australia in multilateral trade, disarmament, Asia-Pacific, and human rights meeting points was jeopardised by confrontational tactics currying domestic support at the expense of intergovernmental co-operation. Other governments did not take kindly to Australia's threat to walk out made prior to the Kyoto deliberations.

Towards the future, Australia faces a task of charting greenhouse gas reduction policy for ongoing negotiations for many years ahead. Immediate national goals gained at Kyoto bought some time, but not much. This 'successful' outcome won local support, but did little to begin the attitudinal changes needed to move Australia towards a more energy efficient economy. By concentrating heavily on the economic costs of cutting back on fossil fuels, Australia neglected the longer-term costs of global warming. To a continent of deserts and coastal dwellers, those costs are not minor.

Notes

1 Svante Arrhenius, 'On the Influence of Carbonic Acid on the Air upon the Temperature of the Ground', *Philosophical Magazine*, 41, 251, 1896, pp. 237-76.
2 *News Release*, World Resources Institute, Washington DC, 17 November 1997.
3 Australian Department of Primary Industry and Energy. Address delivered on behalf of Senator Parer, World Energy Council, Asia Pacific Regional Forum, Beijing, 22 April 1997.
4 Michael Grubb, 'The Berlin Climate Conference: Outcomes and Implications', Royal Institute of International Affairs Briefing Paper, No. 21, 1995.
5 Negotiating text at the fifth session of the Commission on Sustainable Development: Proposed Outcome of the Special Session, 8-25 April 1997, pp. 22-23.

6 'While the world hots up', *The Economist*, 1 November 1997, p. 55.
7 Statement of Environment Minister Robert Hill, 23 June 1997, delivered to the Special Session of the United Nations General Assembly reviewing Agenda 21.
8 *The Australian*, 29 September 1997.
9 *The Australian*, 5 May 1997.
10 Australian Conservation Foundation, *Greenhouse Briefing Paper*, May 1997. (online, http://www.peg.ac.org).
11 *Climate Change 1995. Impacts, Adaptations and Mitigation of Climate Change: Scientific-Technical Analyses*, Cambridge: IPCC, 1996, p. 39.
12 Cited by Kenneth Davidson, 'No leg to stand on Over Greenhouse Gas', *The Age*, (Melbourne), 28 June 1997.
13 G. Skehan, *The Australian*, 30 April 1997.
14 'Gittins on Saturday', *Sydney Morning Herald*, 28 June 1997.
15 Greenpeace International, Briefing Paper, Sixth Session ad hoc group on the Berlin Mandate, 3-7 March, 1997, (online, www. Greenpeace.org/home/).
16 *The Australian*, October 17 1997.
17 Ibid.
18 *Weekend Australian*, 13-14 December, 1997.
19 *The Australian*, 12 June 1997.
20 *The Australian*, 7 October 1997.
21 *Reuters*, 20 November 1997; *AAP Press*, 30 November 1997.
22 At the 1995 Berlin FCC conference of parties, Pacific Island countries believed that neither Australia nor New Zealand did sufficient to support the AOSIS position. *Ciri Yawa*, (Quarterly Newsletter of the Fiji Mission to the United Nations), 2, 2, 1995, p. 3.
23 *Reuters*, Rarotonga: 19 September 1997.
24 Ibid.
25 For fuller details about this episode, see infra p. 192.
26 Australian Broadcasting Corporation, 23 October 1997.
27 Comments of Mark Diesendorf of the Sustainable Energy Industries Council of Australia, *Nature*, 390, 27 November 1997, p.323.
28 Media statement of Senator Meg Lees, Australian Democrats Parliamentary Leader, 22 March 1998, reference no. 98/176.
29 On the One Nation Party, see infra p. 156.
30 Sir Ninian Stephen, 'Making Rules for The World', *Australian Lawyer*, 30, 2, 1995, p. 14.
31 Commonwealth v Tasmania 1983, 158, CLR 1; Richardson v Forestry Commission 1988, 164, CLR 261; Queensland v Commonwealth 1989, 167, CLR 232.
32 For relevant commentary, see Clare Breidenich et al., 'Current Developments: The Kyoto Protocol to the United Nations Framework Convention on Climate Change', *The American Journal of International Law*, 92, 2, 1998, pp. 315-331.
33 Clive Hamilton, 'Land-use Change in Australia and the Kyoto Protocol', The Australian Institute, 1998.
34 Statement of Paul O'Sullivan, Deputy Chief of Mission Australian Mission to Washington, in address entitled 'The Case for Differentiation: Australia's Position on Climate Change', 2 September 1997.
35 Sustainable Energy Industries Council of Australia, statement of 17 December 1997.
36 Secretary of State Albright's address to the Australasian Centre of the Asia Society, 30 July 1998, US Department of State Release.

37 Warwick Parer, Australian Minister for Resources and Energy, *Pacific Report*, 11, 19, 29 September 1998.
38 *Greenpeace Australia*, 'Government Takes "Agenda of Evasion" to UN Climate Change Conference', 2 November, 1998.
39 *The Australian Greenhouse Office*, 'Outcomes from Buenos Aires and the Implications for Australia', 14 December, 1998.
40 *Greenpeace Pacific*, 'Pacific Islands Want Real Action on Climate, Not Just Handouts', news release, Suva, 18 December, 1998.
41 See infra pp. 229-30.
42 *Greenpeace Australia*, 'Environmental legislation back to the Stone Age', 5 March 1998.
43 Howard oral statement to the Press, 28 April 1997, cited by Wayne S. Gumley, 'Legal and Economic Responses to Global Warming – An Australian Perspective', *Environmental and Planning Law Journal*, 14, 5, 1997, p. 349.
44 *The Australian* online, 7 October 1997.
45 *The Australian*, 12 December 1997.
46 National Greenhouse Response Strategy, Canberra, 1992, Part I: Goal, Key Elements and Guiding Principles.
47 *International Trading in Greenhouse Gas Emissions. Some Fundamental Principles*, Canberra: ABARE, 1998.
48 Statement of Paul O'Sullivan op. cit., 2 September 1997.
49 Address of Dr Wendy Craik, Executive Director National Farmers' Federation, APEC Study Centre, Melbourne, 12 February 1998.
50 Senator Robert Hill, letter published in *The Australian*, 31 December 1997.

References

ABARE (1997), *International Climate Change Policy*, Current Issues (April), (online, http://www.abare.gov.au).
Burns, Thomas J., Davis, Byron L. and Kick, Edward L. (1997), 'Position in the World-System and National Emissions of Greenhouse Gases', *Journal of World Systems Research*, 3, 3, 1-19 (online, http://csf.colorado.edu/wsystem/jwsrl).
Climate Change: Australia's Second Report to the UNFCCC, November 1997, (1997), Canberra: Commonwealth of Australia.
Cline, William R. (1992), *The Economics of Global Warming*, Washington DC: Institute for International Economics.
Edmonds, J. (1998), 'We Need Some New Ideas', *Climate Change*, 38, 2, pp. 129-32.
FCCC/IDR (1995), Framework Convention on Climate Change, *In Depth Review: Australia*, unpublished report, 14 December.
Gumley, Wayne S. (1997), 'Legal and Economic Responses to Global Warming: An Australian Perspective', *Environment and Planning Law Journal*, 14, 5, pp. 341-55.
Hanf, Kenneth and Underdal, Arid (1995), 'Domesticating International Commitments: Aligning National and International Decision-Making', in Arid Underdal (ed), *The International Politics of Environmental Management*, Dordrecht: Kluwer Academic Publishers.
Harris, Paul G. (1998), 'Understanding America's Climate Change Policy: Realpolitik, Pluralism, and Ethical Norms', OCEES Research Paper, No. 15, Oxford: UK.

Hasselmann, Klaus (1997), 'Climate Change Research after Kyoto', *Nature*, 39, 20, pp. 225-26.
Hempel, Lamont C. (1996), *Environmental Governance: the Global Challenge*, Washington DC: Island Press.
Henderson, Judy (1995), 'An Environmentalist Perspective', in Philip Alston and Madelaine Chiam (eds), *Treaty-Making and Australia. Globalisation versus Sovereignty?*, Leichhardt: Federation Press and Centre for International and Public Law, ANU, pp.236-42.
Hendy, Peter (1996), 'Intergovernmental Relations: Ensuring Informed Cooperation in Strategic Policy Development', *Australian Journal of Public Administration*, 55, 1, pp. 111-17.
Hurrell, Andrew (1995), 'A Crisis of Ecological Viability? Global Environmental Change and the Nation State', in John Dunn (ed), *The Contemporary Crisis of the Nation State*, Oxford: Blackwell, pp. 146-65.
Intergovernmental Panel on Climate Change (1995), *Climate Change 1995. Impacts, Adaptations and Mitigation of Climate Change: Scientific-Technical Analyses*, Contribution of Working Group II to the Second Assessment Report, Cambridge: Cambridge University Press.
Lipschutz, Ronnie D. (1997), 'From Planet to Planet: Local Knowledge and Global Environmental Governance', *Global Governance*, 3, 1, pp. 83-102.
Lunn, S. (1997), *The Australian*, 21 November.
McEachern, D. (1993), 'Environmental Policy in Australia 1981-91: A Form of Corporatism?', *Australian Journal of Public Administration*, 52, 2, pp. 173-86.
Nakicenovic, N. et al., (1998), 'Emission scenarios database and review of scenarios', *Mitigation and Adaptation Strategies for Global Change*, 3, pp. 95-120.
Ombudsman (1998), *Report of the Investigation into ABARE's External Funding of Climate Change Economic Modelling*, Commonwealth Ombudsman's Office, Canberra.
Pakulski, J. Tranter, B. and Crook, S. (1998), 'The Dynamics of Environmental Issues in Australia: Concerns, Clusters and Carriers', *Australian Journal of Political Science*, 33, 2, pp. 235-52.
Pears, Alan and Wilkenfeld, George (1997), *Develop Australia Bonds: Establishing a Balance Between Energy Service Options*, Paper of the Sustainable Energy Council of Australia.
Peterson, M. J. (1998), 'Organizing for Effective Environmental Cooperation', *Global Governance*, 4, 4, pp. 415-38.
Pockley, Peter (1997), 'Australia Plays Hard to Get', *Nature*, 390, 27 November, p. 323.
Ramakrisna, Kilaparti (1996), 'Building an Effective Climate Regime', in Oran Young, et al., (eds), *Global Environmental Change in International Governance*, Hanover: University of New England Press, pp. 219-28.
Repetto, Robert and Lash, Jonathan (1997), 'Planetary Roulettte: Gambling with the Climate', *Foreign Policy*, 108, (Fall), pp. 84-98.
Saddler, Hugh (1996), 'Greenhouse Policies and the Australian Energy-Supply Industries', in W.J. Bourma, G.I. Pearman and M.R. Manning (eds), *Coping with Climate Change*, Collingwood: CSIRO Publishing.
Sands, Philippe (1995), *Principles of International Environmental Law 1: Frameworks, standards and implementation*, Manchester: Manchester University Press.
Skærseth, Jon Birger (1995), 'The Fruitfulness of Various Models in the Study of Environmental Politics', *Cooperation and Conflict*, 30, 2, pp. 155–78.
South Pacific Forum (1997), *Communiqué*, Heads of Government Meeting, Rarotonga, The Cook Islands, September 1997, Suva: Fiji.

Stewart, Jenny and Jones, Grant (1997), 'The Green Battlefield: Conflict Resolution in Australian Environmental Management', in G. Crowder et al., (eds), *Australasian Political Studies 1997: Proceedings of the 1997 APSA Conference*, Vol. 3, Adelaide: Flinders University, pp. 953-54.

Taylor, Lenore (1997), 'Australia's Greenhouse Triumph', *The Australian Financial Review*, 12 December.

Toyne, Phillip (1994), *The Reluctant Nation: Environment, Law and Politics in Australia*, Crows Nest, NSW: ABC books.

Tsamenyi, Martin (1995), 'The Domestic Consequences of International Environmental Imperatives', in Philip Alston and Madelaine Chiam (eds), op. cit., pp.163-73.

Victor, David (1995), 'On Writing Good Histories of Climate Change and testing Social Science Theories', *Climate Change*, 29, 4, pp. 363-69.

Victor, David (1998), 'The Use and Effectiveness of non-binding instruments in the management of complex international environmental problems', *American Society of International Law. Proceedings of 91st Annual Meeting, 1997*, Washington DC: American Society of International Law, pp. 241-50.

Walker, Ian J. (1996), 'Carbon Dioxide from the Australian Energy Sector: An Energy Efficient Scenario', in W.J. Bourma, G.I. Pearman and M.R. Manning (eds), op. cit., pp. 478–91.

Wilkenfeld, George (1997), 'Kyoto's No Carbon Copy', *The Australian Financial Review*, December 1997, p.15.

4 The Bougainville Conflict

'Today, mipela finisim war bilong Bougainville'.

('Today, I have ended the war in Bougainville'.) Sam Kaouna, Commander Bougainville Revolutionary Army at the formal ceasefire signed 30 April 1998.[1]

Introduction

The conflict on the island of Bougainville in Papua New Guinea (PNG), was easily the worst to befall the Southwest Pacific since World War II. It took between ten and fifteen thousand lives, traumatised and uprooted many others, and left the social and economic structure of the territory devastated. By any reckoning, Bougainville's decade of upheaval from 1988 represented a gross failure of politics at all levels – international, regional, national and local. An abdication of political, administrative and ethical responsibility by state and insurgent operatives alike was painfully evident. Since 1997, a peace process has progressed, but many years of physical repair, social reconstruction, and psychological healing are needed before Bougainville can consign its tragedies to the past.

This chapter investigates the conflict and attempts to settle it. It relates these developments to a framework evaluating domestic and international interactivity utilised throughout this study. Domestic and international influences contributed to the settlement process, and subsequent attempts to sustain a durable peace for the island. While outside settlement formulations had to operate within Bougainville's domestic constraints, local inhabitants appreciated that a lasting peace required external supports.

Bougainville: The Roots of Strife

Located approximately 990 kilometres due east of the PNG capital Port Moresby, Bougainville has a land area of 9,300 square kilometres (slightly smaller than Lebanon) and a population of approximately 160,000. It comprises the main island of Bougainville, the smaller northern island of Buka, and still smaller islets including Nissan. Bougainville's southeastern tip is barely 20 kilometres from the Solomon Islands, peoples on either sides of this border sharing marked cultural affinities that include a distinctive black skin colouring differentiating them from peoples elsewhere in PNG. With nineteen main languages, and several distinct ethnic groups, the development of a Bougainville identity is as problematic as attempts to inculcate shared national loyalty (Levine, 1997: 484). Nevertheless, Bougainville has common customs; they include complementarity of gender relations permitting women relatively better status than elsewhere in PNG.

As a colonial entity, the territory was a relative latecomer. Initially subject to Australian trading and labour recruiting interests, Bougainville fell under German influence during the latter part of the nineteenth century. Control was formalised through an exchange of notes between Berlin and London in 1899. German administration continued until the outbreak of World War I. When those hostilities ceased, Bougainville was designated a mandated territory of Australia, ostensibly accountable to the League of Nations for these responsibilities. Under Australian control, the plantation economy begun by the Germans expanded to facilitate an inception of basic services, but dislocated customary ethnic and social affiliations. Mission services – prominently the Catholic Church – provided valued social, medical, and educational facilities. For lengthy periods, Australia treated the territory as a backwater.

Although isolated from mainland PNG, Bougainville's people are innately Melanesian through an all-encompassing conception of land that is fundamental to identity. To those on Bougainville, this is 'our physical life; it is marriage; it is status; it is security; it is politics; in fact, it is our only world ... We have little or no experience of social survival detached from the land. For us to be completely landless is a nightmare which no dollar in the pocket or dollar in the bank will allay'.[2] Amidst persisting affinity to land, other aspects of the Melanesian social universe exhibit volatility. They include a 'perpetual struggle between leadership contenders operating within limited circumferences (that have) contributed to instability' (Dinnen, 1998: 41).

Autonomy demands intensified following the discovery of a large deposit of low-grade copper in 1960. Upon completion of feasibility studies, a major mining operation initiated under Bougainville Copper Limited (BCL) auspices began developing a major extraction facility at Panguna in 1967. This enterprise was two thirds owned by Conzinc Riotinto of Australia, and one third Broken Hill Proprietary. Enabling legislation formulated with inadequate local consultation, authorised compulsory land acquisition. Although gaining some compensation, landowners were denied status as mineral owners. Citing an Australian High Court ruling, Australian officials told local owners that sub-surface materials belonged to the government. This ruling exacerbated grievances once the scale of the enterprise and its attendant social and environmental dislocation emerged. Under mineral boom conditions during the 1970s, the operation's immensity, rawness, and unforeseen impacts disfigured familiar physical landscapes and fractured trust within social systems. An imported work force of mine site and service operatives from other parts of PNG inflamed already sensitive inter-ethnic relations.

Contract terms re-negotiated in 1974 reduced BCL's generous tax and depreciation exemptions, but did not allay landowner grievances over the mine's negative social impacts, and evident despoliation of landscapes, rivers, and customary food gathering locations. Local resentments festered over the inequitable apportionment of mine revenues. In the decade that preceded the conflict's 1988 eruption, this saw 60 per cent going to the PNG government, 35 per cent to foreign shareholders, 5 per cent to the Bougainville provincial government, but only 0.2 per cent to local landowners as royalties (McDougall, 1991: 108). During peak performance, the operation provided approximately 16 per cent of PNG's annual national income and 44 per cent of the value of its exports.

On the eve of PNG's September 1975 independence, the Republic of North Solomons unilaterally declared itself independent under leader Moses Havini. A May 1975 constituent assembly, supported by traditional leaders, had concluded there was little hope of gaining a just share of the revenue now being earned by Bougainville. Representatives Momis and Teosin unsuccessfully attempted to lobby the UN for support, shocked by rebuffs that left the secession unrecognised internationally (Griffin, Nelson and

Firth, 1972: 216). The independence impetus faltered; after eleven months negotiations, the entity duly returned to PNG as the North Solomons province under an agreement that granted it considerable governance and financial autonomy. This was legitimised under a nationwide system of provincial government where the North Solomons emerged as one of the better administered entities. Gradual decay through corruption, and mutual mistrust between the provinces and the central government, led to this system's demise by the mid-1990s.

By 1980, the Panguna Landowners Association (PLA) had mobilised militant opposition to the BCL. The company attempted to reduce this hostility by expanding compensation payments for environmental damage. Dispute about how to divide funding between community benefit trusts and individual entitlements exacerbated clan frictions. Failure of 1985 attempts to augment compensation worsened inter-generational strife, and PLA clan and class differences (Filer, 1990: 97). They heightened when a scheduled 1987 mine contract reconsideration failed to eventuate. These differences related to longer running dispute about appropriate forms of development. This pitted a modified form of corporate capitalism, favoured by former Provincial Premier Leo Hannett, against a grassroots, participatory, local enterprise mode favoured by the loosely coalesced Melanesian Alliance (Layton, 1992: 316).

In April of 1988, a 'New' PLA executive headed by younger representatives Perpetua Sereo and her first cousin Francis Ona, both disillusioned with compensation distribution policy launched a series of public demands. Supported by Bougainville provincial governor Joseph Kabui, these comprised a damages claim of 10 billion kina (then nearly equivalent to US $10 billion) for environmental damage; 50 per cent share of BCL profits; consultation on all new projects; and localisation of BCL ownership within five years. The extravagance of these demands indicated prior expectation of their rejection, a predictable response designed to further weaken the BCL's local standing.

By November 1988, violence and sabotage against mine facilities erupted. Major insurgency had spread by early 1989, with three companies of regular Papua New Guinea Defence Forces (PNGDF) deployed. The mine closed shortly thereafter, and in June 1989, the PNG government declared a state of emergency. After failing to quell the resistance, the PNG government agreed to a shaky ceasefire arrangement in March 1990 under which it withdrew forces and halted government services. A unilateral declaration of independence was announced in May 1990 by the Bougainville Interim Government (BIG), affiliated to the Bougainville Revolutionary Army (BRA). Ona and the BRA declared that Bougainville was now the independent Republic of Mekaamui. This was rejected out of hand by the PNG government, which then instituted an economic and communications blockade of the province. A mid-1990 agreement (the *Endeavour* Accord), approved a resumption of services, but deferred issues of Bougainville's eventual political status. Failure to implement the *Endeavour* Accord intensified mistrust between the BRA and the PNG government.

Consequential dislocation worsened the incidence of indirectly related political violence (so-called 'payback' killings), human rights abuses, economic decline, and a degradation of health and educational services. Crime rates also increased in number and variety (Premdas, 1998: 30). A localised dispute had now spiralled out of control into a conflict embroiling the national government, and subjecting its international credibility to increasingly critical scrutiny.

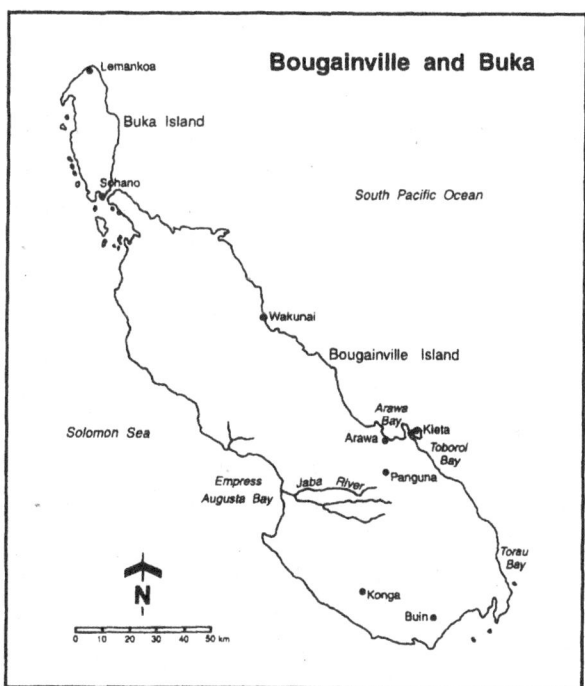

Map 4.1 Bougainville

Internal Conflict as a Generic

Although distinct, Bougainville's strife illustrates the contemporary security dilemma of most states at peace with each other, far fewer at peace with themselves. A 1996 study indicated that of 96 armed conflicts since 1989, only five comprised conventional wars between states, the rest internal with most reflecting ethnic differences (Stremlau: 1998, 1-2). That ratio has not altered. Internal conflicts are protracted; destructive of economic life, trade, and essential infrastructure; conducive to crime and lawlessness; and destabilising of adjoining regions. They devastate the lives of civilians who suffer large-scale displacement and the brunt of casualties. These afflictions magnify tensions between respect for sovereignty and justifications of external intervention; between human rights and state authority; and between territorial integrity and internal autonomy demands. Belligerents exploit the reluctance of outside governments to intervene by flouting international humanitarian law principles designed to protect non-combatants in armed conflict. This evasion is widespread. It has confronted the international community with acute legal, moral, and political dilemmas that will persist.

Internal war literature identifies causal factors that include persisting cleavages among ethnic groups; use of repression by power-holding élites and their discriminatory allocation of rewards for loyalty; recent serious political or revolutionary upheaval; and exclusionary ideologies that define target groups as expendable (Gurr and Harff, 1994). Rupesinghe regards identity conflicts as pervasive in driving internal wars, identity defined as an abiding sense of selfhood that imparts social meaning and functional predictability to the lives of individuals. More than a psychological sense of self, secure identity conveys notions of physical, social, and even spiritual safety. Once these moorings are uprooted, constraints curbing the contagion of violence disintegrate (Rupesinghe, 1992: 57).

Difficulties identified in bringing internal wars to peaceful settlement include endemic tensions within and between combatant factions. Here coalitions form and collapse, previous allies become sworn enemies, and little neutral ground is available from which to negotiate a settlement. Refusing to negotiate, but able to veto potential outcomes, combatants battle on with short-term gains uppermost (King, 1997: 33-36). Under these conditions, a culture of violence runs rife as combatants and civilians enhance their armed capabilities through easily obtained, relatively cheap light weapons. During prolonged stalemates, combatants lack reliable information about whether they are 'winning' or 'losing', their relative bargaining strengths, or levels of public support should they forfeit capacities to coerce, control or intimidate. Should the fighting stop, an absence of impartial institutions needed to monitor and enforce truces, cease-fires, or negotiated settlements, constitutes a further impediment (King, 1997: 51).

Bougainville's Protracted Stalemate

These findings are cited for their pertinence to Bougainville's near decade of conflict when disorder and lawlessness took more lives than overt hostilities. Death toll estimates vary, an accurate figure unlikely to emerge. Some put it as high as twenty thousand, others at between ten and twelve thousand. Bougainville Premier Gerard Sinato claimed the conflict took fifteen thousand lives, including unlawful killings and those who perished through lack of health care facilities.[3] Whatever the true figure, the ratio of those lost to the total population of the territory was horrific. Dislocation of educational, medical, and administrative facilities was extensive. The conflict left the mining location, its centre at Arawa, and related port facilities either destroyed or rendered inoperable. Perversely, this encouraged some protagonists into believing international awareness about Bougainville's destruction would elevate its standing as an entity deserving self-determination. This proved as misleading as information they received indicating some governments would recognise the May 1990 unilateral declaration of independence.

During hostilities, a gradual return by the PNGDF in 1991 to North Bougainville and Buka, then further South, precipitated two significant developments. A first was the establishment of 'care centres', intended for those displaced from rebel-held area by BRA intimidation, or PNGDF destruction of villages. Local statistics indicated that, by the end of 1996, 67,300 internally displaced people were in these locations.[4] Pro-secession interests publicised their unsatisfactory conditions before international forums. These concerns were raised at the UN Human Rights Commission (Crook, 1994: 812). At the UN's Working Group on Indigenous Populations, BIG-affiliated Mike Forster insisted that the centres were little better than 'concentration camps'.[5] Conditions in these locations added to war weariness and social pressure for settlement.

Box 4.1 Bougainville: The Key Entities

BRA: Bougainville Revolutionary Army, the main secessionist grouping.

BIG: Bougainville Interim Government, the political arm of the BRA.

BTG: Bougainville Transitional Government established after agreement between PNG authorities and Bougainville leaders. Abolished December 1998.

Bougainville Reconciliation Government: The entity authorised by the 1998 Lincoln agreement to represent the people of Bougainville following the conduct of free and democratic elections.

PNGDF: The Papua New Guinea Government Defence Forces.

Resistance: Government backed and equipped militia engaging the BRA.

TMG: Truce Monitoring Group: the unarmed regional force that performed truce monitoring functions.

PMG: Peace Monitoring Group that replaced the TMG in April 1998 to ensure cease-fire compliance, and to assist civil restoration, constabulary training, and local promotion of the peace process.

A second effect was a strengthening of the so-called Resistance, a militia that received equipment and allowances from PNG authorities. Initially Resistance objectives were indistinguishable from those of its PNG backers, some of its elements sustaining heavy casualties.[6] Resistance involvement with PNGDF units occurred in the October 1996 assassination of Theodore Miriung, Premier of the Bougainville Transitional Government. This was verified by government appointed Sri Lankan Justice Suntheralingham's findings, through an investigation convened under Commonwealth auspices.[7] By contrast, some Resistance factions extended feelers to the BRA about negotiating possibilities. Central here was Samuel Akoitai, whose 1994 contacts with the BRA led to discussions about cease-fire modalities, resumption of essential services, and conditions needed for a political settlement.[8] Although abortive, this initiative was not wasted. Followed by others, it helped slowly erode hostility, mistrust, and animosity between parties.

How did an interplay of domestic and international factors affect this embryonic dialogue process? At times an impediment to settlement, elsewhere it created space that was utilised productively. Both are considered, the more negative aspects first. Barriers included sovereign sheltering, tendentious interpretation, and illegitimate recourse to force.

Sovereign Sheltering

A consequence of PNG's Bougainville blockade was the constriction that this placed upon information and reporting about the territory's security, political and social conditions. Although news media outlets operating under difficult conditions reported egregious outrages and conflict events, opinion in neighbouring Australia and New Zealand lacked the continuous coverage needed to gauge the accumulated damage that years of violence and neglect had sustained. Nor did Bougainville have a 'CNN factor', where television coverage of strife and suffering can galvanise domestic publics abroad into demanding immediate relief responses from governments and aid agencies.

At diplomatic levels, the PNG government insisted to its South Pacific Forum partners that Bougainville was an internal problem. This succeeded to the extent that Bougainville's 'declaration of independence' went unrecognised. At the Forum's 1992 Heads of Government meeting in Honiara, the Solomon Islands, delegates refused to hear Bougainville representatives on the grounds that the matter was internal to PNG (Perry, 1996: 212). This suited the Australian and PNG governments, not wanting conflicts in Irian Jaya or East Timor treated as any other than internal to Indonesia.

This position grew less tenable as humanitarian concern about Bougainville's social toll mounted. Prime Minister Bolger of New Zealand began informal soundings about the scope for an assisted settlement at South Pacific Forum Heads of Government meetings. Claims that the issue was purely internal weakened once the neighbouring Solomon Islands was involved as a haven for refugees and the war wounded, including BRA personnel. Solomons territory was also a target for 'hot pursuit' operations, conducted against suspected BRA personnel and their facilities. Nevertheless for a lengthy period, the PNG government was cushioned by the international community's preparedness to extend the 'benefit of the doubt' to Port Moresby's suspect handling of the conflict.

Distortions

Bougainville's conflict was subject to contrasting external interpretations that 'read' the situation to suit different purposes. Generalisations about the conflict's nature, promoted for international consumption, included its characterisation as:

- A struggle where indigenous peoples were asserting cultural and political rights following the destruction of customary lifestyles, land practices, and resource uses. This saw support from the Unrepresented Nations and Peoples' Organisation (UNPO), whose tactics included releases attacking the reporting of events considered unfavourable to secessionist aspirations. The conflict was portrayed for international purposes as a denial of indigenous rights for which a number of sympathetic international interests existed.
- A conflict caused by the obstruction of a legitimate drive for political self-determination leading to the creation of a sovereign and independent Bougainville. The often publicised, frequently controversial Australian lawyer Rosemary Gillespie, who maintained links with Francis Ona, promoted this interpretation.
- An upheaval consequential upon the forces of transnational mining capital colliding with local class and kin formations. This claimed that the PNG government was effectively little more than an auxiliary to external commercial interests, forces that it might influence but never control.
- A war prolonged by Australian determination to maintain 'stability' to its North. This had resulted in generous economic and military assistance to PNG grossly abused to prosecute a war against helpless civilians on Bougainville.

At times, metaphor characterised these interpretations. Some were romanticised, simplified, and conveyed readily assimilated images to external audiences unsure of Bougainville's complexities. Interests involved highlighted particular images. For the first item above, the cameo was that of the permanently poisoned Jaba river flowing from the mine operation; for the second, Gillespie's photographed presence in Bougainville; for the third, the vast gaping hole comprising Panguna's disused mine site; and for the fourth, Australian supplied Iroquois helicopters flying above defenceless villages. Although selective, these images carried sufficient conviction to activate official responses to the conflict – whatever their nature.

Illegitimate Recourse to Force

Concerns about PNGDF deployment of Australian supplied Iroquois helicopters to attack Bougainville's civilians were never satisfactorily denied. This compounded growing unease about ill discipline among the PNGDF and police operating on Bougainville, their poor morale and conditions of service, and sharpening local hostility towards PNG personnel viewed as no better than interlopers. Aggravated by that scourge of internal conflict – impunity from prosecution – PNGDF human rights violations faced mounting censure. Documentation of those violations began surfacing internationally.[9] They were treated seriously by the Australian and New Zealand governments whose apprehensions about rights violations were deepened by the so-called 'Sandline' episode of March 1997.

Failure by PNG Prime Minister Chan to weaken the BRA through various negotiating stratagems, saw him resort to the services of Sandline International, a subsidiary of Executive Outcomes and self-described 'security consultancy' operation. Once news of this initiative entered the public domain, Chan's administration faced censure from counterparts in Australia and New Zealand. Australian Prime Minister Howard warned that any deal involving Sandline would sustain long term damage to PNG's international standing since 'any use of mercenaries would be totally unacceptable'.[10] Chan retaliated by claiming that, in representing a sovereign state, his government had the authority to hire whomsoever it wished to deal with an internal insurgency (Ivarature, 1998: 202). Proposed contract terms indicated that the state of PNG 'engulfed in a state of conflict with the illegal and unrecognised Bougainville Revolutionary Army (BRA) requires such external military expertise to support its Armed Forces in the protection of its Sovereign Territory and regain control over important national assets, specifically the Panguna mine. In particular, Sandline is contracted to provide personnel and related services and equipment to ... conduct offensive operations in Bougainville in conjunction with PNG defence forces to render the BRA militarily ineffective and repossess the Panguna mine' (Macmillan, 1998: 4).

Although the Sandline initiative collapsed amidst acrimony, it provoked easily the worst crisis in PNG's civil-military relations since independence. Disregarding Australian advice, Commonwealth Secretary General Chief Emeka Anyaoku visited Papua New Guinea in the immediate aftermath of the episode. He warned PNG's military and civilian leaders that in many Commonwealth countries 'the disregarding of constitutions has led to great troubles'.[11] The affair damaged relations with Australia, and precipitated Chan's replacement as Prime Minister by Bill Skate. Attacking the deal, subsequently sacked PNGDF chief Brigadier Singarok repudiated it as professional and ethically improper, especially when local security services could be re-equipped and their moral boosted for the same amount of money (Ivarature, 1998: 212). Most damning, the Chan government stood exposed as giving greater priority to the use of hired external force, than committing resources to an internally negotiated settlement, and Bougainville's reconstruction. Overall, the Sandline episode sounded a 'wake-up call' about the extent of PNG's policy disarray and political mismanagement of Bougainville's situation.

The Rocky Road to Peace

What of more positive domestic/international interactivity assisting the peace processes? The issue was delicate – particularly the role of outsiders in assisting towards a settlement. Previous settlement attempts did not result in overt intervention, but its possibility engendered suspicion among belligerent parties. Those attempts included the abortive 1990 *Endeavour* Accords and the January 1991 Honiara Declaration. The latter attempted to rescind the secessionist unilateral declaration of independence; restore services cut by the blockade; introduce a multinational supervisory team to supervise a truce, arms surrender, and amnesty to the BRA. Like its predecessor, this initiative also failed.

After assuming office in 1994, Prime Minister Chan attempted to break the stalemate by signing a ceasefire agreement with BRA military leader Kaouna. A regional monitoring force comprising units from Tonga, Fiji, and

Vanuatu initially designed to oversee this agreement did not perform that function, but provided security for negotiations conducted in October 1994. While not producing a commitment to settle, those talks formulated framework principles designed to shape a continuing dialogue. Scope for continuing association in the peace process by the offices of the UN Secretary General and of the Commonwealth was provided. When faced by faltering initiatives, Chan sought to isolate the BRA by building a peace momentum among other Bougainville factions. BRA fears about the security of its representatives attending proposed talks then arose as a barrier to progress. These concerns were real: returning from talks held in Cairns during late 1995, rebel representatives were attacked by the PNGDF.

New Zealand's Role

After the Sandline debacle, New Zealand Foreign Minister McKinnon judged the timing as good as any to begin moving the peace process beyond stalemate. Facilitating factors included ample evidence of war weariness on Bougainville, the Sandline episode's discrediting of Chan and the PNGDF, and worries that the conflict was biting ever more deeply into PNG's integrity as a viable sovereign entity. Australia's financial commitment towards implementing a settlement was solid, but diplomatically Canberra could not afford further rebuffs to peace initiatives that it hosted. Given New Zealand's commitment of forces to UN operations in Bosnia as an act of global citizenship, McKinnon reasoned regional needs and responsibilities demanded nothing less. His visits to Bougainville left him appalled at the conflict's toll upon the education and life chances of an entire generation of young people.

In determining his strategy, McKinnon weighed relative advantages and challenges. Advantages included New Zealand's standing as an actor playing a disinterested role, unencumbered by substantial previous involvement in the conflict. Unlike Australia, it had no major commercial or military involvement in either Bougainville or PNG. Experiences from the *Endeavour* accord negotiations confirmed that a substantial Maori presence within New Zealand's armed forces enhanced their acceptability on the island. This was borne out subsequently, as Bougainville representatives expressed a preference for New Zealand rather than Australian forces in the territory. According to Kabui, this was because of New Zealand's relatively better record in treating its indigenous people through Treaty of Waitangi settlement processes, Pacific islander representation in its Parliament, and willingness to extend the human touch.[12] These forces were sufficiently resourceful, prepared to improvise under difficult conditions, willing to communicate with local residents, and trained to patrol in difficult terrain.

New Zealand's limited capacity to contribute substantial resources to a settlement and reconstruction process on Bougainville imparted credibility to an appeal consistently sustained. This emphasised that an effective outcome was crucially reliant upon the determination and co-operation of those on Bougainville itself. The key task lay in ascertaining whether parties to the conflict were serious about making peace and prepared to act in good faith to that end. Keeping this uppermost was a reason why New Zealand officials rejected numerous external offers to assist with mediation and conciliation (McMillan 1998:6). No matter how well conceived, the mechanics of mediation were no substitute for knowledge of actual conditions on Bougainville.

Advantageous was the accumulated knowledge, experience and contacts established by senior official John Hayes. He performed an effective low-profile role, exemplified by deliberately shunning publicity about the personal risks he experienced in a helicopter shooting incident over Bougainville. In discussions, Hayes sought to persuade, cajole, build consensus, and exert pressure to sustain a settlement momentum. The peace process itself was a crucial ingredient in solidifying the eventual agreement; where for a conciliating interest, 'it is a question not only of correctly identifying the right times to move but also of moving the times with skill' (Zartman, 1989: 273).

New Zealand's challenges lay in determining how far to widen the exploratory dimensions of the peace process initiative, as distinct from conducting a 'need to know' policy about its status and progress. Key PNG Ministers were consulted before initiatives began in early 1997. This entailed contacts established with BRA and BTG representatives abroad. They included private meetings in Auckland with Martin Miriori, Secretary to the BIG, and then domiciled at The Hague under refugee status. Another challenge was to proceed as if a viable peace plan was ready, even when no such formula actually existed. Realistically, that could emerge only after sufficient dissipation of mistrust between the parties had occurred to allow agreement over settlement framework principles. This meant assembling those most involved on neutral ground under secure conditions, a logistical task of magnitude. Incentives for participation included the interest shared by contesting factions in speaking with a single voice to the PNG government over matters of common concern, something the Solomon Islands government proved willing to expedite.

The Burnham Talks

In July 1997, the New Zealand government hosted a remarkable cross section of Bougainville representation at Burnham military camp near Christchurch in the South Island. To facilitate this initial confidence building exercise, credentials, agenda and timetable stipulations were relaxed. Avoiding the risk that absence might provide an excuse for future non cooperation, New Zealand offered generous terms for participation: to a projected total of 180 participants came an additional one hundred, importantly a number of women prominent in the community.

In revitalising the peace process, New Zealand faced a problem concerning the legal status of insurgents. Normative guidelines regarding external interests dealing with insurgents are weak (Wilson, 1988: 24). New Zealand officials, however, believed that ignoring the political presence of the BRA would render the peace process nugatory. A conspicuous absence was Francis Ona, maintained for subsequent meetings but to declining effect. (With a hard core of supporters, Ona retained a potential to upset the peace process. His standing then suffered through opportunistic links that he developed with gun lobbyists and fringe extremists in Queensland, moves that Australian BRA representative Havini described as regrettable.[13])

When transported by the Royal New Zealand Air Force delegations were separated, on occasion physically restrained by accompanying security personnel breaking up fistfights. Choosing a neutral offshore venue was important. It diminished apprehensions that the initiative was an intervention into Bougainville's space. The meeting provided appropriate security and hospitality, while generally competent organisation assisted the climate of discussions. To those who had experienced years of privation and isolation, this was an opportunity to adopt fresh perspectives. A more intangible benefit lay in participants' opportunities to witness the novelty of daily routines in a society unhindered by overt conflict and strife.

New Zealand indicated that it would not use the discussions to advance proposals over the future political status of Bougainville, or possible resumption of operations at the Panguna mine. Left largely to their own devices, Bougainville participants concluded a Declaration that committed the parties to seek an internal reconciliation, and work with the PNG government towards establishing a negotiating process. A significant marker towards progress immediately followed with the release of five PNGDF personnel held hostage by the BRA for over a year.

A second phase of talks held at Burnham in October 1997 saw added representation from the Australian, PNG, and Solomons governments. The Solomons Home Affairs Minister and Chairman of the Solomon Islands Bougainville Peace Committee, Leslie Boseto, played a key role in chairing sessions. Some of them saw shouting episodes and cathartic outpouring of pent-up recrimination and bad faith. That out of the way, and following intensive back-room encouragement and persuasion, these deliberations produced the Burnham Truce. This acknowledged the necessity to cease armed conflict; restore normalcy and essential services; lift previous restrictions on freedom of movement and services; monitor the cease-fire and resolve incidents threatening its continuation; and institute proceedings designed to immediately invite a neutral, unarmed regional group to monitor the terms of this agreement.

The specifics of the final point were settled during a third round of discussions held in Cairns in November 1997. At that meeting, the 250 personnel, unarmed Truce Monitoring Group led by New Zealand, but with added contributions from Fiji and Vanuatu, gained approval for prompt deployment to Bougainville. This was succeeded by a post-April 1998 Peace Monitoring Group led by Australia. A delay at Cairns emerged when the PNG government opposed demands by secessionist leaders for immediate PNGDF withdrawal. The PNG government believed that this could be construed as an abandonment of sovereignty. Terms of withdrawal were eventually agreed.

The Lincoln Agreement

A formal peace agreement for Bougainville was signed at Lincoln University, near Christchurch, on 23 January 1998. This was concluded by representatives of the PNG government; the Bougainville Transitional government; the Bougainville Interim government; the Bougainville Revolutionary Army; the Resistance forces; and Bougainville members of

PNG's Parliament. Added legitimacy was provided through the agreement's witness and endorsement by South Pacific representatives of standing, and Australian Foreign Minister Downer. Key elements included:
- A 'permanent and irrevocable cease-fire' scheduled from 30 April 1998 with an extension of the existing truce monitoring group to that date.
- Agreement to the phased withdrawal of PNG forces subject to the renewal of civilian authority.
- Appointment of a UN special observing mission to monitor peacekeeping arrangements.
- An offer by the PNG government to remove bounties and grant amnesties and pardons to 'persons involved in crisis-related activities'.
- Agreement to co-operate in the restoration and development of Bougainville.
- Agreement to discuss Bougainville's political future and elect a Reconciliation government before the end of 1998.

Pragmatism thus prevailed by not attempting to resolve the future of the Panguna copper mine and Bougainville's future political status. On 30 April 1998, the cease-fire was duly signed allowing the truce monitoring group under Australian direction to begin its peace monitoring and reconstruction functions.

New Zealand's effectiveness in promoting the peace process lay in its capacity to work within principles ostensibly separating internal from external political conduct. Before dealing with BRA external representatives on a basis of confidence, it secured prior PNG government consent to do so. Unlike Australian Prime Minister Howard's statement (subsequently modified by Foreign Minister Downer) that it was essential for Bougainville to remain within the PNG fold, New Zealand kept silent on that question.[14]

Differences of position between New Zealand and Australia were viewed as an advantage in some quarters on Bougainville. In a speech welcoming McKinnon to BRA controlled territory in central Bougainville, BIG Vice President Kabui had some advice for his visitor. Do not 'allow the Australian influence, perhaps seeing itself as bigger brother, to push you around and perhaps try and redirect the spirit of Burnham in some other way that we in New Zealand came up with'.[15] Overall, the pragmatism and experience of key New Zealand figures involved saw them follow a patient, listening role attuned to Bougainville's fluid internal political dynamics. When telling

Bougainville's representatives that the outcome was in their hands, New Zealand's position carried credibility. This confirms a comparative finding suggesting that the more likely talks are to succeed on their own, the less likely will high costs, mediation, or outside guarantees exert any effect on the outcome (Walter, 1997: 344).

Profile of Interests

Many interests – some longstanding, others ephemeral, many denying categorisation – were caught up in the Bougainville conflict. Consideration here is based on salience to the conflict, its settlement, and relevant domestic/ international interactivity. State-based, factional, and humanitarian interests were important, mining and commercial representation less so since they did not assume a direct role in peace settlement and rehabilitation processes.

State-based Interests

As the main state actors concerned, Australia, New Zealand and Papua New Guinea all sought a permanent, durable settlement to the Bougainville conflict. They sought to quarantine secessionist influence by urging denial of international recognition to any Bougainville entity claiming independent status. This was not difficult, but did little to advance the peace process. Settlement initiatives by Australia and New Zealand saw diplomatic conventions observed, and the PNG government informed in advance. Australia and New Zealand moved beyond treating the conflict as primarily an internal matter following PNGDF incursions into Solomon Islands territory.

All three governments identified shared memberships within the South Pacific Forum, the Commonwealth, and the United Nations. The Bougainville conflict occurred at a time when these and other international organisations displayed greater readiness to confront domestic human rights violations, unsustainable development, and breakdowns of governance. This strengthened Australian and New Zealand apprehensions towards PNG conduct over the Sandline controversy. Related concerns were longer-standing — PNG's state legitimacy, territorial integrity, and economic dependency (MacQueen, 1993: 149).

Elsewhere, these state interests differed: PNG grew increasingly defensive about the ill-discipline of its forces, human rights violations, and the harmful social consequences of the blockade. Recovering economic harm sustained by the conflict, and offering an eventual prospect of mining resumption on Bougainville was a further PNG interest. It needed the external legitimacy that continuing integration into the international economy could provide, enabling its survival in the face of diminishing internal legitimacy (Dinnen, 1998: 58). This related to the perceived need to recover standing and flexibility lost during the conflict's stalemate.[16]

Australia regarded its regional security interests and its relations with PNG best served by keeping the conflict's bilateral political tensions under control. It simply dismissed as unhelpful Chan's 1996 attacks saying Canberra had to accept guilt for Bougainville deaths because it failed to control rebel spokesmen in Australia.[17] Nor did Canberra respond to BRA attempts to portray the conflict as one of Bougainville's David pitted against an Australian Goliath. A major difficulty for Australia lay in maintaining a close defence relationship with PNG, while insisting that equipment supplied was not abused by its use against civilians. Where this occurred, the PNGDF 'contravened the end use conditions agreed to with Australia and sharpened domestic concerns over human rights abuses, thus undermining Australia's attempt to limit its involvement and avoid controversy' (Henningham and Woodman, 1993: 130).

New Zealand's interest lay in maintaining regional cohesion: the longer the conflict persisted, the greater its potential damage to the South Pacific Forum and associated intergovernmental co-operation. This collaboration was imperative for future Pacific Islands trade, resource management, Law of the Sea, and political needs. Nor did New Zealand want the Bougainville conflict disturbing indigenous rights and national reconciliation with Maori. As settlement attempts fell at their fences, New Zealand upgraded its interest as potential interlocutor willing to step in to facilitate a settlement.

Bougainville's Insurgent Factions

The conflict on Bougainville fractured identity and support structures across several dimensions: between generations, across gender, and throughout the territory. With economic life heavily disrupted, even primary systems of social relations such as traditional pig exchange were shattered. This created a void filled by BRA elements drifting in and out of criminal conduct within a volatile 'rambo' gun culture. Violence was handmaiden to complex admixtures of crime, political motivation, and unresolved clan feuding. Defectors from the BRA spoke of their disillusionment as it contorted the goals of self-determination and independence into an unstable, dictatorial, anti-western populism.[18]

Known identity symbols and cultural practices dissipated under these pressures, confronting the BRA's potential support base with major questions about future conditions under its hegemony. While independence was the eventual goal, insurgent interests were dominated by tactical considerations: gaining limited zones of security, surety of supply in weapons, food, or medicine, and local alignments of convenience. Retaliating for the failure of collapsed agreements and broken alignments between leaders meant diversion from essential goals. For whatever reasons – mistrust of the PNGDF, internal disputes, or ill discipline – the BRA gained a reputation for bad faith over adhering to agreements. This was not surprising; only part of the insurgency was political, others elements including cargo cultists, young unemployed itinerants, and criminal elements beyond BRA control.

Nevertheless, some shared objectives existed. They included full restitution for damage sustained by the mining operation, and a future political status that would never again subject the territory to the commercial contract, labour importation, and revenue extraction experienced under BCL. External projection of the independence cause was difficult; while it had some of its people in other countries, the BRA's civilian counterpart lacked an exile constituency abroad that could mobilise public sympathy or support. Generally the PNG government proved effective in blocking access by BRA and sympathisers to official delegations attending South Pacific Forum meetings. This directed the search for legitimacy to other avenues. Access to the UN was one means of internationalising interests and included passage of resolutions at the United Nations Human Rights Commission.[19] However this tactic was double-edged: external human rights investigations revealed culpability for violations on all sides of the conflict. Following an October 1995 visit, UN Special Rapporteur Bacre Waly N'Diaye had reported human rights violations on Bougainville, easy access to arms, excessive use of force by the PNGDF, civilian suffering aggravated by collapse of essential services, and decline of traditional authority within a culture violence and reprisals.[20]

Humanitarian Interests

Humanitarian interests initially concentrated upon mission survival under difficult conditions, a goal at times disappointed. The relief aid agency *Médecins Sans Frontières* withdrew in November 1993, citing obstruction of its medical personnel by the PNGDF. Some humanitarian agencies ran to procedures that owed more to headquarters requirements, than the improvisation and co-operation demanded by Bougainville's chronically reduced circumstances. Some agency positions reflected wider uncertainty evident throughout the development assistance community about how relief, rehabilitation, and development objectives should function in harness.

Assistance is required to rebuild essential human capacity in technical fields that include data and census compilation, local level training of nursing and para medical staff, primary schooling, and small business activity. With approximately A$70 million committed to assistance projects on Bougainville, Australian official assistance has been vital. However it is 'constrained by ... an uncertain and fluctuating security situation, the lack of a clear co-ordination mechanism acceptable to all parties, weak public and private sectors with low absorption capacity and unreliable transport structure, which has made aid delivery very difficult and expensive'.[21] Another difficulty is that Bougainville's external funding demands may subtract from needed national allocations. Throughout PNG resentment accumulated towards Bougainville as the province that, having broken the rules, now attracted a disproportionate share of external assistance. This engendered retaliatory suspicions from Bougainville that Port Moresby might siphon assistance intended for the territory towards other interests or regions in the country.[22] Following the 1999 East Timor crisis, concern also intensified that this might divert resources and attention from Bougainville.

Once the Lincoln Agreement was in place and the peace process underway, humanitarian agencies broadened the scope of their activities. This included developing skill training among younger former combatants on a counterpart basis, assisting the establishment of local welfare organisations, and enhancing the role of women in the community. Among the approximately 3000 who fled Bougainville to the Solomon Islands, most had returned by 1999 bring some infusions of aptitude and vigour. Development assistance officials reported post-Lincoln improvements in

Bougainville's atmosphere and confidence to home capitals and interested publics. This encouraged programme maintenance. Abiding difficulties included lack of funding for even very basic service restoration; food, medical, and clothing shortages in remote areas; and frictions in local administration.

Post-1998 Developments

From 1998, violence on Bougainville subsided as services, limited economic activity, and schooling made a hesitant start. Some districts remained unsettled, while alcohol abuse, boredom, and joblessness persisted among young people. Bottlenecks in the distribution of assistance gradually eased, but persisting problems of substance included inadequate weapons surrender, lack of police training, and delayed economic reconstruction.

In late 1998, the PNG Parliament failed to muster the two thirds parliamentary majority needed pass amending constitutional legislation enabling establishment of the proposed Bougainville Reconciliation government scheduled for instalment in 1999. In January 1999, the PNG government suspended the territory's Provincial government, ostensibly to facilitate the establishment of the planned Reconciliation administration. This decision was unsuccessfully challenged on legal grounds by long standing Bougainville Member of Parliament John Momis, who lost political ground through the suspension.

In May 1999, a 69 member Bougainville Peoples Congress was elected to provide a firmer basis for local representation in negotiations with the PNG government regarding the territory's future political status. Ona's faction refused to join the Congress. President of the Congress, Joseph Kabui, indicated that it regarded independence from PNG as an ultimate goal. The PNG government continued to reject this option, although in October 1999 Bougainville Affairs Minister, Sir Michael Somare, announced it was willing to grant Bougainville greater autonomy. Kabui welcomed this announcement as an important step, but indicated a surrender of arms would not occur without the guarantee of a referendum to determine whether Bougainville would opt for total independence.

Rules and Norms

To help ensure its durability, Bougainville's peace process faced rule formation requirements that comprised internal and external dimensions. Key internal requirements concern future constitutional relations with PNG, and the administration of justice. Although the future constitutional relationship with PNG was undetermined in 1999, significant determinants about its likely direction were evident. They included PNG's capacity to survive its many economic and social difficulties without reversion to non-constitutional rule, and systems of representation needed to perform effectively as public institutions on Bougainville.

The administration of justice, and maintaining the rule of law on post-conflict Bougainville, required international and domestic supports. External assistance and appropriate investment were required to generate the work practices needed to wean people from habits of crime, resort to violence, and liquor abuse. Parties to an internal conflict encounter difficulty establishing a working justice system, and require external assistance to make it function as a reality. That entails accurate assessment of what outside assistance can provide. Some external help was provided for informal mediation services, and the restoration of judicial administration. Technical assistance for police training remain limited and left large areas of Bougainville unsupervised.

Common to PNG, Bougainville faced major educational gaps, a 1996 UNICEF report indicating a nationwide 45 per cent literacy rate compared to an average 85 per cent in other Pacific Island countries.[23] Without work activity, law enforcement, and literacy improvements, Bougainville's basis for civil order remained problematic. Circuit court sittings had not been regularised in 1999, their infrequency indicating the lack of a permanent legal structure to hear human rights abuses cases.[24] Those deficiencies have sustained negative attitudes obstructing the establishment of civil, rule-governed conduct on Bougainville.

Externally, there is the challenge of incorporating Bougainville within an appropriate framework of dispute settlement. Even should the territory not attain full independence, a semi-sovereign status could necessitate this requirement. In this regard, it is a puzzle why Senator Evans, Australian Foreign Minister for much of the Bougainville conflict period, remained reluctant to apply principles outlined in his widely noted publication,

Co-operating for Peace.[25] Building on UN Secretary General Boutros-Ghali's 1992 *An Agenda for Peace*, these proposals set out a blueprint about how to handle the multifarious problems of post-conflict peace reconstruction. Readers of that study search in vain for any indexed reference to Bougainville or, for that matter, East Timor – easily the biggest regional settlement challenges confronting Australia's final decade of the century. But why did the Australian government not try to apply these principles to the Bougainville conflict smouldering on its doorstep?

A possible answer rests with the reluctance of governments to follow normative prescriptions for order in settings of immediate proximity to them. The role that Australia played over Cambodia in the early 1990s was not replicated in PNG and Bougainville. This required a perspective difficult to achieve for historical reasons. Australian awareness of Bougainville's social complexities, advanced and astute in some quarters, could not penetrate established foreign policy perspectives emphasising the primacy of sovereignty considerations, existing security alignments, and military capability as the dominant arbiter in conflict.

The Institutional Dimension

Decisively affecting Bougainville's peace and reconstruction process is the extent to which emergent representative and governmental institutions function without fragmentation. Factional contest between the long standing, if chameleon-like Bougainville parliamentarian John Momis, and a grouping headed by Joseph Kabui and Gerald Sinato assumed prominence. To Momis, the best eventual option for Bougainville remains an autonomy status. Kabui on the other hand has seen the proposed Reconciliation government as a vehicle 'to take us to the ultimate goal ... an independent homeland for Bougainvilleans'.[26] Division between these two positions is unresolved, a polarisation that persisted amidst progress under the Lincoln peace process.

To promote peace on Bougainville, leaders from other parts of PNG, including the well regarded Stephen Pokawin (Manus Island) have indicated an interest in mediating these differences.[27] The suspension of the Bougainville provincial government at the scheduled December 31 1998 expiry of the Bougainville Transitional government was not life threatening to the peace process, but added uncertainty to recovery timetables. Were that to continue, public faith in formal political processes risks erosion. Although establishing operative representative institutions of legitimacy is crucial to an enduring peace, for a source on Buka most local people were not unduly concerned as to the form of governance adopted. Rather 'the main worry people in the rural villages of Bougainville have are about roads, schools, health services and the guarantee of lasting peace, security, and freedom to lead a normal life. The establishment of the BRG is no big deal to them'.[28]

Although isolated and leaderless during the conflict, enough grassroots support for peaceful co-operation exists to allow a consolidation of the post-1997 peace process. Overarching commitments to Christian principles persist, enshrined in the Lincoln Agreement's Preamble 'praying for the Almighty's forgiveness, guidance and blessing for ... common endeavours'. Deeply rooted is a firm belief in Bougainville's intrinsic territorial, cultural, and historical distinctiveness. Remarkable as well is a physical and emotional resilience in the face of debilitating setbacks.

Whatever the options for self determination generated by the post-1998 peace process, Bougainville's future status is subject to the volatility of PNG's parliamentary politics. Nationwide dispute over an unresolved determination of provincial governing functions continues unabated. Seemingly clear-cut as an internal constitutional matter, external economic and commercial considerations are potential determinants shaping provincial status outcomes. Apposite is the claim that this is a setting where 'the market integrated the people more with the outside world than internally' (Ghai, 1996: 178).

Transformative Factors

Did the peace process instituted in 1997 succeed through Bougainville turning the corner towards a stable peace and effective political settlement? As indicated, New Zealand consistently emphasised the importance of local impetus to the peace process. A central question is whether Bougainville's war weariness and subsequent peace process did enough to raise qualitatively different expectations among Bougainville's key players about future options and opportunities. Several factors directly bearing upon domestic/international interactivity assume relevance. Viewed as a physical, environmental, and cultural dislocation of the first order, the BCL mine operation at Panguna epitomised to many the malign impacts of penetration facilitated by globalisation. It exposed PNG's exposure to the harsher impacts of foreign capital under inadequately formulated or enforced legal, environmental, and fiscal restraints.

A more incipient transformation was constitutional. The observations of Barkin and Cronin, cited in the Introduction, deserve reiteration: how sovereignty is publicly constituted can provide a significant pointer to the way that it alters.[29] As the peace process developed, previous assertions that Bougainville's future of necessity had to remain with PNG began modifying. Between the lines of statements from BTG representatives, emerged hints that something less than total independence need not face outright dismissal. Bougainville's neighbourhood includes New Caledonia, where a constitutional arrangement could evolve signifying something less than complete independence. In all locations, public support for whatever formulation eventually emerges will more likely determine outcomes than a force of arms determining the limits of territoriality.

The Bougainville conflict and settlement process contributed to a continuing reappraisal of objectives and modalities in development assistance, particularly among Australian aid circles. This relates to the philosophy of the Burnham/Lincoln peace process that consistently recognised Bougainville's people as the centre of recovery and change, regardless of previous political affiliations or conduct potentially subject to incrimination. The Lincoln Agreement's call for the PNG government to seek appropriate assistance from international organizations, foreign governments, and organisations for Bougainville's restoration and development underlined the need for its administration to promote local participation.

The challenge now lies in rebuilding an identity, previously fractured by exclusion and conflict, and that is capable of taking responsible ownership of the peace process. Destabilising forces include excessive personalism, and abuse of the electoral process to secure private access to state wealth creating functions (Dinnen, 1998: 58). Should Bougainville's power holders stay neither subject to the law nor constitutionally derived standards of accountability, then the public support that they gain through identity appeals will prove erratic. If nothing else, the territory's conflict has taught that lesson.

Finally, the peace process effected a transformation that avoided the distortions inherent in a characterisation of the conflict as essentially a

BRA-directed struggle for self-determination. To Ghai, if the BRA claims were accurate 'they would constitute a strong case for self-determination. The difficulty with the BRA's position is that many of the claims are unsustainable. They have no mandate from the people, they have destroyed the provincial government (enjoying a wide measure of autonomy) which was fairly elected by the people, they have not negotiated in good faith (as they are not willing to abandon the cause of independence), they have perpetrated atrocities against innocent people and terrorised the population. Their case would be even weaker but for the ineptitude of the central government and the atrocities inflicted on innocent people by the armed forces, conduct which, if not knowingly allowed, was certainly condoned' (Ghai, 1996: 195). While some forms of domestic/international interactivity perpetuated a BRA mythology, others weakened it, in particular once the monitoring and reporting of human rights violations emerged more fully.

Conclusions

What has this case illustrated about the interaction of domestic and international politics? A reason for the Bougainville conflict's prolonged stalemate was that diplomatic convention, hazardous access, and ambiguous interpretation of the territory's events, restricted impartial external evaluations that could have assisted conflict settlement. Formal internationalisation of the situation through the Solomons involvement, and PNG's perceived violation of regional security norms by its abortive hiring of Sandline, provided circuit breakers that added timeliness to the McKinnon intervention. This initiative worked to get the peace process underway because key New Zealand officials operated in relative seclusion, utilised knowledge of Bougainville's key personalities and factions, and understood why previous peace attempts had faltered. No preconceived notions or formula was advanced; Bougainville's representatives were told that the peace process was in their hands.

Further variants of domestic/external linkage affecting Bougainville include the accumulation of non-governmental and UN-based information about human rights abuses. As this increased, PNG government insistence that Bougainville was an internal matter grew less tenable. This coincided with growing international demands that governments discharge international accountability for human rights conduct within their borders. However one effect of publicising BRA violations by means of external scrutiny was to heighten an ever more difficult question. At what price came self-determination beyond terms acceptable to the PNG government? By 1999, a consensus had developed that moves to determine political status could not proceed outside the circumference of a continuing dialogue between Bougainville and PNG authorities. This did not alleviate possible resort to force, but reduced its probability.

And what of Bougainville's future? Interactions between Bougainville's key personalities, and the relations that they develop with those of influence elsewhere in PNG will remain fluid, important, and unpredictable. That volatility need not destabilise the peace process provided it assists, not degrades institutionalisation commanding local respect. Considerations include leaders' relative levels of clan and broader public support, legitimised representation as a source of acknowledged status, and the legality of links public authorities develop with commercial and private interests. A durable peace on Bougainville will necessitate political accountability, and office-holding that is subject to the rule of law. Public supports will shape, but also remain subject to Bougainville's eventual political status. That could evolve towards something less than complete independence but more than provincial autonomy – an 'autonomy plus'. The conduct of that debate will influence PNG's national constitutional evolution. The philosophy, direction, priorities and management of Bougainville's post-conflict recovery will remain unresolved for some time yet. That will matter the longer a social and economic recovery takes to build the community cohesion that is needed to consign a return to arms to the past.

Domestic/international interactivity, whether by design or selective perception, distorted representations regarding the nature of the Bougainville conflict. As hostilities ceased and the security situation improved, a variety of external interests gained access to interpret the situation in a more nuanced fashion than that previously offered. This helped place human need and civil reconstruction priorities ahead of political status determination, deliberately left in abeyance. How exogenous and internal interests interact to frame that debate will prove vital for the future of the territory.

Notes

1. Cited Raymond Apthorpe, 'Bougainville Reconstruction Aid: What are the Issues?' *State Society and Governance in Melanesia*, Discussion Paper, 7, 1998, Canberra: ANU/RSPAS, p. 1.
2. The comments of Bougainville students cited by Chris Ballard (1997), 'It's the land, Stupid! The moral economy of resource ownership in Papua New Guinea', in P. Larmour (ed), *The Governance of Common Property in the Pacific Region*, Pacific Policy Paper No. 19, National Centre for Development Studies, ANU, p. 52.
3. *The Nation*, PNG, 24 March 1998.
4. Figure cited by Amnesty International, *Papua New Guinea. Bougainville: The Forgotten Human Rights Tragedy*, London: Amnesty International, 1997, p. 25.
5. UN doc. E/CN.4/1996/Add.2.
6. *Sydney Morning Herald*, 13 July 1996.
7. For details of this Enquiry facilitated by the Commonwealth Secretariat, see Amnesty International, op. cit., 1997, pp. 13-17.
8. Comments of Samuel Akoitai to 22-24 June 1995 seminar entitled *The Bougainville Crisis; The Search for Peace and Rehabilitation*, Canberra, (mimeo), p. 7.
9. Ibid. See also UN doc. E/CN.4/1996/Add. 2.
10. *Post Courier*, Port Moresby, 25 February 1997.
11. Derek Ingram 'Commonwealth Update', *The Round Table*, 342, 1997, p. 168.
12. Comments of Joseph Kabui on Radio New Zealand International Programme, *Tangata O Te Moana*, 6 March 1999. Reported *The National*, Port Moresby, 8 March 1999. On Treaty of Waitangi, see infra pp. 157-158.
13. Greg Roberts, 'Bougainville Peace: Noumea Accord Used as Model', *Sydney Morning Herald*, 28 July 1998.
14. Prime Minister Howard, statement to the September 1997 South Pacific Forum Heads of Government meeting, Rarotonga, the Cook Islands. *The Australian*, 19 September 1997.
15. Joseph Kabui speech in 'Roreinang', *Asia Pacific Network*, 29 August 1997, (online, http://acij.uts.edu.au/cafepacific/resources).
16. These costs were already evident by 1991. Norman MacQueen, 'New Directions for Papua New Guinea's Foreign Policy', *The Pacific Review*, 4, 2, 1991, p. 172.
17. *Pacific News Service*, 31 July 1996.
18. *Bougainville: A Pacific Solution*. Report of the Australian Parliamentary Delegation to Bougainville of April 1994, Canberra: Government Publishing, p. 23.
19. Comments of BIG representative Moses Havini, *The Guardian* (UK), 9 December 1998.
20. UN doc. E/CN.4/1996/4/Add. 2, 17-18.
21. Foreign Affairs and Trade, Australia, *Bougainville: Bougainville Peace Process*, Canberra: Commonwealth of Australia, 1999.
22. This was the gist of a news media release of 29 January 1999, by Moses Havini regarding Prime Minister Skate's abolition of the Office of Bougainville Affairs and its replacement by a Ministry headed by Samuel Akoitai reporting to the Prime Minister.
23. *The Nation*, Port Moresby, 16 July 1998.
24. UN doc. E/CN.4/1996/Add. 2.
25. Gareth Evans, *Cooperating for Peace. The Global Agenda for the 1990s and Beyond*, Australia: Allen and Unwin, 1993.
26. Jospeh Kabui's comments as quoted in the *Post Courier*, Port Moresby, 26 October 1998.

114 *The Domestic Politics of International Relations*

27 *The Nation*, Port Moresby, 19 February 1999. This move signified the possibility of an informal alliance between PNG's outer islands based on shared expectations of greater autonomy. This is not new and was the subject of a provincial premiers' meeting in 1994.
28 *The Independent*, Port Moresby, 23 October 1998.
29 See Introduction p. 7.

References

Crook, John R. (1994), 'The Fiftieth Session of the UN Commission on Human Rights', *The America Journal of International Law*, 88, pp. 806-21.

Dinnen, Sinclair (1998), 'In Weakness and Strength - State, Societies and Order in Papua New Guinea', in Peter Dauvergne (ed), *Weak and Strong States in Asia-Pacific Societies*, Australia: Allen and Unwin, pp. 38-59.

Evans, Gareth (1993), *Co-operating for Peace. The Global Agenda for the 1990s and Beyond*, Australia: Allen and Unwin.

Filer, Colin (1990), 'The Bougainville rebellion, the mining industry and the process of social disintegration in Papua New Guinea', in R. J. May and Matthew Spriggs (eds), *The Bougainville Crisis*, Bathurst: Crawford House Press, pp. 73-112.

Ghai, Yash (1996), 'Self-Determination in the South Pacific', in Donald Clark and Robert Williamson, *Self Determination: International Perspectives*, London: Macmillan, pp. 173-99.

Griffin, James, Nelson, Hank and Firth, Stewart (1972), *Papua New Guinea: A Political History*, Victoria: Heinemann Education.

Gurr, Ted Robert and Harff, Barbara (1994), *Ethnic Conflict in World Politics*, Boulder: Westview Press.

Henningham, Stephen and Woodman, Stewart (1993), 'An Archilles heel? Australian and New Zealand Capabilities for Pacific Islands Contingencies', *The Pacific Review*, 6, 2, pp. 125-43.

Ivrature, Henry (1998), 'The Sandline International Controversy', in Peter Larmour (ed), *Governance and Reform in the South Pacific*, Canberra: ANU National Centre for Development Studies, pp. 200-52.

King, Charles (1997), *Ending Civil War*, Adelphi Paper No. 308, London: IISS.

Layton, Suzanna (1992), 'Fuzzy-Wuzzy devils: Mass media and the Bougainville Crisis', *The Contemporary Pacific*, 4, 2, 1992, pp. 299-324.

Levine, Stephen (1997), 'Culture and Conflict in Fiji, Papua New Guinea, Vanuatu and the Federated States of Micronesia', in Michael E. Brown and Sumit Ganguly (eds), *Government Policies and Ethnic Relations in Asia and the Pacific*, Cambridge: MIT Press, pp. 457-508.

MacQueen, Norman (1993), 'Island South Pacific in a Changing World', *The Pacific Review*, 6, 2, pp. 145-53.

McDougall, Derek (1991), *Studies in International Relations. The Asian Pacific, the Superpowers, Australia*, Melbourne: Edward Arnold.

McMillan, Stuart (1998), 'Bringing Peace to Bougainville', *New Zealand International Review*, XXIII, 3, pp. 2-9.

Perry, Richard J. (1996), *From Time Immemorial. Indigenous Peoples and State Systems*, Austin: University of Texas Press.

Premdas, Ralph (1998), 'Secession and Decentralisation: The Bougainville Case', *Canadian Review of Studies in Nationalism*, XXV, pp. 23-36.

Regan, Anthony 'Causes and Course of the Bougainville Conflict', *The Journal of Pacific History*, 33, 3, (1998), pp. 269-85.

Rimoldi, Max and Rimoldi, Eleanor (1992), *Hahalis and the Labour of Love*, Providence: Berg.

Rupesinghe, Kumar (1992),'The Disappearing Boundary Between Internal and External Conflict', in Elise Boulding (ed), *Conflict and Security Examined*, Boulder and London: Lynne Rienner Publishers, pp. 43-64.

Stremlau, John (1998), *Human Rights, Humanitarian Action and Preventing Deadly Conflict*, New York: Carnegie Commission.

Walter, Barbara (1997), 'The Critical Barrier to Civil War Settlement', *International Organization*, 51, 3, pp. 335-64.

Willett, Susan (1999), 'The Economics of Security in the Developing World', *Disarmament Forum*, 1, pp. 19-30.

Wilson, Heather A. (1988), *International Law and the Use of Armed Force by National Liberation Movements*, Oxford: Clarendon Press.

Zartman, I. W. (1989), *Ripe for Resolution*, New York: Oxford University Press.

Zartman, I. W. (1995), 'Introduction: Posing the Problem of State Collapse', in I. William Zartman, (ed), *Collapsed States: the Disintegration and Restoration of Legitimate Authority*, Boulder: Lynne Rienner, pp. 1-11.

5 Decolonisation

Introduction

Decolonisation and its protracted processes have continually entangled domestic politics with international relations. In their struggles for independence, activists from dependent territories traditionally looked to the international arena for education, solidarity, and support. This provided knowledge of the political processes, law, and public sentiment needed to advance national self-determination. Subjecting administering powers to international pressure was an essential element of these strategies. Within territories under foreign control, colonial rule strengthened cultural allegiances, centralised administration, and made ethnic groups interact as they faced international forces of modernisation (Aldrich and Connell, 1998: 239).

Where decolonisation was bloody and attenuated, it penetrated the administering power's domestic politics with volatility. Kahler's astute comparison of French and British decolonisation saw it affected by the metropole's domestic politics, including party assessments of electoral costs incurred through disengagement (Kahler, 1984: 361). Furthermore 'actors on the periphery, settlers or bureaucracy, could ally themselves with domestic political opponents of decolonisation' (Kahler, 1988: 363). Conflict in Indo-China and Algeria cut to the heart of the French Republic's proclaimed indivisibility. Into the 1980s, less traumatic but revealing disturbances occurred in what Paris euphemistically termed New Caledonia's 'events'. Described soon, these conflicts mirrored significant fissures within France over the role of the state and the army, structural inequities, and ethnicity (Aldrich, 1993: 282).

Even more telling was system collapse at the centre, as in the *coup de grâce* that military deposition of the Caetano dictatorship delivered to Portugal's ramshackle colonial edifice in April 1974. Twenty months later, East Timor was forcibly 'incorporated' into Indonesia, a status unrecognised by the UN through Portugal's failure to discharge internationally legitimised processes of decolonisation. By ironic inheritance, the territory next climacteric also followed an external dominator's internal upheavals when the Suharto regime disintegrated in 1998. As the Fourth Republic's collapse in 1958 signalled France's beginning of the end in Algeria, so Indonesia's upheavals four decades later heralded its East Timor nemesis.

Under the UN, decolonisation expanded from a problem primarily preoccupying European powers to an issue of global dimensions. Although now regarded a relic, the UN's Trusteeship Council performed vital legal functions of state creation by facilitating UN Charter 73 reporting and petitioning functions. In 1960, the UN General Assembly approved its landmark Resolution 1514, widely known as the Declaration on Decolonisation. This asserted the subjugation of any people was a denial of fundamental human rights; reaffirmed a universal right of self determination; repudiated inadequacy of social, economic, educational, or political advancement as a pretext for delayed independence; demanded immediate transfer of powers necessary for complete independence; and upheld national unity and territorial integrity. Although adopted without dissent, administering powers other than New Zealand recorded abstentions. The American abstention followed pressure from the British government, unwilling to support the Declaration, but sensitive about divergence in Anglo-American UN voting conduct.[1]

The same UN General Assembly session passed Resolution 1541. This established principles that obliged administering powers to transmit information to the UN through regular General Assembly review under the aegis of the 'Committee of 24'. Under 1541, a non-self governing territory was deemed to have reached effective self-government by its emergence as either a sovereign independent state; free association with an independent state; or integration with an independent state. This range of possibilities has retained its relevance. It assumes interactivity between external and internal factors shaping relevant choice. For example, when the Cook Islands chose free association with New Zealand, both countries acknowledged the former dependency's domestic conditions might alter to allow a move to full independence.

While the UN offered a route to orderly, phased decolonisation, elsewhere the process faced unrestrained volatility. Sometimes the turbulence generated within metropolitan states disturbed international relationships. France's internal parliamentary and constitutional crises over Indo-China and Algeria shook Western Europe and the Atlantic alliance. The United

Kingdom's handling of Rhodesia's violent decolonisation, and its trade and investment policies towards *apartheid* South Africa, polarised British parliamentary politics and the Commonwealth. New Caledonia's troubles in the 1980s aroused passions within France, unsettled the South Pacific, and damaged France's relations with Australia and New Zealand.

Skilled at castigating France's colonial misadventures from the safety of opposition, Francois Mitterrand warned the French Assembly in 1979 about New Caledonia. He claimed: 'We have had enough experience over the last quarter of a century of the problems of decolonisation to know how desperate and then how angry peoples can become when they do not know when or where to turn, or when knowing where to turn – to the French government – they find neither interest, nor vigilance, nor consideration, nor understanding' (cited Maclelland and Chesneaux, 1998: 143). Given the widely noted French aphorism that the more things change, the more they stay the same, how do Mitterand's observations now appear? Does the burden of his message echo elsewhere? And what do the frustrations of denied decolonisation suggest regarding the role of domestic/international interactivity as alleviating or aggravating considerations?

Cases Considered

A mistaken view is that apart from such isolated 'confetti of empire' as Norfolk Island, the Melanesian Pacific's colonial chapter has concluded. Yet it is remarkable that entering the 21st century, colonialism remains inadequately discharged within territories not without importance. East Timor was an international time bomb that ticked ominously for decades, to explode with fury in 1999. By any reckoning, the region's bungled and belated decolonisation has proved a gross impediment to the advancement and welfare of peoples concerned, and their opportunities to participate within the comity of nations.

Table 5.1 Dependent Status in Oceania and Greater Melanesia

Territory	Status	Land area Sq. km.	Population	
New Caledonia	French overseas territory	19,103	196,000	(1996)
French Polynesia	French overseas territory	3,521	219,000	(1996)
East Timor	Unresolved[a]	14,500	800,000[b]	
West Irian	Indonesian province	256,000	2,058,000[b]	(1997)
Guam[c]	US	541	153,700	(1996)
Tokelau	New Zealand dependency	10	1600	(1996)
Wallis & Futuna	French overseas territory	255	14,800	(1996)
Norfolk Is.	Australian territory	35	2,285	(1991)
American Samoa	US[c]	195	58,900	(1996)

a   as of 1999
b   estimated
c   unincorporated US territory

Source: UN; South Pacific Community.

Most attention in this chapter is devoted to New Caledonia, East Timor and West Irian, South Pacific examples occasionally cited to illustrate contrasting approaches to decolonisation. East Timor and West Irian are important not just for their regional and wider political and economic significance, but the Melanesian heritage that they share with New Caledonia. That heritage has produced social formations challenging contemporary state formation. All cases illustrate the mixed political impacts incurred by domestic/international interactivity. Evaluation of those impacts follows commentary on political developments and identity aspirations within each location. That leads to a discussion of normative, institutional and transformational aspects. Decolonisation options are assessed prior to a conclusion.

New Caledonia

When France won football's World Cup in 1998, few outside his native New Caledonia noticed that Christian Karembeu, a key mid-field player, refused to sing the national anthem. His gesture symbolised the *systematised cleavage* that has divided the social world of New Caledonia, and manifest in the territory's demographic composition. By the mid-1990s, this comprised 43 per cent indigenous people, or Kanaks; 38 per cent French settlers (including an influential minority of long time settlers, or *caldoches*); twelve per cent from other French Pacific territories, mainly Wallisian migrant labour for nickel mining and services; the remainder comprising some Asian minorities. Representation before the UN's General Assembly Decolonisation Committee in 1998 by the National Socialist Front for the Liberation of the Kanak People (FLNKS), a pro-independence coalition of parties, warned about a future leaving the Kanaks a minority in their own land. Noted was a 20 per cent increase, totalling about 20,000 non-Kanak peoples in New Caledonia during the preceding 20 years.[2] Whatever the ultimate demographic arithmetic, dispute about its potential electoral consequences will not abate. However to some Kanak activists, undue fixation with these questions risks obscuring deeper issues of unaccountable power such as unequal land ownership.

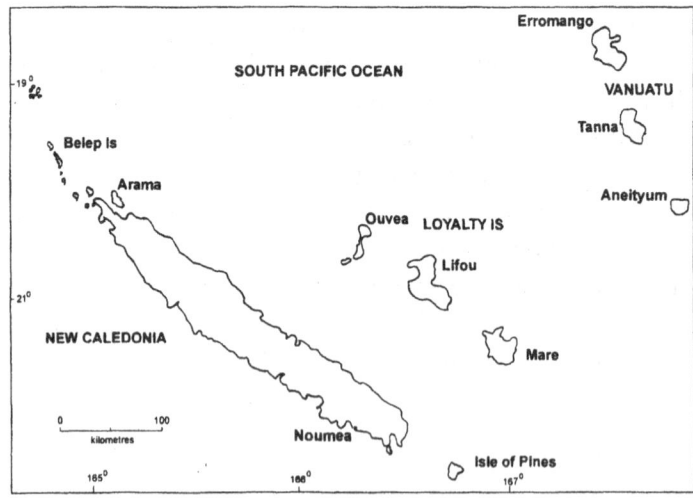

Map 5.1 New Caledonia

New Caledonia's demography relates to its constitutional identity. Here 'the root of the problem has been that France has not considered its Pacific possessions as colonies: rather, that they are overseas territories, and so while there might be a case of reforms of various kinds, independence has not been negotiable' (Cambell, 1989: 205). Between 1947 and 1986, France refused compliance with UN Charter Article 73 provisions requiring transmission of information about dependent territories. Non-compliance was justified on grounds of New Caledonia's self-government within the French Republic, the Quai d'Orsay flatly stating it was 'the sole judge of the state of emancipation reached by the peoples under its administration'.[3] Reinscription in 1986 to the list of countries subject to UN scrutiny, disavowed French claims that this was essentially an internal issue. This step was significant, strengthening calls that other conduct in the Pacific Paris defended as 'internal' – in particular nuclear testing – warranted systematic external scrutiny.

Throughout, Paris has subjected the territory's governing statute arrangements to constant revision and alteration. This included the 1985 Pisani Plan offering a choice between the status quo, and 'independence in association with France'. Although scuttled by local loyalist sentiment, actively backed by Chirac and Le Pen who campaigned in New Caledonia's territorial elections as a 'dry run' for the March 1986 election in France, the association option retained its visibility. Possible sweeteners included French citizenship, budgetary support, non-Kanak land placed under leasehold to Kanak owners, and security assistance (Ross, 1993:142). New Caledonia's possibly maintaining a long term relationship with France through a treaty safeguarding rights and long-term French financial support, was also floated (Henningham, 1992: 233).

French officials viewed self-government in association as a mechanism to ease an increasingly embittered polarisation over independence that emerged after 1980. The settler/indigenous divide was the most prominent, although schisms existed within factions to either side. Radicalisation of the Kanak movement coincided with in-migration from France, and from former or existing French territories, including regional neighbours Wallis and Futuna. Kanaks lost relative numerical strength, diminishing prospects for an electoral outcome delivering majority support for outright independence. Faced with loyalist insistence that the territory was not a colony but part of France,

Kanak frustration erupted to spark easily the worst years of violence in memory between 1984 and 1989.

In January 1985, violence took the lives of a key pro-independence figure, Eloi Machoro, and his deputy Marcel Nanaro. September 1987 saw the passage of referendum which allowed voters with at least three years' territorial residence the choice of either full independence, or remaining within the French Republic. In a climate of jingoism, the option of staying with France was carried with 98 per cent of the electorate voting to favour remaining with France. Estimates of Kanak participation ran as low as 16 per cent.

In May 1988, during the charged atmosphere immediately preceding the first round of a French presidential election, Kanak militants killed four French gendarmes and took further French security personnel hostage within caves on the island of Ouvea. French troops then stormed these caves, killing 19 Kanaks but losing two of their forces dead. These events convulsed New Caledonia, took it to the brink of civil war, damaged France's international standing, and inflamed its internal politics. That was aggravated by Chirac's negative campaigning on the issue prior to 1988 Presidential elections that he lost to incumbent Mitterand.

Retracting from the crisis, the newly installed, more moderate Rocard government instituted the 1988 Matignon Accords. They bought time by setting out a ten year programme of regional development, Kanak management training, judicial decentralisation, accelerated land redistribution, and a semi-autonomous tripartite representative provincial framework. Positive developments under the Matignon process included some land reforms, investment for infrastructural development, and commitments to the Kanak cultural renaissance authoritatively articulated by the late independence leader Jean Marie Tjibaou. Assassinated in 1989, this moderate's political and intellectual legacy bequeathed a philosophy of indigenous selfhood. To him, 'France looks at itself, and through itself looks at the world. From this basis it is difficult for France to allow a certain autonomy, to accept that other people can take pride in existing by themselves' (cited Bensa and Wittersheim, 1998: 376). He saw the Kanak identity not as a reconstruction of tradition, but evolving into the future. Through French finance, local solemnisation, and Pacific indigenous peoples' support, the Tjibaou legacy was hallowed through a major cultural centre built in his name and opened in 1998.

The Kanak cultural renaissance challenged, but could not lessen the totality of French social and economic impacts. Driven by economic need and job insecurity, integrationist Kanak sentiment aligned with majority settler preferences in uneasy consensus to support continuing ties with France. Some estimates indicated that between 15 and 20 per cent of the Kanak population favoured a continued French presence in the territory (Berman, 1998: 62). This allowed France the leeway it sought to maintain a policy of delayed decolonisation. A supposedly definitive referendum on the territory's constitutional future, foreshadowed under the Matignon Accords, saw further delay. Duly conducted in November 1998, this recorded a 74 per cent turnout of 106,000 eligible electors. They voted a 71 per cent approval to the 1998 Noumea Agreement that prescribed a twenty-year programme of gradual, irrevocable transfer of sovereignty, with final status subject to a referendum due between 2013 and 2018.

This prolongation was agreed in order to stabilise conditions, attract investment, reduce settler/Kanak economic disparities, and build common ground for constitutional stability. In outline, this could allow settler sentiment an opportunity to appreciate the advantages of enhanced autonomy from France, and the independence movement benefits of continued association. Bernard Lepu, President of the largest party in the pro-independence Front, viewed the transition as the 'only way to reconcile the Kanak desire for independence with the desire of Loyalists and Paris for French representation in the region'.[4] This conveys a modernist conception of material and social advancement that ignores the territory's abiding ethnic, social, and cultural schisms.

East Timor

While cleavage has polarised identities in New Caledonia, they have encountered *severe social dislocation* in East Timor. Following Indonesia's December 1975 invasion, the territory suffered a decade of social devastation. Within five years of 1975, an estimated one seventh of a 700,000 population died, most at hands of the Indonesian military. In the following five years, as many again died – either violently, through starvation, or from disease.[5] While opposition to Indonesian rule built comradeship among East Timorese exiles, this was less evident among those remaining within the territory.[6] For mixed motives, a component of the population, not just recent settlers, have supported integration. They have done so for economic reasons, fear of retribution following previous contacts with the Indonesian military, and from political affiliations hardened by the legacies of violence that erupted following Portugal's hasty departure and Indonesian invasion.

In 1994, local Roman Catholic Bishop Carlos Belo had signified his preparedness to work with all parties, including the Indonesian government, towards defining a 'special status' for the territory. Although details remained undisclosed, Belo believed it was the best eventual solution.[7] This position reflected prudence between militant local nationalism, pro-intergrationist sentiment, and the Suharto regime's suspicions that this future Nobel Peace Prizewinner was meddling in politics. In 1995, the head of the East Timor military command indicated to the visiting Australian Ambassador that granting the territory 'special status' remained under consideration.[8] The Suharto regime did not advance this proposal given its potential as a precedent threatening supposed state integrity and national ideology. Nor did Indonesia want its standing among Association of Southeast Asian Nations (ASEAN) partners weakened by granting concessions to insurgents supported from abroad. The regime's authorities continued to detain Timorese speaking to representatives from visiting foreign delegations.[9]

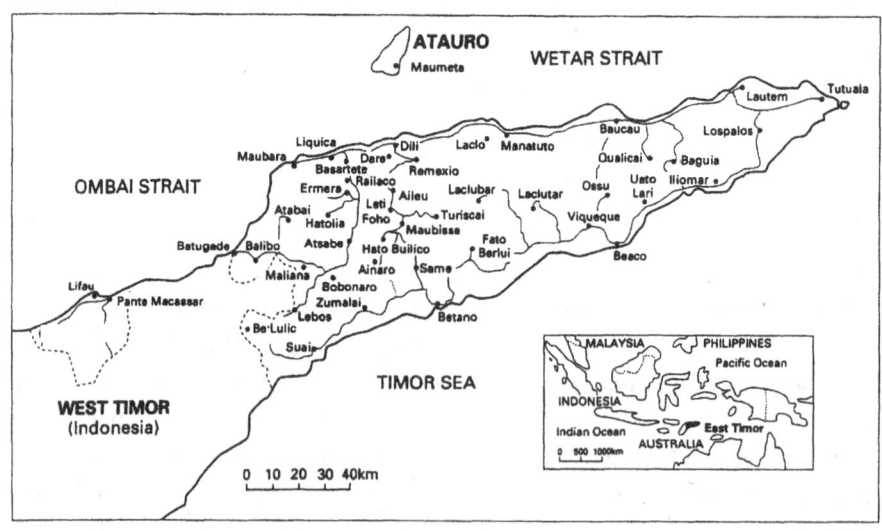

Map 5.2 East Timor

Following the Suharto regime's collapse, the Habibie government announced in January 1999 that the East Timorese could choose either broad autonomy or independence. Recession-hit Indonesia's heavy reliance on international assistance was a key factor in this sudden change of policy. In March 1999, Indonesia and Portugal agreed on a UN-sponsored ballot for the people of East Timor. This included those living abroad in a decision about whether to accept autonomy within the Republic of Indonesia or independence. The move worsened already tense relations between pro-integration sentiment and independence activism. Prospects for the territory's fuller autonomy heightened insecurity, particularly between those backing para-military formations engaged in irregular combat against pro-independence movements. From March 1999, this polarisation deteriorated into outright conflict with numerous deaths, rapes, forcible relocations, and kidnappings reported. This occurred at the hands of the militia groupings such Besah Merah Putih ('Red and White Iron' and based in Liquica), Aitarak (Dili) and Mahidi (Suai) that comprised transmigrants, some West Timorese, paid conscripts, and criminal elements armed by the Indonesian military.[10]

Although not designated a formal referendum, the political significance of the planned ballot was unmistakable. Indonesian Foreign Minister Alatas confirmed that East Timorese independence activist Xanana Gusmao under house arrest, would be released once an overall settlement was agreed. Even without hindsight, the UN's decision to proceed to a late August 1999 referendum, conducted under its auspices, represented a monumental miscalculation of timing. Indeed, the preceding April, when army backed militia killed 45 refugees in a church compound, senior UN officials voiced grave apprehensions via internal memoranda about going ahead with the planned referendum.[11] In the event, this saw 78.5 per cent of the territory's 430 000 voters rejecting autonomy within Indonesia to favour independence. Given the territory's poor transport and communications infrastructure, it was a remarkable feat of electoral logistics to register voters and achieve a 98 per cent turnout.

UN personnel received significant assistance from the over 400 UN volunteer electoral supervisors, non-governmental representatives, and Australian, Japanese, British, American, and New Zealand officials. That assistance and relative polling efficiency, enraged the militias. Once the result was announced, they launched a pre-planned campaign of killing and destruction flagrantly aided and abetted by the Indonesian military, in particular the US-trained elite special forces or Kopassus.[12] This occurred for a variety of motives: fears East Timorese independence would further fuel separatist aspirations in Aceh and West Irian; beliefs the territory's independence betrayed previous military sacrifices; incredulity at the 78 per cent vote favouring independence; and internal military manoeuvring against the Habibie administration. For this study's purposes, Indonesia's internal civil military relations doubtless provided a major dynamic driving international response to the crisis.

Within ten days of the poll, thousands had died, the main centre of Dili and most other towns and villages systematically torched, many thousands put to flight into the hills to suffer acute deprivation, and homes, properties and commercial facilities looted and ransacked. Apart from fears about refugees within East Timor, grim reports surfaced about the tens of thousands forced or in flight into the neighbouring Indonesian province of West Timor. Within a month, the entire island had confronted a full scale humanitarian crisis.

These events occurred as the Asia Pacific Econonmic Cooperation (APEC) summit met in Auckland. Governments previously eschewing political issues under these auspices faced a crisis that had the potential to either make or break APEC's international credibility. Sufficient pressure was exerted upon the Indonesian government for it to 'invite' an international force into the territory to restore order, and allow it the opportunity to rebuild towards independence. President Clinton's support for this step was decisive at APEC, but so was the arrival of Ramos Horta who quickly assumed high public and international media focus as the conscience of the East Timorese people.

A UN Security Council mission visited Jakarta and East Timor, followed shortly by UN High Commissioner for Human Rights, Mary Robinson. The Security Council mission's written report indicated that the role of Indonesian troops and police in organizing and backing militia violence in East Timor had 'become clear to any objective observer'.[13] This was confirmed by High Commissioner Robinson and virtually all journalists and UN personnel directly involved. Both added pressure on the Habibie government, itself under increasing influence from the military, to accept international assistance. From late September 1999, a UN multinational force in East Timor slowly restored order to the battered province that remains a continuing charge on the guilt of the international community. These events left Indonesian/

Australian relations badly damaged, and endemic instability sustained throughout the Indonesian archipelago.

West Irian

In West Irian (or West Papua) identity formation opportunities faced pressure from *sustained fragmentation*. Temporary UN authority facilitated an accommodation between Netherlands and Indonesia facilitating Dutch withdrawal from the territory in 1962. The new status quo of de facto Indonesian control was confirmed in a rigged 'Act of Free Choice' in 1969. This restricted participation to 1025 Indonesian hand-picked tribal male leaders 'representing' a population of some 800,000. Under the gaze of the military, they opted to support integration with Indonesia. Australia played an active role in ensuring that the 'Act of Free Choice' gained acceptance without debate at the UN General Assembly later in 1969. Its Ambassador to the UN, Sir Patrick Shaw, cabled Canberra expressing Australian and Dutch hopes that the issue would move through the UN quietly.[14] Although not opposed by the UN, the travesty that this procedure represented did not entirely escape censure. At least some governments recognised that Jakarta's grounds for demanding departure by the Dutch – because they were not Indonesians – required that the demonstrably non-Indonesian Papuans not come under its control either.[15]

Aggravating subsequent hostility towards Indonesian rule was an extensive transmigration programme of Javanese and Bugis people facilitated by World Bank funding. (Of a 1.8 million population, approximately 43 per cent are transmigrants). Jakarta's forcible attempt to subordinate existing loyalties to a greater Indonesian identity, even outlawing the word Papua, was aggravated by official insistence on the use of Bahasa at the expense of the more than 250 languages spoken in the territory.

This fomented deep anti-Indonesian sentiment that lacked effective political focus. Impeding its subsequent formation remained formidable barriers of linguistic heterogeneity, localised clan custom, and the territory's rugged terrain. Political vulnerability is aggravated in a battle to survive by subsistence under conditions of educational and social neglect. Although shared attachment to the land maintains a strong social and spiritual hold, development of a common territorial loyalty is stunted. Activists have sought to establish territorial co-ordinators, but regional differences and personal rivalries impede territorial political unity while their military capability is limited. The territory's insecurity is heightened by religious differences, the divide between Muslim transmigrants and local Christian affiliations more threatening as its death toll has mounted elsewhere, including neighbouring Ambon.

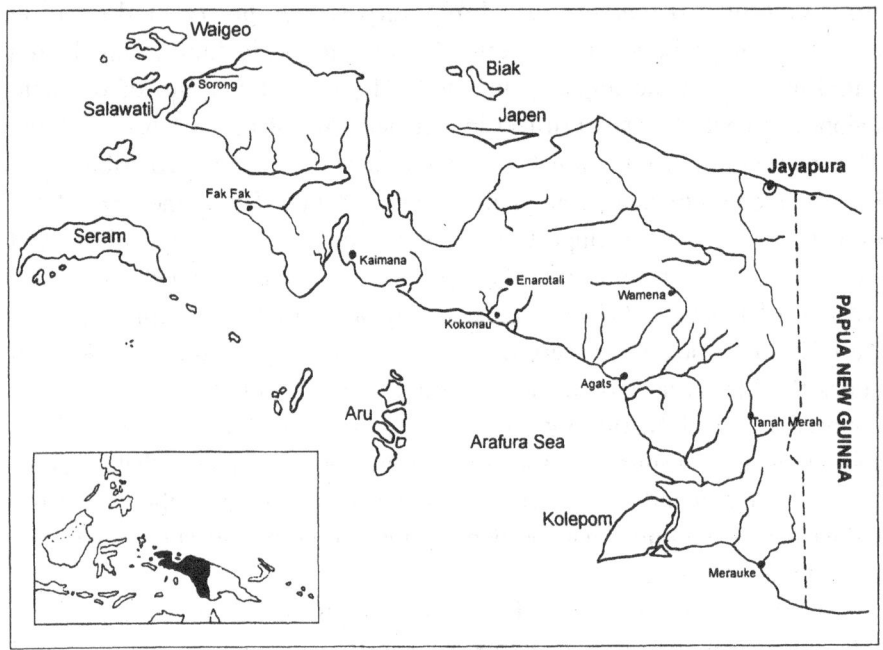

Map 5.3 West Papua

Longstanding factionalism according to regional location has inhibited formation of external support linkages (Wesley-Smith, 1987: 33). Indonesia's non-aligned credentials, and its support from Third World majorities in the UN General Assembly, helped shield its conduct in Irian Jaya from effective international scrutiny. This weakened opportunities to build international support by publicising Indonesia's negative conduct in the territory. Operating since 1969, and dominating the territory's economic activity, the huge Freeport McMoran copper and gold mining complex accounts for 88 per cent of the province's exports. It benefited from close links to the Suharto regime, but has a record of poor environmental stewardship. Gold and copper reserves estimated at its locations are among the highest in the world.[16]

In a January 1996 hostage taking incident, 13 conservationists were incarcerated by Operasi Papua Merdeka (OPM) leader Kagoya and his Nduga tribal adherents at Mapnduma, Jayawijaya district. Staged near the massive Freeport gold and copper mine, the capture was designed to highlight grievances regarding 'fundamental human rights of self determination' against Indonesian rule, and the environmentally damaging operation of the mining facility. Further demands articulated for international purposes included repudiation of the 1969 'Act of Free Choice'; an end to Indonesia's military presence and controversial transmigration programme; a halt to environmentally damaging mining; and international recognition of the national liberation struggle.[17]

The Sydney-based Australian Papua Association believed the kidnapper's demands were driven by local anti-mining and social concerns, although their political nature suggested a search for international diplomatic support as well.[18] A 1996 OPM statement sought 'to obtain international recognition for West Papua independence through international forums such as the United Nations, the Non Aligned (sic) Movement of Nations, the South Pacific Forum, and the Association of Southeast Asian Nations'.[19] Following rescue of the hostages, where mercenaries and even the Red Cross played a role, reprisals and human rights abuses by the Indonesian military intensified. Added difficulties included Indonesia's serious drought of 1997-98 that precipitated famine in a territory badly hit by the declining value of the Indonesian rupiah.

Since the Suharto regime's collapse, sporadic pro-independence rallies have clashed with security forces. In July 1998, Indonesian security forces killed between 60 and 70 people during incidents surrounding an illegal flag raising that proclaimed West Papuan independence. These killings were verified by a Christian Evangelical Church investigation.[20] West Irian's remoteness and modest international support, meant this outrage gained little international publicity.

After detailing these atrocities, a solidarity committee, *Komite Solidaritas Rakyat Irian Kosorairi* appealed directly to the UN Secretary General calling for the UN to 'take the necessary actions to intervene'.[21]

Following the 1996 hostage taking, and amidst growing alarm at Indonesia's security conduct in the territory, independence demands gained enhanced international publicity. Links included Minority Groups International, Survival International, the British-based human rights organisation TAPOL, and support from members of the United States Congress. Eni Faleomavaega, American Samoa's Delegate to the US House of Representatives, called on colleagues in September 1998 to urge the Indonesian government to cease human rights violations 'and take immediate steps to review the political status of West Papua'.[22] The West Papua Peoples' Front, operating from Utrecht, has lobbied the UN Human Rights Sub-Commission on Prevention of Discrimination and Protection of Minorities over transmigration and settlement relocation grievances, while the Unrepresented Peoples' Organisation included West Papuan concerns within its brief when appearing before the UN.[23] The PNG Council of Churches has stated West Papua's concerns should go before the UN on grounds of human rights abuse, rather than as a case for self determination.[24] Survival International has appeared on behalf of West Papua's interests before the UN Commission on Human Rights, attacking transmigration and the population displacement effects of Indonesian military conduct in the territory.

In 1999, the Habibie administration permitted a subsequently inconclusive 'dialogue' with leading West Irianese, the latter concluding that the former was not serious about changing the territory's status. In brief, then, the politics of identity has offered little but frustration to Irian Jaya. The territory has not attracted East Timor's international publicity, nor the scrutiny needed to exert international pressure on Jakarta to alter its political status and improve material and social conditions.

Identity and External Linkages

Decolonisation processes have generally provided the catalyst to forge a national identity through political emancipation. That identity is required to underpin and legitimise emerging statehood, an aspiration that helped to drive the great wave of post-World War II decolonisation. But what of its relevance now? Viewed broadly, a predominantly statist interpretation of self determination '*is blind to the demands of ethnic groups, and national, religious, cultural or linguistic minorities*' (Cassese, 1995: 328, italics original). From cases considered here, the need for self-determination has retained its centrality, but there is less certainty about its capacity to achieve national identity. Ensuring coherent territorial integrity has complicated self-determination, given the region's share of colonial demarcations paying scant heed to ethnic or social complementarities. Furthermore, in an environment of immense linguistic heterogeneity (PNG alone has approximately a quarter of the world's languages), the colonial experience instituted economic, settlement, and lifestyle disparities that reinforced urban/hinterland, and capital location/outer island divisions. As essentially a French city in the South Pacific, Noumea's domination of New Caledonia is the most telling example. Faced by forces causing internal compartmentalisation, identity aspirations have looked to external supports that are now assessed.

In *New Caledonia*, attempts to validate the Kanak identity by international means saw independence demands aggregate grievances over lost land, violated cultural integrity, and continuing economic servitude. These appeals reverberated around the South Pacific, land dispossession the strongest point of reference. These links grew despite poor comprehension of French among the region's English speaking countries. The Tjibaou legacy continued to build on this figure's role in inspiring the landmark South Pacific cultural festival of 1975.

Other measures helped register Kanak identity abroad, as in 1986-87 when its activists manipulated Western Cold War susceptibilities by establishing links with Libya for so-called training purposes. This manoeuvre was primarily designed to draw international attention to local grievances. It also provided the pretext for a curious episode, when Australian Foreign Minister Hayden visited New Zealand at short notice to brief Prime Minister Lange, at an early morning air base meeting. This concerned the supposed Libyan threat in Melanesia, particularly Vanuatu. Presumably unintended, this high level animation distracted attention from moves then afoot to topple the Fiji government in a military coup following soon after.

East Timor's quest for effective decolonisation amplified identity demands, but without bridging local cleavages. The Cold War's demonisation of the Soviet Union declined as an excuse to ignore the territory's increasingly exposed human rights violations. The 1991 Dili massacre, the arrest and incarceration of East Timorese leader Gusmao a year later, and continued asylum seeking forays into Western embassies in Jakarta, provided high visibility international news media events. Like Nelson Mandela, Gusmao's incarceration attracted international news media attention. Ramos Horta gained increasing access to governments during numerous forays abroad. He reinforced international images of a territory denied its fundamental rights under external subjugation. This drew support from a broadening community of sympathetic non-governmental humanitarian, relief, and human rights groups. Behind the headlines, however, the territory's internal schisms proliferated amidst mistrust and poverty.

Jakarta's claims about East Timor's effective incorporation as the 27th province of Indonesia failed to block the territory's distinctive political identity aspirations. Although it impeded scrutiny by UN rapporteurs, the Suharto regime's final decade faced critical international scrutiny over East Timor. This included UN Human Rights Committee investigations; Portugal's regular itemisation of the territory's affairs before the European Parliament; visiting EU and parliamentary delegations; and close attention by Amnesty International and Human Rights Watch/Asia.[25] Specific international support groups included the Netherlands-based International Platform of Jurists for East Timor, the US-based East Timor Action Network, the Asia-Pacific Coalition on East Timor (APCET), and Lord Eric Avebury's British Parliamentarians for East Timor. Information dissemination by concerned groups expanded rapidly during the 1990s by exploiting advances in electronic communication.

East Timorese abroad are regarded as performing a valid future role in the territory's future. APCET stated to ASEAN representatives that: 'Let it be noted ... that there have been initiatives of the East Timorese diaspora together with counterparts inside the territory and in the international community to already evolve mechanisms for the socio-economic, political, judicial and cultural development of the territory in the post colonised future'.[26] The August 1999 UN supervised ballot offering autonomy within Indonesia or separate independence, relied upon external non-governmental agencies to assist in polling preparation. That external presence helped counteract internal pressures attempting to intimidate voters from exercising freely determined voting choices. Central to that purpose was the relevant UN Security Council Resolution's stipulation for effective information dissemination. This would be 'responsible for explaining to the East Timorese people, in an impartial and objective manner without prejudice to any position or outcome, the terms of the General Agreement and the proposed autonomy framework, for providing information on the process and procedure of the vote and for explaining the implications of a vote in favour or against the proposal'.[27]

West Irian's scope for building a distinctive territorial identity was dealt a bad hand by decolonisation. Because its suspect 1969 'Act of Free Choice' gained UN support, the territory's indigenous political aspirations languished through international neglect. The subject had no place as an item before intergovernmental forums, indigenous representatives rarely had access to governments, and international non-governmental involvement in the territory was episodic. Among South Pacific governments, Vanuatu attempted without success to have West Irian's self determination demands heard by the UN.

More progress was possible once Indonesia's 'national identity' policy began to buckle with the demise of the Suharto regime.

Indonesian subjugation to one side, accommodating local custom (*kastom*) to national identity needs under statehood has been problematic throughout Melanesia. Lack of traditional affiliations beyond the ambit of established communities has historically impeded formation of a national identity (Davidson, 1971: 4). The factionalism evident in West Irian's remote, and parochial environment is replicated elsewhere in Melanesia. Working within those constraints has been a significant challenge for the administering powers. It has required them to adjust to different social worlds and scales of value. Doing so has normally required some reckoning of past conduct. New Caledonia's 1998 Noumea Accords, legitimised by referendum, acknowledged that colonialism had disfigured the Kanak indigenous identity. No such *mea culpa* was forthcoming from Jakarta towards either East Timor or West Irian however.

Decolonisation's Wider Political Agenda

A prominent PNG activist, Powes Parkop, has characterised decolonisation throughout the South Pacific and wider Melanesia as a contest across three fronts. These include old colonial rule, as in French Polynesia and New Caledonia; south-south colonialism, as practised by Indonesia in East Timor and West Papua; and recolonisation by the International Monetary Fund and transnational companies.[28] The first is viewed as subject to gradual erosion by historical forces ineluctably reducing the European colonial presence. The second reflects disillusionment with developing country domination of the UN decolonisation agenda. Hence 'in the 1990s a new type of colonialism thrives in Melanesia ... there are peoples of Melanesia who have never been given the right of a free unimpeded vote on the issue of self determination.

The extent to which the Committee of 24 closes its eye to this reality is the extent of failure and hypocrisy of the world community'.[29]

Indonesia has provided the focus for this censure, a factor encouraging East Timor and West Irian to regard their Melanesian credentials as justifying their future membership in the South Pacific Forum. This orientation has gained active support from Vanuatu, while the former President of Nauru, Bernard Dowiyogo, has asserted that 'our brother Melanesians ... have been cut off from us by the vagaries of colonial map-making. We should give support to their attempt to achieve self determination and to their interest in joining the South Pacific Forum'.[30] In 1999, Fiji and PNG offered forces to East Timor ahead of the decision to send an international mission.

The third component – international financial and corporate influence – has gained salience as a target for protest in New Caledonia and West Irian. However, challenging that influence requires civil interest infrastructures, supported by traditional collectivism that can furnish viable alternatives. That mix has not emerged in any of the cases considered, current civil components either stretched financially or organisationally weak. New Caledonia's experience under the Matignon Accords suggests that local and transnational interests, interacting through no other medium than the market, have constricted the formation of a national collective identity able to satisfy Kanak material and symbolic needs. Indigenous clan-based communalism, based on traditions of gift exchange, have not adapted to the buying and selling of capitalist enterprise without dislocation.

Nevertheless younger public figures throughout Melanesia, less wedded to custom or externally derived material blandishments, have begun confronting the challenge of demarcating national, issue-based identities. They regard cultural preservation and natural conservation goals as growth points; developing them is considered as important as gaining formal representation via electoral means.

Decolonisation Options

So far, most attention has been directed to territorial dependency interests and values, but what of administering power options? Once propelled towards self-determination, seams within long static colonial systems start opening to permit new pressures to shape outcomes. Choices may also depend upon the availability of appropriate institutional settings and legitimised forms of reference. This includes prescriptive norms and expectations developed through state conduct, and evolving customary rules about principles of state formation. Practical difficulties accrue by attempting to mesh distinctive local group identities within national constitutional systems through decolonisation (Ghai, 1996: 184). Appeals based on cultural loyalties, and designed to maintain indigenous political systems, may selectively preserve positions of élites (Lawson, 1994: 92). Identity appeals calling up tradition are usually genuine, but also subject to political manipulation.

In some instances, domestic/international interactivity may assist by making a previously rejected decolonisation option more acceptable. This may result from internal upheavals of a fundamental social, political, or ideological kind that coincides with substantial external policy, or international system re-orientations. Previous engagement within internal situations by external actors not performing colonial functions may affect subsequent self-determination priorities. And local actors pursuing self-determination may pitch their demands according to likely or future international economic support. Overall, decolonisation options are shaped by prevailing international political trends. Relevant is the extent of perceived urgency, including possibilities of settling for something less than outright independence, as well as normative, institutional, and transformative aspects. Choices are also shaped by situational determinants that include pressures to accommodate the special needs of distinctive, sub-state social, ethnic, or minority configurations.

The decolonisation record in New Caledonia and East Timor (and arguably Bougainville) supports claims that the most vehement demands for immediate self-determination have occurred in locations where they have been longest thwarted. As in East Timor, pro-independence Kanak interests demanding unconditional independence established international linkages, although not to any immediate effect. Some domestic/foreign interactions formed to accelerate independence, helped advance French decolonisation. They capitalised on international hostility to France's continued nuclear testing in the South Pacific, and insisted upon the reinscription of its territories before the UN Committee of 24. Demands for a relative acceleration of decolonisation occurred in locations considered, but faced substantial constraints. Some were regional, much of the South Pacific treading a hesitant path to independence. In PNG and Fiji, both important examples,

The 'Qualified' Independence Option?

UN Resolution 1541's guidelines, included free association with another state as an option.[31] Adopted by New Zealand for the Cook Islands (1965), and Niue (1974), this permitted New Zealand citizenship, financial assistance, and relief from the expenses of formally conducting foreign relations. Free association did not limit executive or legislative competence; although not sovereign independent countries as traditionally recognised in international law, these entities can assume an international personality for treaty purposes.

Attempts to balance domestic and international considerations has pointed towards the option of what could be termed 'autonomy plus'. The possibility of an emergent political status other than independence, free association (as in the Cook Islands), or integration, is alluded to in the 1970 UN Declaration on Principles of International Law Concerning Friendly Relations and Co-operation Among States.[32] The 1975 Helsinki Final Act of the Conference (now Organisation) on Security and Co-operation in Europe, claimed: 'all peoples always have the right, in full freedom, to determine when and as they wish, their internal and external political status, without external interference, and to pursue as they wish their political, economic, social and cultural development'.[33]

Without prejudice to the degree of independence entailed, this may include subordination to another entity, common citizenship, delegation of competence in foreign relations or defence, and participation in economic arrangements such as customs unions (Hannum and Lillich, 1981: 249). Politically, much may depend on the conditions surrounding the inception of a status of sustained autonomy. An essential element is the achievement of a self-governing status that results from the freely, democratically expressed wishes of the people concerned. Instances of decolonisation tending towards 'autonomy plus' have revealed contrasting domestic/international interactivity. They reveal tactical, constitutional and representational considerations.

There are tactical instances of a decolonising power floating variants of autonomy in order to weaken potentially damaging domestic opposition. Administering power reluctance to decolonise usually reflects strategic priorities of retention. Negotiating the terms of a proposed self determination may assist postponement, France's tactics of delay by persistently reformulating New Caledonia's governing statutes is an example. Grist to that slow grinding mill was also the self-interest of state functionaries. New Caledonia's bureaucratic interests fought Paris tenaciously to safeguard generous occupational, service, and lifestyle advantages. Further spokes impeding New Caledonia's wheel of full independence included insertions about electoral participation in future referenda, relationship of custom to legal codes, and differing timetables for devolving powers to local institutions.[34] For some territorial leaderships, the autonomy option's tactical advantages have promised an opportunity to accrue development assistance benefits, or forestall unwanted final constitutional determinations.

Rules and Norms

How have the often controversial rules and norms guiding decolonisation been affected by the intersection of domestic and international considerations? What do these cases reveal? Relevant issues include self-determination, international accountability, non-intervention, and the status of so-called 'autonomy plus'.

Viewed as a principle but not a right, the standing of individual *self-determination* claims are subject to the vagaries of what the international community deems tolerable. That may depend upon the international support that domestic groups asserting these claims can accumulate. The durability of sovereign territorial integrity principles cannot obscure shortcomings of self-determination as a state-based formulation. Individuals may seek and find international protections for rights they hold dear, but groups claiming such rights have fared less well (Cassese, 1995: 329-30). For example, objections to the 1969 Act of Free Choice in West Irian lacked the political impetus needed to force reconsideration and conduct an act of self determination in accord with international practice.

After insisting New Caledonia was essentially an extension of metropolitan France, Paris allowed referenda determining future status. This followed international pressure to end South Pacific nuclear weapons testing, cease manipulating New Caledonia's difficulties for electoral ends, and commit to the indigenous community's belated social and economic rehabilitation. The Kanak agenda abroad was furthered following New

Caledonia's reinscription on the UN decolonisation list. This followed South Pacific regional pressure, while Vanuatu's membership of the Non-Aligned Movement provided developing country support. Reinscription facilitated New Caledonia's continuing scrutiny by the South Pacific Forum where its pro-independence front gained observer status.

Political considerations operated differently for East Timor, where western power strategic interests, acquiescing in Indonesia's forcible incorporation of the territory, helped shut down the self-determination option. These interests accorded higher priority to bilateral relations with Indonesia than concerns about its breach of customary principles of international law, or acknowledging the rights of self-determination to colonial peoples under foreign military occupation (Cassese,1995: 226-27). However this forced some contortions, Australian policy towards East Timor during the Suharto period was described by Portuguese lawyer, Pedro Leite, as a 'legal centaur – half integration and half self determination'.[35] To the pro-independence movement, the life-line remained UN refusal to accept self-determination had occurred.

Accountability to the United Nations over decolonisation has been more consistently applied than the principle of self-determination. Where they gain standing, domestic interests have not hesitated to reprimand colonial powers for failing to meet these obligations including UN Charter Article 73 provisions. These include regular transmission of information concerning conditions in non-self governing territories. In East Timor, human rights concerns forced the Suharto regime to confront, although not accept, accountability demands. It rejected most visiting mission recommendations, but accepted one which resulted in the 1992 establishment of a national human rights commission. Contrary to numerous doubts, this body proved resilient and independent in its procedures and recommendations. In 1999, it began investigating human rights violations in West Irian.

Indonesia and France emphasised the norm of *non-intervention* to limit domestic/international interactivity anxious to further decolonisation. Indonesia has relied on sovereign integrity principles to deflect human rights investigations that non-governmental interests, and the UN, have insisted are intimately linked to peaceful progress towards decolonisation. At the UN in 1996, the Indonesian government maintained that 'as a sovereign state, we reserve the right to refuse access to any organizations, cloaked with human rights premises while their real purposes are actually political'.[36]

During the Suharto regime's final years, Jakarta usually succeeded in dismissing human rights concerns expressed at the ASEAN Regional Forum as unwarranted interference (Human Rights Watch, 1997: 168). That defence steadily weakened following the 1991 Dili massacre, the Asian financial crisis, and the Suharto regime's collapse, all developments assuming consequence beyond Indonesia's borders.

Finally, how robust is the norm of *'autonomy plus'*? Although lacking secure moorings through international instruments (Alfredsson, 1996: 72), the concept is under active consideration in a variety of settings, if often reluctantly offered and ungratefully received (Dinstein, 1981: 302). The 1998 Noumea Accords are open-ended in that the 'evolving sovereignty' envisaged does not rule out an eventual status where, following an act of free choice, the option chosen permits voluntary subordination of powers exercised from Paris. France continues to insist that a referendum on self-determination is not subject to UN supervision and monitoring, although by insisting this is an internal matter France risks violating the outcome's integrity (Berman, 1998: 72).

In East Timor, the 1999 referendum on the territory's future included an option for either a form of autonomy within the Indonesian Republic, or outright independence. As seen over Bougainville's stuttering progress towards greater autonomy, the dictates of pragmatism and reconciliation of political interest have overshadowed normative appraisals. To East Timorese leader Ramos Horta, Indonesia needed to drop its 'insistence on the precondition that we first accept its illegal annexation before it proceeds with granting genuine autonomy to the region. The conflicting views on the legal status of the territory should not be an obstacle to the fundamental changes that must occur on the ground for Indonesia to gain international credibility and for a degree of peace to prevail'.[37]

Institutions

Decolonisation in the South Pacific facilitated the formation of national representative and regional intergovernmental institutions Those formations resulted from interplay of domestic and external factors. Regarding national institutions, administering power consultation with domestic interests over constitutional formulation was conducted effectively in some instances, partially in others, and poorly elsewhere. This range might be characterised by placing Samoa's effectively promoted and conducted plebiscite processes at one end of a continuum, Portugal's lamentable failure in East Timor at an opposite pole, and numerous consultations utilising traditional, male-dominated cultural systems somewhere between.

The South Pacific's constitutional development preceding decolonisation often encountered difficulties over land, customary law, the role of chiefs, and devolution functions (Ghai, 1996: 184). Foreign experts, rather than visiting UN missions or concerned non-governmental bodies, exerted greatest influence. The challenges they faced lay in devising institutions explicable for international purposes, yet consonant with distinctive, localised social practices, customs and traditions. An international dimension of importance comprised long term assistance agreements negotiated at independence.

Compared to an earlier phase (1962-80), the region's more recent decolonisation attracted a broader constellation of concerned constituencies – indigenous, gender, and civil rights; environmental; entrepreneurial; commercial; and newer wave denominational religious influences. This generated strains within New Caledonia's independence movement, the Matignon Accords process dividing those who favoured utilisation of what the new investment structures offered for entrepreneurship, from those attaching higher priority to grassroots schooling and co-operatives (Berman, 1998: 61-2). To each, an international dimension existed to provide supports and incentives.

In expectations of moves towards enhanced autonomy, East Timorese see domestic institutional building as a direct responsibility of the international community. A transitional government process, supervised by the UN, but creating the basic institutional infrastructure needed for operable independence was canvassed by Xanana Gusmao.[38] This structure was established in 1999 to build from the ashes of the territory's devastation. This has entailed a substantial 'shopping list' including electoral, judicial, police, educational, health and communications requirements. World Bank involvement is probable.

Regional intergovernmental institutions have assisted decolonisation. In 1971, independent and self governing states formed the South Pacific Forum established to promote regional trade, economic development, technical and political co-operation. The Forum's annual heads of government meetings maintain open agendas and a commitment to reach decisions by consensus. Over New Caledonia, the Forum conducted visiting missions (1991, 1993, 1996, 1999) where it heard non-governmental witnesses and prepared reports drawing upon their evidence. The 1996 report indicated the Independence Front's willingness to negotiate an arrangement for transition to independence, and that it understood 'the possibility of an associated state with France is a likely option for that transition period to full independence' (Forum Report, 1996: 33). The Front recommended Forum member countries build contact with all communities in New Caledonia, assist in training and education, and ensure UN attention was maintained on the future political status of the territory (Forum Report, 1996: 38). The South Pacific Forum is guided by conventional state practice regarding access to its proceedings and deliberations. New Caledonia Independence Front representation occurred only following reinscription of the territory by the UN Decolonisation committee.

ASEAN side-stepped East Timor and West Irian as decolonisation issues. ASEAN governments have followed developments in both locations closely, although not admitting this publicly. More than the South Pacific Forum, ASEAN is firmly anchored to principles of sovereign prerogative, its decentralised nature confirming the state-centric conduct of its members (Peou, 1998: 447). Regionally, ASEAN provided a firebreak that helped buffer the Suharto regime from domestic/international interactive processes threatening its hold over East Timor. With the backing of fellow governments, it was easier for the Suharto regime to dismiss external concerns about its East Timor human rights violations as unwarranted foreign meddling. In 1994, the Suharto regime successfully pressured the Philippines to cancel a proposed conference dealing with East Timor and attracting major names that included Danielle Mitterand. Although a public relations reversal affording non-governmental interests bonus publicity, Indonesia's handling of the episode underlined its insistence that self determination was inherently incompatible with principles of national unity and territorial integrity.

Transformations

France's South Pacific nuclear testing and security forces conduct in *New Caledonia* galvanised public responses that helped move decolonisation policy of indefinite delay to one of phased, but irrevocable disengagement.

Although domestic/international linkages amplified independentist demands, they could not unify domestic Kanak sentiment. On the contrary, New Caledonia's international publicity strengthened settler insistence for metropolitan backing of the territory's existing status within the Republic.

Social and economic demarcations reflecting commercial penetration and settler migration did not alter. They comprised demographic and economic realities that the accelerated independence option could not ignore, at least in the short to medium term. In the event, what occurred through implementation of the 1988 Matignon Accords, and the 1998 Noumea Agreement's ratification, was a process of *negotiated* transformation. The domestic/international linkages, operating in support of different interests assisted in both setting boundaries to such outcomes while imparting momentum to their resolution. Although the process was protracted, the more it progressed the greater the realisation that indefinite delay was unsustainable. The state of France, settler interests and their Wallisian supporters, Kanak accommodationists, and pro-independence activists – all accepted a time-bound compromise.

Over *East Timor*, foreign policy interests accommodated Indonesia because its de facto control of East Timor was not reversible. This restricted, but did not reduce local and international interactive pressures asserting demands for the territory's demilitarisation by Indonesian forces in order to facilitate an act of free choice. UN retention of East Timor as an item of unfinished decolonisation business offered a fastening point – a common reference around which domestically driven initiatives for East Timor's decolonisation could coalesce internationally. This exploited the opportunities that emerged after the Suharto regime collapsed, and as the legitimacy of decolonisation demands gained added urgency. International apprehension over the Suharto regime's human rights conduct in East Timor turned to alarm and then anger at the conduct of the Indonesian military in the territory.

Although the forces driving Indonesia's 1998 upheaval grew manifest in *West Irian*, the territory's divided domestic political formations and restricted international linkages did not effectively exploit them to promote self determination. Although West Irian's supposed self determination was as suspect as that followed by Jakarta in East Timor in 1976, it had received a UN endorsement of sorts when the organisation 'took note' of the 1969 outcome. The petitioning, advocacy and monitoring functions that allow domestically-based interests to utilise international means to further decolonisation were not possible here. The scope for domestic/international interactivity to mobilise transformation prospects were occluded. This continues despite the OPM's objectives of getting the 1969 outcome rescinded, putting West Papua on the UN decolonisation list, and gaining international oversight pending full self determination and independence by 2005. The transformation envisaged is one of rebuilding the new nation of West Papua within Melanesian perimeters.

When viewing domestic/international interactivity as a handmaiden resisting or impeding decolonisation, asymmetrical features were evident. Where injections of skill, capital, force, political dominance, or commercial and extractive penetration perpetuated dependencies, then local security, rent seeking, and employment needs were enlisted or manipulated. Examples have included nickel smelting in New Caledonia, the array of semi-civilian service activities associated with the military in East Timor, and major concentrations of finance capital and infrastructure accompanying West Irian's resource exploitation. In these instances, civil society capacity was either impoverished, driven underground, or forced to subsist by the funding, encouragement, and propaganda coming from abroad.

Overall, the domestic/international nexus facilitated formal decolonisation transformations. However as New Caledonia's women would attest, constitutional transformation has not equated with social emancipation. Dependencies aggravated by weak national civil society formations and state deformations remained. Closer international links built pressure for domestic emancipation from violence within families and clans, unsustainable resource depredations, and a fuller spectrum of human rights observance and promotion.

Conclusions

These cases revealed domestic/international interactivity performing contrasting functions. One was a vivid, but inconsistent representation of otherwise remote societies and their needs before international audiences. External familiarisation of territorial conditions expanded through implementation of UN Charter principles mandating accountable decolonisation. These functions were distorted in West Irian, delayed in New Caledonia, but belatedly expanded in East Timor. Self determination demands within colonial territories began assuming sharper focus, urgency, and political direction. Facing increasingly rigorous international scrutiny, administering powers appeared less unaccountable to those they governed.

All cases revealed how administering power strategic, military, and internal security interests impeded decolonisation. Melanesian social structures displayed ambiguity towards incipient national identity formations, eventually intended to underpin future statehood. Colonial economic and administrative structures institutionalising settler/indigenous differences emerged as deeply embedded in New Caledonia. Indonesia's forcible incorporation of East Timor delayed its decolonisation by twenty five years. International acceptance of a dubiously delivered decolonisation outcome denied self-determination in West Irian. Domestic/international interactivity helped publicise conditions, rights and expectations of those within the territories considered. Effectively communicating that need in the cause of decolonisation required attachment to a high profile international issue. This was evident through claims made by Kanaks that French nuclear testing violated cultural and environmental norms and human rights violations in New Caledonia.

Governments wanting their decolonisation policies internationally legitimised have had little problem in subject peoples utilising the UN's petitioning and monitoring processes – indeed, encouraged them to do so. Australia and New Zealand consistently used these mechanisms, anxious to convince the international community of their standing as responsible decolonisers. This suited their foreign policy interests including maintenance of close relations with major western states. That consideration did not affect French policy, more preoccupied with the national republic's integrity than deliberations before the UN Committee of 24. Domestic integrity justified possession and refinement of a nuclear deterrent or *force de frappe*, international security coinage employed for colonial retention in the remote South Pacific. Indonesia's conduct over East Timor was shielded by Cold War exigencies – including mid 1970s alarmism of its possibly becoming the Cuba of Southeast Asia.

Decolonisation within these territories has pitted social worlds against one another, placing imported institutions in potential conflict with local webs of kinship and leadership allegiance. That conflict need not dominate, but grows acute when unfamiliar public and organisational norms are inadequately inaugurated. They include instrumental bargaining, individuated business skill acquisition, national goal setting, electoral competition, legislative representation, and formal public office-holding. These innovations have occurred in New Caledonia, but their acceptance and utilisation by Kanaks has been tentative and ambivalent through their perceived weakening of local clan ties. Decolonisation as state making can thus threaten the primacy of traditional social space – whether conceived through neighbourhoods, within families, between sexes, or towards customary authority. It can raise, but disappoint expectations for the emancipation of women and advancement of social equity. Overall, it is a process carrying potentially profound implications for the social location of individual and group identity.

Protest about the violation of custom and dispossession of land furnished some basis for popular support. However, with the possible exception of Vanuatu, the Southwest Pacific has not seen local land grievances translate into territory-wide movements of nationalist anti-colonialism. At élite levels, the region was physically and politically isolated from these forces. Conservative leaderships were often unsympathetic to a politics of drastic recasting, favouring appropriate indigenisation of colonial systems. Identity formations struggling to build nation wide loyalties, had to contend with not just colonialism's historically induced cleavages. Pressure also came in the form of a state security presence, and transnational resource extraction interests. In Irian Jaya and New Caledonia, identity sentiment was inflamed yet eroded by powerful transnational mining and state security pressures.

France as a resource rich state was better positioned than Indonesia to attenuate decolonisation. French capital and access to European Union funding, allowed Paris to offer material incentives under the Matignon Accord process that diluted pro-independence Kanak sentiment. The French state remained arbiter between settler/indigenous interests; their contrasting cultural and ethnic backgrounds were maintained through the different relationships that each maintained towards that central role. By contrast, Indonesia's bayonets were not for sitting on: the force used to take East Timor was never sufficient for its retention once the Suharto regime collapsed. The barrenness of Indonesian state functions in East Timor was revealed by the insecurity and violence perpetrated by the pro-Jakarta militias before and after the August 1999 referendum. In West Irian a similar vacuum of state responsibility was evident.

Sovereignty and national security imperatives revealed their capacity to bypass domestic/international interactivity as irrelevant to state policy regarding the timing and content of decolonisation. Globalisation and modernisation, so-called, exerted divisive impacts. Indonesia and France exploited an international environment ignoring egregious state violations of individual rights and basic social entitlements. Appeals to the international community regarding rights violations often received short shrift; responses claimed that these demands comprised insurgency against state integrity. Principles of non-intervention, allied to Cold War exigencies, helped shield human rights abuses and the neglect of social, economic, and political advancement.

To shape decolonisation, domestic/international interactivity needed footholds to exert an impact. Reinscription of New Caledonia as a territory subject to UN decolonisation investigation was one opportunity. More emphatic was the Security Council resolution authorising a UN role in East Timor's 1999 referendum, which helped legitimise non-governmental electoral observation and humanitarian relief, and eventually peace enforcement. That expedited a future of domestic/international interactivity required before East Timor can secure any semblance of sovereign viability. Other cases considered are relevant, but East Timor stands as the most glaring example of how decolonisation's unfinished business can poison relations between peoples, within countries, and throughout regions.

Notes

1. This was because of anti-American sentiment evident among some backbenchers over the proposed US Holy Loch nuclear submarine base (Scott, 1991: 125).
2. UNGA, Fourth Committee, Press Release, 9, GA/SPD/134, 4th Meeting, 7 October 1998.
3. Fourth Committee, UN General Assembly, official records 4th Session, 4 November 1949, para 18, p. 135.
4. Radio Australia News, 9 February 1997.
5. UN Commission on Human Rights. Report of Special Rapporteur Bacre Waly N'diaye, UN doc. E/CN/1995/61/Add. 1, para 17.
6. Accurate totals of East Timorese abroad do not exist, but 1999 estimates were 20,000 in Australia, 3000 in Portugal, with small numbers dispersed elsewhere, including Macau, Mozambique and the United States. *The Australian*, 29 March 1999. In the August 1999 referendum, more than 13,000 votes were cast abroad.
7. *The Star*, Kuala Lumpur, 29 October 1994.
8. 'New Approach in Timor Needed', *Jakarta Post*, 15 March 1995.
9. East Timor: UN Secretariat Working Paper, doc. A/AC/109/1187, p. 11.

Decolonisation 147

10 These concerns were addressed in the UN Secretary General's Report, *Question of East Timor*, 22 May 1999, S/1999/595, section 23.
11 Steven Mufson and Colum Lynch, 'E. Timor Failure Puts UN on the Spot', *Washington Post*, 26 September 1999.
12 *Far Eastern Economic Review*, 162, 37, 16 September 1999, p. 11. On US training of Kopassus, see Ed Vulliamy and Antony Barnett, 'US trained butchers of East Timor', *Guardian Weekly*, 23-29 September 1999, p. 2.
13 *Reuters*, 14 September 1999. The Report is UN doc. S/1999/976.
14 Files released by Australian Foreign Affairs to SBS 'Dateline' television programme, broadcast Australia 25 August 1999.
15 Official records 16th Session of the UN General Assembly, 1153rd meeting, 1962, p. 507.
16 Chris Ballard, 'Irian Jaya', *The Contemporary Pacific*, 10, 2, 1998, pp. 438-39.
17 *Pacific News Bulletin*, 11, 1, January 1996.
18 John McBeth, 'Now Hear This: Irian Jaya Rebels Learn to Play Hardball', *Far Eastern Economic Review*, 18 April 1996, p. 24.
19 The Free West Papua Movement. OPM, (online, http://www.converge,org.nz/wpapaua/opm).
20 Message of KOSORAIR to UN Secretary General Annan 7 August 1998 (online, http://www.irja.org).
21 Pacific Islands Report 15, 8 August 1998, (online, http:// pidp.ewc.hawaii.edu/PIReport).
22 US House of Representatives, Washington DC 11 September 1998 (online, http://pidp.ewc.hawaii.edu/PIReport).
23 See infra p. 161.
24 Statement of PNG Council of Churches Secretary Leva Kila Pat, *Post Courier*, Port Moresby, 6 February1998.
25 See for example Amnesty International, East Timor: *Broken Promises – Implementation of the Recommendations of the UN Special Rapporteur*, 1998. Human Rights Watch/Asia, *Deteriorating Human Rights in East Timor*, New York: Human Rights Watch/Asia, 1995.
26 APCET statement for the ASEAN Ministerial Meeting, Guy Miclat, 22 July 1998, (online, http:// www. pactok.net.au/docs).
27 UN Security Council Resolution 1246, 11 June 1999, section 4(c).
28 Statement of Powes Parkop, General Secretary of Melanesian Solidarity (MELSOL) to the Asia Pacific Solidarity Conference, Sydney 10-13 April 1998, (online, http://www.3.silas.unsw.edu.au).
29 *The Times of Papua New Guinea, Editorial*, 10 June 1993, p. 4.
30 'Nauru's Dowiyogo Supports East Timor, West Papua Self-determination', Pacific Concerns Resource Centre Media Release, Suva, 15 August 1999.
31 UNGA Res. 1541, (XV), doc. A/4634, 29.
32 *Declaration on Principles of International Law Governing Friendly Relations and Co-operation Among States in Accordance with the Charter of the United Nations*. New York: United Nations, 1970.
33 Conference on Security and Co-operation in Europe. *Final Act: Helsinki 1975*, (online, http://www.1.umn.edu/humanrts/osce).
34 *From the Matignon Accords to the Noumea Accord*. Government of France, Secretariat d'Etat à l'Outre-Mer, July 1998.
35 Cited by Gerry van Klinken, 'Peacemaking for East Timor', *Inside Indonesia*, 44, 1995, p. 10.
36 Statement Ambassador Agus Tarmidzi, UNHRC, Geneva, 18 April 1996.

37 Statement of Ramos Horta to the UN Decolonisation Committee, 30 June 1998.
38 *Reuters,* 'Timor rebel wants UN to step in', 1 March 1999.

References

Aldrich, Robert (1993), *France and the South Pacific Since 1940*, Honolulu: University of Hawaii Press.

Aldrich, Robert and Connell, John (1998), *The Last Colonies*, Cambridge: Cambridge University Press.

Alfredsson, Gudmundur (1996), 'Different Forms of and Claims to the Right of Self-Determination', in Donald Clark and Robert Williamson (eds), *Self-Determination: International Perspectives*, London: Macmillan, pp. 58-86.

Bensa, Alban and Wittersheim, Eric (1998), 'Nationalism and Interdependence: The Political Thought of Jean-Marie Tjibaou', *The Contemporary Pacific*, 10, 2, pp. 369-90.

Berman, Alan (1998), '1998 and Beyond in New Caledonia: At Freedom's Gate?', *Pacific Rim Law and Policy Journal*, 7, pp.1-76.

Boyd, Mary (1987), *New Zealand and Decolonisation in the South Pacific*, Wellington: New Zealand Institute of International Affairs.

Bush, Kenneth D. and Keyman, Fuat (1997), 'Identity-Based Conflict: Rethinking Security in a Post-Cold War World', *Global Governance*, 3, 3, pp. 311-28.

Campbell, I.C. (1989), *A History of the Pacific Islands*, Christchurch: University of Canterbury Press.

Cassese, Antonio (1995), *Self Determination of Peoples. A Legal Reappraisal*, Cambridge: Cambridge University Press.

Davidson, J. W. (1971), *The Decolonization of Oceania – A Survey 1945-70*, Wellington: New Zealand Institute of International Affairs.

Dinstein, Yoram (ed) (1981), *Models of Autonomy*, Tel Aviv: Tel Aviv University.

Forum Report of Ministerial Visit to New Caledonia (1996), Report to the 27th South Pacific Forum (South Pacific Forum document).

Ghai, Yash (1996), 'Self-Determination in the South Pacific', in Donald Clark and Robert Williamson, (eds), op. cit., pp. 173-99.

Hannum, Hurst and Lillich, Richard B. (1981), 'The Concept of Autonomy in International Law', in Yoram Dinstein (ed), op cit., pp. 215-54.

Henningham, Stephen (1992), *France and the South Pacific: A Contemporary History*, North Sydney: Allen and Unwin.

Human Rights Watch (1997), *World Report 1997*, New York: Human Rights Watch.

Kahler, Miles (1984), *Deolonization in Britain and France*, Princeton: Princeton University Press.

Lawson, Stephanie (1994), 'Culture, Democracy, and Political Conflict Management in Asia and the Pacific: An Agenda for Research', *Pacifica Review*, 6, 2, pp. 85-98.

Maclellan, Nic and Chesneaux, Jean (1998), *After Moruroa. France in the South Pacific*, Melbourne: Ocean Press.

May, R.J. (1982), 'Political Style in Melanesia', in R. J. May and Hank Nelson (eds), *Melanesia: Beyond Diversity*, Canberra: RSPAS, Australian National University.

Peou, Sorpong (1998), 'The Subsidiarity Model of Global Governance in the UN-ASEAN Context', *Global Governance*, 4, 4, pp. 439-59.

Ross, Ken (1993), *Regional Security in the South Pacific: The Quarter Century 1970-95, Canberra Papers on Strategy and Defence*, No. 100, Canberra: RSPAS, Australian National University.
Scott, John (1991), 'Getting off the Colonial Hook: New Zealand's Record of Decolonisation at the United Nations', in Malcolm McKinnon (ed), *New Zealand in World Affairs, Volume II 1957-1972*, Wellington: New Zealand Institute of International Affairs, pp. 122-44.
Smith, Roy H. (1997), *The Nuclear Free and Independent Pacific Movement*, London: Tauris.
Spanier, John W. (1967), *World Politics in an Age of Revolution*, London: Pall Mall Press.
Wesley-Smith, Terence (1987), 'Lost Melanesian Brothers: The Irian Jaya Problem and its Implications for Papua New Guinea', *Pacific Studies*, 10, 3, pp. 27-51.

6 Indigenous Rights

Introduction

Indigenous rights issues straddle domestic and international politics across several dimensions. They are junctures where *legacies of colonialism*, demands for *internal decolonisation*, and imperatives of *globalisation* meet. All are relevant for a chapter that considers how a mix of domestic and international determinants has affected indigenous rights developments in Australia, New Zealand and Fiji. It evaluates identity aspects, mobilisation of interests and supports, emergent rules and norms, institutional dimensions, transformational aspects, and a final summation. In each country considered, indigenous rights issues are in flux. This reflects uncertainties evident elsewhere about accommodating indigenous aspirations and entitlements.

The way governments handle indigenous rights issues affects their foreign relations and the external standing of the societies that they represent. Although they do not normally favour formal secession, indigenous rights interests interrogate the premises of state and nationhood. Calls for enhanced autonomy, stronger self-governance, and options of self-determination by indigenous peoples attract international publicity and the attentions of governments. Some outcomes, such as Canada's Nanuvut designation, invite positive comparison. Failure to manage indigenous demands can incur reputational damage that threatens attainment of external objectives. Pertinent are unresolved questions about whether 'outsiders', however defined, can make determinations 'for' indigenous peoples, or reach 'final settlements' over their continuing concerns (Fletcher, 1997: 419).

More than 900 million people (almost one sixth of the world's population), identify with some 270 significant ethnic and communal groups. Thousands of smaller entities exist. Neglect of these interests can upset the domestic and international relations of states. Although usually country specific, the needs and grievances of indigenous peoples impart messages that readily cross borders to form bonds of empathy. This facilitates the determination of common objectives and mobilisation of international pressures and concerns (Coates, 1998: 12).

Self perceptions of insufficiency accrue from shared tragedies of land loss under colonialism. This deprivation ravaged social structures, brought spiritual bereavement, and uprooted identity moorings. The resulting social void left fertile ground for a proliferation of negative social phenomena: alcohol abuse; violence among kin; poor educational, health, and housing conditions; high solo parent family numbers; crime; heavy welfare dependency; and chronic unemployment. Atonement for these grievances through appropriate remedies is a driver that motivates the international politics of indigenous rights.

Indigenous groups seek international support and publicity to maintain or retrieve access to customary resources (Perry, 1996: 39). This is hazardous since governments may regard restrictions in utilisation of communal resource systems an impediment to modernisation. Furthermore, indigenous groups may divide between those opting for immediate local gain from resource exploitation, and those wanting it 'banked' as collateral.

Contrasting Agendas

Nineteenth century French historian, Ernest Renan, once characterised nationalism as the right to exist and have a name. He also observed that national identity involves forgetting the past as much as remembering it (cited Kymlicka, 1995: 189). Both observations are pertinent for indigenous peoples: first, demands for self-definition have assumed growing significance in national and international affairs (Stavenhagen, 1996: 10-11); second, capacity to forget need not mean neglect of the past, but a willingness to challenge those who might monopolise political power to define 'tradition'. From this, it appears a form of double debate is underway. At one level, indigenous rights demands are challenging the conventional precepts of state sovereignty. At another, tradition and how it is constructed, faces revision and reinterpretation from within indigenous movements. At both levels, these challenges are unresolved and widening; both assume importance for domestic/ international interactivity. Accommodating contending identity structures within state systems is now an abiding international question. At one extreme is dread that viable statehood is threatened by ethnicity and tribalism generating abiding schisms, disintegration, and violence (Maybury-Lewis, 1997: 99).

Yet to some indigenous groups, the fears just described are part of the problem. Rather than expecting cultures to adapt to state systems, the onus should rest with sovereignty constructs to alter and accommodate indigenous demands. Since transnational forces are diluting sovereignty from above, why not concede that pressures from below do likewise and adjust accordingly? A respected Maori jurist believes indigenous groups do not regard themselves as creations of states, but akin to them by possessing an inherent autonomy (Durie, 1995:3). Further, it is 'arguable that there is a duty on the state not just to permit aboriginal autonomy but to support it as a positive way of improving internal peace, national performance and individual freedoms' (Durie, 1997: 1).

Added contention surrounds definitional disputes about the nature of indigenous identity. Emphasising self-identification as the essential criteria, many indigenous group representatives regard objective stipulation as neither necessary nor desirable. A study by J. R. Martinez Cobo, distinguished indigenous communities, peoples, and nations as possessing historical continuity to pre-invasion and pre-colonial societies, but distinct from societal formations subsequently prevailing in their territories. Indigenous groups were non-dominant, typically determined to preserve, develop, and transmit ancestral territories and ethnic identity to future generations. This was the basis of a continued existence as peoples with distinctive cultural patterns, social institutions, and legal systems (Cobo, 1986: section 379).

Eschewing ethnic criteria, Erica-Irene Daes identified indigenous peoples according to traditional land associations and historical continuities. They are native to specific ancestral territories, rather than native generally to a region in which a state is located.[1] To assist general application of international legal instruments, 'relatively unproblematic' criteria identified have included self-identification; historic disruption, dislocation or exploitation; long connection with a region; and the wish to retain a distinct identity (Kingsbury, 1998: 453).

Although assimilationist in orientation, International Labour Organisation (ILO) Convention 107 (1957) acknowledged the rights, needs and priorities of indigenous peoples. This was superseded by ILO Convention 169 *Concerning Indigenous and Tribal People in Independent Countries* (1989). This endorsed self-identification as a determining criterion of indigenous peoples, with rights to decide development 'as it affects their lives, beliefs, institutions and spiritual well being and the lands they occupy or otherwise use' (section 7.1). Looking to state interests, the Convention indicated that its use of the term 'peoples' did not imply implications beyond any currently applying under current international law's territorial concept of people; that is, all the inhabitants of a state or a colony (Quane, 1998: 571). Inclusion of this provision during the Convention's June 1989 deliberations, provoked a walkout by indigenous peoples' representatives already smarting from the observer status granted to them in proceedings. Some organised a boycott of ILO Convention 169 and recommended its non-ratification to governments (Iorns Magallanes, 1999: 241).

Elsewhere, ILO Convention 169 recognised indigenous rights to retain customs and institutions provided 'these are not incompatible with fundamental rights defined by the national legal system and with internationally recognised human rights.'[2] As a framework identifying indigenous peoples' needs, and as a statement of relevant principles guiding ownership, entitlements and obligations, ILO Convention 169 represents 'international law's most concrete manifestation of the growing responsiveness to indigenous people's demands' (Anaya, 1996: 45). As an ILO instrument, agency compliance obligations extend beyond governments to include employers and trade unions. Of relevance for Asia-Pacific settings, Article 20: 3 (a) asserts indigenous peoples' rights and protections as migrant, seasonal, agricultural, and casual workers. Fiji is among the 13 states that have ratified this Convention, but not Australia or New Zealand, although the latter began reviewing its position in 1999.

The Cases Compared

The colonial experience of Australia, New Zealand and Fiji witnessed wilful economic, social and educational neglect of indigenous peoples. These failings were serious in Fiji, highly damaging to Maori in New Zealand, but devastating for Aboriginals and Torres Strait Islanders in Australia to the extent grievance is now considered a function of identity (Mulgan, 1998:191). All three countries have witnessed vigorous, contrasting assertions of indigenous identity that have utilised domestic/international interactivity to highlight their claims.

All countries experienced British rule which, notwithstanding the special status granted the indigenous community in Fiji, propagated common law principles of justice and individual rights before the law. Rights granting group property entitlements required authorisation by statute, rather than approval through recourse to customary principle. As countries adopting the essential features of the Westminster parliamentary system, representation of indigenous interests fared poorly. The 1867 Maori Representation Act, creating four Maori electorates, remained effectively unrevised for over a century. It took until 1962 before Australia amended the Commonwealth Electoral Act to enfranchise all Aboriginal and Torres Strait Islanders. Indigenous Fijians did not receive full enfranchisement until 1963.

Table 6.1   Australia, New Zealand, Fiji: Indigenous Populations and Land Tenure

	Population millions	% Indigenous Population	Area sq.km.	% Indigenous tenure
Australia	19.0	1.6	7,687,300	8.3
New Zealand	3.8	9.7	266,000	5.6
Fiji	0.77	51.0	18,350	83.0

Sources: Australia, New Zealand and Fiji Census data

Identity Contrasts

Australia

In Australia, indigenous cultural affiliations are manifest through claims to ancestral lands. Despite social and physical upheaval afflicting Aboriginals, these links are intimate, pervasive and enduring. Complex ties that evolved around spatial, spiritual and social modes of organisation link to marriage, economic exchange, and reciprocities evolved through the transmission of animist beliefs and religious knowledge. These cultures were devastated following settler discovery, conquest and session, and as alcohol, disease, and violence took their toll. Currently, Aboriginal people in Australia 'are the poorest, sickest, most homeless, least literate and hungriest ... the most oppressed, repressed and depressed; most arrested, imprisoned and convicted' (Tatz, 1994: 167). Given the considerable exposure and resource allocations involved, 'these outcomes are disgraceful' (Fletcher, 1997: 418). Most Australians are aware that, in relation to resources allocated to Aboriginal advancement during the last three decades, actual results are unsatisfactory.

Unlike New Zealand, resistance to colonisation in Australia was fragmentary, disorganised and in perpetual retreat. Lack of aboriginal resistance reinforced settler beliefs that Australia was essentially an uninhabited continent. Indigenous peoples were perceived as not just nomadic, without fixed attachment to the land, but a lower order of humanity incapable of assuming the rights and duties of private property ownership identifiable in law. This laid the ground for the *terra nullius* doctrine – land belonging to no one – a concept overturned by the landmark 1992 *Mabo* (No. 2) decision. That ruling recognised the compatibility of possessed communal native title (although not native tenure) with common law principles. *Mabo* extracted native title from legal limbo, and confirmed the Crown's express power of native title extinguishment by valid executive act or statute. Extinguishment was also possible through land alienation by the Crown, or exercise of powers inconsistent with the continued existence of native title, for example by freehold grant. In effect, *Mabo* meant native title's continued existence in those parts of Australia neither closely settled nor subject to inconsistent land grants (Mason, 1997: 819). In response, the Keating government enacted the Native Title Act in 1993. This complex statute devised ways to determine claims to native title, recognise continuous native use and possession, and limit conditions under which native land rights could be extinguished.

Mabo acknowledged Australia's obligations to comply with international standards accepted upon ratification of the 1966 International Covenant on Civil and Political Rights (ICCPR). Hence 'the common law does not necessarily conform with international law, but international law is a legitimate and important influence on the development of the common law, especially when international law declares the existence of universal human rights. A common law doctrine founded on unjust discrimination in the enjoyment of civil and political rights demands reconsideration' (per Brennan, J. cited Nettheim, 1998: 198). Relevant here was a 1975 ICJ Advisory Opinion on the *West Sahara* case – namely that under decolonisation principles, indigenous peoples have the right to self-determination, the acquisition and occupation of their territory as *terra nullius* rejected.³ Indigenous peoples were 'now legitimate *objects* of international law and could even become *subjects* of international law in the right circumstances' (Iorns Magallanes, italics original, 1999: 239).

In a further case of significance (*Wik Peoples v. Queensland*), the Australian High Court ruled in 1996 that granting pastoral leases did not necessarily entail extinguishment of native title. The equivocation was understandable given variable individual circumstances within and between states, and uncertainty as to whether the 'lease' concerned was more a license of permissive occupancy (Mason, 1997: 825). The High Court held that, in the event of inconsistency between the rights of pastoralists and those of native title holders, the rights of the former would prevail.

Political controversy followed when the Howard government moved to dismantle 'right to negotiate processes' over compulsory acquisitions and mining on native land by amending the 1993 Native Title Act. Indigenous rights groups responded with hostility to controversial 1998 amendments designed to enhance security of tenure for mining and pastoral activities. Placing barriers to the protection of native title left those holding it with less security than other landowners. Indigenous groups vehemently insisted that this opened the door to discriminatory action by governments. They fought these changes with claims that they contravened Australia's commitments under the International Convention Eliminating all Forms of Racial Discrimination (ICERD).

A complicating factor was the 1997 formation of Pauline Hanson's One Nation Party campaigning on tariff protection, an end to Aboriginal welfare benefits, reduction in Asian immigration, concessions to small businesses, and abolition of bodies dealing with multicultural affairs (McAllister, 1999: 45). Appealing to rural workers and those disadvantaged by worsening economic conditions in Asia, One Nation created difficulties for the Australian government's land title policy, particularly in Queensland. It exposed unresolved cross-pressures between farming and mining interests, indigenous rights, domestic law, and international obligations.⁴ Developments following *Wik* indicated that the Howard Federal Coalition government's response was 'overwhelmingly framed in terms favouring non-indigenous interests' (Grose, 1997: 87). Foreign news media coverage of Hanson and One Nation harmed Australia's image abroad, especially in Southeast Asia. Political controversy to one side, these developments indicated the distance Australia had yet to travel to ensure the effective recognition and protection of native title interests.

Nevertheless, judicial rulings that domestic law could not ignore international practice helped strengthen indigenous identity claims in Australia. In supporting human rights internationally, Australian governments have normally sought to ensure their domestic handling of indigenous rights issues does not expose them to charges of inconsistency. Aboriginal groups have sought to exploit this sensitivity. The increased internationalisation of indigenous rights questions expanded opportunities to exert leverage on the Australian government by subjecting it to unwanted publicity and advocacy. Indeed, an 'ability to disturb the conscience of the nation and unsettle its government is one of the few weapons available to Aboriginal people and one they are unlikely to surrender lightly' (Mulgan, 1998: 190). Identity-based grievances projected locally and internationally regularly included claims to self-determination and autonomy over local needs, relevant policy determination and programme design, management of service delivery, and control over land futures. Notwithstanding immense regional differences, cultural particularities, and the weight of accumulated social degradation, Aboriginals have slowly won stronger political backing for their entitlement demands.

New Zealand

When the Treaty of Waitangi (1840) was signed, the subordination of indigenous Maori to British 'order' was authorised. Signing chiefs were assured that existing chiefly structures (*te tino rangatiratanga*) would remain undisturbed. Treaty Article Two reserved to Maori the full, exclusive and undisturbed possession of their lands, estates, forests and fisheries. However under the Treaty's English version, the transfer of sovereignty from chiefs to the Crown made Maori subjects under British law. Sovereignty and chiefly authority, therefore, were at odds within an agreement also subject to contrasting cultural and linguistic interpretations. Treaty Article Two fell prey to often unscrupulous, increasingly remorseless settler land acquisitions. That expropriation generated conflict, insurgency and violence that engendered legacies of bitterness.

For a lengthy period, indigenous claims for restitution stayed submerged by the dominant culture's preoccupations with national economic security and welfare, wartime exigencies, material expansion, and urbanisation. Grievances festered under assimilationism, apathy, and insularity. Although little heralded at the time, a turning point occurred in 1975 when, under the Treaty of Waitangi Act, the Third Labour government established the Waitangi Tribunal. This was empowered with advisory functions and procedures to hear grievances by Maori against the Crown for breaches of the Treaty's provisions. The Tribunal's scope gradually widened following judicial rulings confirming the Crown's fiduciary responsibilities to make restitution according to principles of equity. In a series of significant cases, the New Zealand Court of Appeal formulated a concept of 'partnership' between the Crown and Maori, each obliged to negotiate reasonably and in good faith. The principle of partnership and contract moved into the public sphere (McHugh, 1999: 460). Only gradually, however, has the dominant Pakeha community accepted that the Treaty is *both* a charter of indigenous entitlements *and* a framework for nationhood.

Treaty of Waitangi developments imparted focus to Maori aspirations. Piecing together the historical evidence required for claims verification helped reconnect dislocated identity. After more than a century's fragmentation through individual ownerships and amalgamations via trusts and incorporations, a statutory means to engage the Crown in claims for land return and redress now existed. Waitangi Tribunal processes orchestrated *local* Maori tribal (iwi) demands through claims advocacy, but also generated *national* divisions within Maoridom. Of the 70 per cent Maori who are urban-domiciled, estimates indicate a fifth cannot reliably trace tribal affiliations (Hayward, 1999: 192-3). Unable to verify these links, urban Maori have resented denial of access to determinations deciding complex land and resource claim settlements.

Exogenous factors encouraging activism have included post-1945 decolonisation, the growth of civil rights movements elsewhere, and UN activities on the environment and human rights. Greater scope for travel, enhanced communications links, and opportunities to gain funding for international conference participation have played a role. It is only a slight exaggeration to claim that 'the imperative to resolve Maori claims owes almost as much to international developments as to domestic protests and demands' (Coates, 1998: 20).

When projecting the national image abroad, New Zealand governments are keen to incorporate a recognisable Maori component. By contrast, the post-1984 embrace of market-driven financial deregulation, restructuring for export efficiency, and downsizing of the public sector carried heavy social and economic costs for the unskilled Maori work force. This is not the result of an ethnic policy, but a combination of policies that, in totality, have hit those most disadvantaged the hardest (Sharp, 1997: 445).

Fiji

Unlike Australia or New Zealand, Fiji's indigenous people can point to neither repression nor dispossession as distinguishing features of their colonial experience. When the country gained its independence from the United Kingdom in 1970, principles of equitable representation for all races were stretched to accommodate demands for Fijian paramountcy. This included dominant Fijian representation in Parliament's 22 member Senate, where any three Great Council of Chiefs' appointees could block changes considered inimical to core indigenous interests, including land-holding arrangements. Formulation of these rules was not subject to public consultation, chiefly élites dominating determination of the indigenous agenda. Nor was the 1970 constitution translated into Fijian; there is little doubt that most Fijians did not know that it protected their rights.

As a predominantly bi-racial society, where race is an acknowledged 'fact of life', communal representation restricted public contest over the indigenous community's economic and social needs. Chiefly élites from the eastern islands of the country dominated Fijian political party formations where urban-based, poorer Fijians were under-represented. This also structured politics in ways that legitimised defence of indigenous interests at the expense of the Indo-Fijian community.

However, the Fijian Labour Party, as the dominant component in the short-lived Bavadra coalition government of 1987, did pledge to alleviate evident social and educational disparities within the indigenous community. Many most in need were urban dwellers, neglected under Ratu Sir Kamisese Mara's increasingly aloof, autocratic, and corrupt Alliance Party administration. One reaction comprised occasional upsurges of Fijian ethnic populism. As an organised political force, this did no more than gain marginal parliamentary representation, an outcome that generated frustrations manipulated in 1987.

In that year, General Sitiveni Rabuka staged two military coups, the first toppling the short-lived Bavadra government; the second rescinding the 1970 constitution, declaring Fiji a Republic, and removing it from the Commonwealth. Claims the coups were justified to protect indigenous rights threatened by the Bavadra government's moderate reformism, ignored existing protections under the 1970 constitution. These upheavals witnessed the abuse of indigenous identity appeals directed to domestic and international audiences.

To some public figures in Fiji, it was 'a matter of shame rather than pride to be associated with the world "indigenous" in Fiji. Since the coup the word has been associated with authoritarianism, racism, fascism and even apartheid. There is a political connotation to the word which democrats and egalitarians feel uncomfortable with. It is that the people of pure indigenous descent or the "pure Fijian" uncorrupted by other races have superior legal, political or other rights to the citizens of Fiji' (Dakavula, 1992: 71). To another prominent public figure, 'indigenousness or ethnicity is not the issue for most Pacific Islanders. It is rather justice has been denied us by our own indigenous leaders and some aspects of our traditional systems' (Rokotuivuna, cited by Smith, 1997: 167). A more detached perspective detected 'an irony in the fact that indigenous institutions that protect the interests, identity, traditions and even the land of indigenous Fijians, actually represents the bureaucratisation of tradition and traditional authority developed during the colonial administration' (Bush, 1999: 758).

Tensions about who spoke for Fiji's indigenous peoples surfaced with acrimony at regional non-governmental, independence movement gatherings convened abroad. At the 1987 Nuclear Free and Independent Pacific (NFIP) conference held in Manila, a complex three-sided clash occurred. For one participant, the movement's divisions had some Pacific islanders campaigning for independence and opposition to nuclear installations, exhibiting little patience towards indigenous rights activists running land rights campaigns. By contrast, anti-nuclear activists, mainly white but including some from Japan, found their calls for independence and anti-nuclear action distrusted by indigenous movement activists who accused them of avoiding more serious issues in their own countries (Wilkes cited by Smith, 1997: 162). In the event, delegations from New Zealand and Hawai'i refused to condemn the Rabuka coups. Self-absorbed and inflamed by personality differences, indigenous rights activism has not always proved a comfortable companion for either decolonisation or disarmament in the South Pacific. Since the cessation of nuclear testing, the NFIP has called on the South Pacific Forum to ensure the UN furthers the self-determination of remaining Pacific non-independent territories.[5]

As Fiji gradually returned to the path of constitutional rule, stridency over 'indigenous interests' in rationalisation of the coups subsided but did not disappear. Under constitutional reforms finalised in 1997, retention of Fijian land rights, the chiefly system, and existing systems of administration helped persuade the indigenous community's representatives to accept restoration of democracy at a national level (Quentin-Baxter, 1998: 31). In its preambular paragraphs, the 1997 Constitution recognised that Fiji is a multicultural society where 'we commit ourselves anew to living in harmony and unity, promoting social justice and the economic and social advancement of all communities, respecting their rights and interests and strengthening our institutions of government'.[6] That advice is endorsed in Fiji, but only reluctantly implemented. Unresolved is the use of indigenous identity to justify exclusion of those not ethnically Fijian, despite generations of occupation and commitment to the country (Robertson, 1998: 205).

The UN Working Group on Indigenous Populations

The international arena has been indispensable for domestically located indigenous groupings to register, explain, and advance their interests. Most attention here is devoted to the UN Working Group on Indigenous Populations. This first met in 1982 under the Sub-commission of the UN Human Rights Commission. Its dual mandate was to review national development affecting indigenous rights, and develop appropriate international standards.

Related deliberations traversed an extensive agenda: sustainable development practices; forestry, bio-diversity, and cultural property rights; deficiencies of national and international representation; a permanent forum for indigenous peoples; indigenous self-government and self-development; language; health; education; economic; and social conditions. The Working Group has seen approximately 700 attend each year, about half from indigenous nations, peoples and communities.[7] Against the objection of some governments, UN accreditation requirements for non-governmental status were relaxed to facilitate indigenous peoples' participation before these proceedings. Although not obliged to report to the working group the Australian and New

Zealand governments have done so. Like other governments, their motivation has been to ensure the Working Group's records 'were not dominated by statements focusing on the shortcomings of state conduct or inaction' (Anaya, 1996: 154).

Indigenous groups increasingly viewed the Working Group as a body lacking sufficient status within the UN hierarchy. They sought a broader platform through which to voice demands over health, education, economic development, and the environment. This has included calls originally sponsored by Denmark for a permanent forum of indigenous people. In 1998, the UN Commission on Human Rights established a working group to elaborate this proposal. It is envisaged that a future body would comprise a mix of indigenous and government representatives, operate as a two-tier body, and pursue a broad mandate extending beyond rights matters.

The UN Draft Declaration on Indigenous Rights

In 1985, the Working Group began preparing a Declaration on the Rights of Indigenous Peoples. Under the direction of Erica-Irene Daes, the Working Group attracted a broad range of witnesses from indigenous peoples groups. Identified as guiding themes were fundamental freedoms, human rights, and the development of international standards on the rights of indigenous peoples.

Following complex exchanges, the Draft Declaration on the Rights of Indigenous Peoples (the Draft Declaration) was released in 1993 to the UN Commission on Human Rights. That body established an open-ended intergovernmental working group to refine the Draft Declaration, a major undertaking uncompleted at the new century. Slow progress has not been surprising given the range and substance of issues on the table: self determination; use of the term 'peoples'; the concept of collective rights; separate legal and judicial systems; forms of autonomy and self-government; as well as land entitlements and intellectual property questions.

The Draft Declaration raises substantive problems of principle for governments, making protracted debate understandable. Accordingly it 'is far from a rhetorical question to ask why a simple declaration of self-determination for indigenous peoples by the international community is not sufficient – why most nation states prefer a document of innumerable articles susceptible to rather different readings' (Rosen, 1997: 249). In addition, numerous governments do not support UN promotion, monitoring, and supervision of human rights norms, let alone facilitate its expansion into indigenous rights issues. They are satisfied to keep the UN Human Rights Commission and Convention committee system under-resourced, and give low priority to its needed institutional reform and associated intergovernmental cooperation.

In October 1996 after seeing previously agreed Draft Declaration language subject to continual revisiting and picking over by government officials, indigenous representatives from the Working Group staged a walkout. They included Maori, the Autonomous Indian movement, and the Masai of Kenya. Their view was that changes made by governments to weaken the Draft Declaration's support for genuine expressions of self determination rendered meaningless the participation of indigenous peoples. In 1998, the Howard government faced excoriation before the UN Working Group from Aboriginal representative Gatjil Djerrkura (Havemann, 1999: 62).

Slow progress at diplomatic levels has mirrored a lack of urgency by governments in tackling the social, health, employment, educational and language attrition problems afflicting indigenous peoples. To varying degrees, these shortcomings are evident in Australia, New Zealand and Fiji where, failing remedial action, the Declaration's goals risk irrelevance regardless of articulation. Nevertheless the Draft Declaration *is* a seminal statement. It synthesises extensive consultation by indigenous groups prepared to cross numerous cultural barriers in search of common ground. It has deliberately staked out 'the high ground' by propounding rights and principles intended to benchmark future relations involving governments and indigenous peoples, and between non-indigenous and indigenous peoples. For this discussion, features of the Draft Declaration pertinent to cases examined include self-determination, intellectual property, and sacred rights.[8] The latter two headings are distinguished for discussion, although indigenous peoples often treat them as inseparable.

Self-Determination

The Draft Declaration's Article Three claims the right of self-determination for indigenous peoples through which they may freely pursue their political status, as well as economic, social, and cultural development. Although stopping short of endorsing independence, the Draft Declaration would limit the authority of states to take measures affecting indigenous peoples except with their informed consent.

Determining these provisions saw unresolved disagreements that have continued into subsequent negotiations. One perspective regards the option of full independence necessarily inherent within existing recommendations, while another envisages enlarged indigenous autonomy falling short of outright sovereignty, independence or secession.

At 1995 Working Group proceedings, Australian officials believed it was possible to formulate broad self-determination principles falling outside attainment of national independence. These principles would acknowledge the search for identity; preserve language, culture and tradition; confer enhanced self-management and autonomy; and resist undue interference from central government (Anaya, 1996: 86). This position was partly the initiative of Foreign Minister Senator Evans, who endorsed a then expansive philosophy of UN peace-building and preventative diplomacy. This supported notions of internal self-determination, the 'content of the right of self-determination for indigenous peoples ... consistent with (this) approach'.[9] Australia's willingness to link philosophies of self-determination to so-called 'peace-building', suggested a tailoring of internal community interest to external state needs.

By 1998 however, the Australian government had moved to a position that endorsed 'self-management' and 'self-empowerment' of indigenous Australians. Despite court rulings, the Howard government viewed Australian external obligations secondary to domestic electoral and economic considerations. Little else explains why, in August 1998, Foreign Minister Downer found it necessary to trail the red herring of secession when he claimed: 'We don't want to see a separate country created for indigenous Australians ... It might be better to use the term self-management rather than leaving an impression that we are prepared to have a separate indigenous state'.[10] Other explanations for this shift include the Hanson factor, the political furore following *Wik*, and concern not to interrupt continued commercial resource development.

In fact, most indigenous groups in Australia and New Zealand favour neither secession nor independent statehood. Some Maori believe the issue died in 1840, when indigenous chiefs repudiated secession by signing the Treaty of Waitangi (Williams, 1998: 188). Yet neither do Maori wish to relinquish advantages that a disavowal of the self-determination option might entail. Keeping it current adds bargaining purchase to a range of claims. Similar reasoning surrounds contention about use of the term 'peoples'. Some governments – including those in Australia and New Zealand – construe this as an implied right of secession, indigenous rights activists by contrast treat its denial as violating the choice of self-determination.

A September 1996 regional Pacific workshop on the Draft Declaration, convened in Fiji, resolved to support Article Three. Opening the meeting with remarks reflecting as much concern about protection of local Fijian paramountcy as promotion of indigenous rights, Prime Minister Rabuka maintained 'we must share our heritage with others. In fact, part of our heritage, often taken away from us against our will, is no longer ours, it belongs to others. That cannot be entirely altered, redress is no longer a practical proposition. We cannot and must not expel others from our midst, that would be contrary to civilised principles, even though the methods used to deprive us of what was wholly ours, were less than civilised' (cited Basawaija, 1997: 208-09). In subsequent proceedings, non-governmental representatives unsuccessfully urged the South Pacific Forum to ask all UN members to support the Draft Declaration without amendment.

South Pacific Forum governments do not want existing intergovernmental agendas, or relations with external dialogue partners such as the United States and France, complicated by indigenous rights demands emanating from non-governmental interests. They have viewed indigenous rights demands in Hawai'i as matters internal to the United States. In response, counter conference activity has ensued, indigenous rights activism combining with developmental and sustainable resource management demands. The Fourth Parallel Non-Governmental Forum of 1998 urged South Pacific Forum governments to endorse and implement the Draft Declaration; oppose the extinguishing of Aboriginal rights to land, law and custom; and support the right of self-determination for indigenous peoples. The international human rights agenda, non-governmental representatives told officials, 'now includes the collective rights of all indigenous peoples, including Hawai'i, in our region'.[11]

Intellectual Property

The Draft Declaration's Article 29 asserts indigenous rights to the full ownership, control and protection of cultural and intellectual property. This includes rights to special measures controlling and developing indigenous sources of knowledge, cultural traditions, or human and genetic resources. The contribution of Maori to an incorporation of cultural and intellectual property rights in the Draft Declaration was substantial (Taiaroa, 1998: 57). Instrumental here was the 1993 Mataatu Declaration, resulting from an international conference held at Whakatane (North Island, New Zealand), on cultural and intellectual property rights of indigenous peoples. This attracted representation from Japan, Australia, India, the Philippines, the Pacific Islands, and Peru.

The Mataatu Declaration outlined framework principles for the control, re-acquisition, preservation, exploitation, experimentation, and research into indigenous intellectual property. A preambular item declared indigenous peoples capable of managing their traditional knowledge alone, but willing to offer it to all provided fundamental rights to define and control such knowledge receive protection by international means. A moratorium on further commercialisation of indigenous medicinal plants and human genetic materials was recommended, pending development by indigenous communities of appropriate protections.[12] Supporting arguments supplied by Maori included claims that there is a *terra nullius* perspective implicit in intellectual property laws that fails to acknowledge existing customary indigenous knowledge (Mead, 1997: 25).

Unresolved issues include application of patent law to indigenous knowledge, the use of western legal systems to secure and defend rights, and pressures for the commodification of intellectual property flowing from global trade liberalisation. Indigenous peoples in Australia, New Zealand and the Pacific share concerns over the collection, screening, and patenting of plant and plant products by pharmaceutical and research companies. They claim that this occurs without regard to indigenous custody of such knowledge, consent to its exploitation, or adequate return.

Intellectual property is a field where conversion of indigenous interest principles into implementation modalities is difficult. Consensus between companies, governments, and indigenous representatives over priorities is often absent. World trade liberalisation, and moves to universalise the United States system of intellectual property, have hardened divisions (Patel, 1996: 315-16). Indigenous representatives from New Zealand have engaged in international conference activity to expedite implementation of the Convention on Biological Diversity (1992), and its Article 86. Subject to national legislation, this calls for the preservation, protection, utilisation and sharing of indigenous knowledge in the interests of sustaining biological diversity. The New Zealand government has reserved its position towards indigenous traditional knowledge provisions extending beyond existing law and international intellectual property Conventions (Graham, 1998: 9-11).

Sacred Rights

The Draft Declaration seeks to further the rights of indigenous peoples to maintain and strengthen the distinctive spiritual and material relationships held towards physical environments. This is to sustain stewardship responsibilities for future generations. Activities that preserve cultural integrity are self-determining; denied custody of artefacts threatens indigenous identity (Stamatopoulou, 1994: 76).

In Australia, 'sacredness' has aggregated otherwise disparate indigenous interests to seek protection of cultural, historical, archaeological, religious and burial sites, and prevent their commercial or mineral exploitation. Those who oppose these claims believe that by bidding up religious, spiritual, or sacred components of development disputes, indigenous rights representatives have politicised grievances in order to gain added compensation. A widely shared view in the dominant Australian culture holds that, while different groups deserve protection against discrimination, freedom to retain ethnic or cultural heritage must remain consistent with the rights of others. Hence the Aboriginal and Torres Strait Islander Protection Act (1984) specified sacredness as but one criterion a Minister must balance with others when designating an area for indigenous heritage. This does not apply to the protection of oral histories and other forms of indigenous intellectual property. Relevant Australian adjudication has determined that cultural heritage is protected provided beliefs are discernible, and indicate an explicable rule.

In June 1998, representatives of an Aboriginal people, the Mirrar, lodged a submission with the World Heritage Bureau of UNESCO requesting protection of sacred sites from a proposed uranium mine facility. The site concerned was the Jabiluka facility in the Kakadu National Park, Northern Territory. Following investigation, the Heritage Bureau in December 1998 endorsed findings that the planned mine threatened the integrity of the National Park, an outcome castigated with vehemence by the Australian government. Mirrar representatives, who in April 1999 won a US$100,000 international environmental award (the Goldman Prize), gained support from national Jabiluka Action committees, international publicity, and environmental protest directed against the project's continuation. In July 1999, UNESCO ruled that the uranium mine site did not threaten Kakadu National Park, but voiced concerns over the development's impact on the cultural values of this location.

New Zealand 'sites of significance' (*wahi tapu*) are places of special historical, spiritual, or cultural associations for Maori. The Crown accepts an obligation to protect such sites under 1993 legislation allowing either Crown retention, reserve creation, or transfer to Maori ownership conditional upon protection by reservation. Maori may nominate 'sites of significance' for protection. If the location is a surplus Crown holding, they may have it 'landbanked' for possible incorporation under future settlement of a Waitangi Treaty claim (Te Puni Kokiri, 1996: 8-9).

Norms and Rules

The interface between international and domestic law is significant for indigenous rights demands. Relevant is the scope and authority of evolving normative frameworks, and what Australia, New Zealand and Fiji cases suggest regarding the role of domestic/international linkages in rule formation. Australia's *Mabo* outcome acknowledged international law as an important and legitimate influence on the common law. Although they may appear in unratified treaties or other non-binding formulations, emerging international standards provide interpretative tools. In 1991, Australia acceded to the First Optional Protocol to the ICCPR. This permitted individuals exhausting domestic remedies to communicate allegations of rights violations to the Convention's Human Rights Committee. This accession occurred before tabling the Protocol in Parliament, an omission described as 'extraordinary ... without any public debate or even public awareness of its existence, let alone scope and significance' (Twomey, cited by Kirby, 1995:87).

An Australian 1995 High Court judgment, the *Teoh* case, raised significant issues about the domestic impact of treaties. In this instance, a deportation order was successfully appealed on the grounds of Australian ratification of the UN Convention on the Rights of the Child (CRC). The ruling indicated that, in general, international treaty provisions do not form part of Australian law unless incorporated into municipal law by statute. Regarding *Teoh* however, ratification had generated a *legitimate expectation* that, absent any statutory or executive indications to the contrary, the government would consider the CRC when acting.

What of more recent Australian development regarding domestic alignment to international human rights Conventions affecting indigenous rights? A leading British lawyer, Lord Lester, has maintained that the ICCPR 'may yet prove to be a sleeping giant in Australia' (cited Mason, 1997: 829). To date, that Covenant has been less significant than ICERD where acrimony regarding Australia's obligations has occurred. Australia's 1999 appearance before the ICERD panel was unusual in that it was called under an 'early warning measure' normally reserved for countries facing gross human rights abuses. Reviewing 1998 amendments to the Native Title Act, particularly those validating pastoral leases during an intermediate period in the mid-1990s, the ICERD Committee expressed concern about their infringing Australia's international obligations under the Convention. Disquiet was also expressed that the certainty the amended Act afforded to governments and third parties had occurred at the expense of indigenous title; lack of effective participation by indigenous communities in legislative formulation; abolition of the post of Aboriginal and Torres Strait Islander Social Justice Commissioner; and restructuring of the Human Rights and Equal Opportunity Commission.

The Australian government was urged to address these concerns by suspending implementation of the 1998 amendments, and re-opening discussions with Aboriginal and Torres Strait Islander representatives for solutions acceptable to the indigenous peoples in compliance with ICERD obligations. These findings belied official claims that the government has 'expanded the treaty-making process to ensure greater consultation with the community' (White Paper, 1997: section 195).

In New Zealand, the judiciary has displayed some readiness to give effect to unincorporated international obligations. Although not going as far as *Teoh*, the New Zealand courts have employed treaties 'as an aid to statutory interpretation, if the statute is ambiguous, or if the treaty is relevant to the legislative policy concerned' (Gobbi, 1998:94). New Zealand Law Commission guidance on unincorporated treaties sees them playing a role on constitutional, common law, declaratory, and public policy grounds (NZLC, 1996: 23-5). In *Tavita* (1994), it was held New Zealand courts could encounter legitimate criticism should they accept that, because a domestic statute giving

170 *The Domestic Politics of International Relations*

discretionary powers does not possess human rights norms or obligations, then the executive is necessarily free to ignore them.[13] The judiciary has also been averse to 'window dressing': that is where New Zealand governments enter treaties, but then fail to secure appropriate implementation (Gobbi, 1998: 94).

Fiji's approach to normative factors has altered since the post-coup regime sought to justify its extra-constitutional practices by claiming they conformed to ILO Convention 169 standards (Dakavula, 1992: 77). More recently, it has complained at the UN that efforts to promulgate legal instruments for the protection and promotion of indigenous peoples rights are ineffectual without matching initiatives to enhance appropriate economic, social and human development.[14] In Fiji, officials have urged the Draft Declaration Working Group to establish a consensus supporting recognition of the principle of collective rights under international law. Government official Graham Leung, who regularly attended the Working Group, was an initial appointee to the Fiji Human Rights Commission formed in 1999.

Fiji's reluctance to fully accede to international human rights instruments is seen by its use of reservations. Ratification of the Convention on the Elimination of Discrimination Against Women maintained operative Convention Article 5 (a) impinged on its cultural values and social norms of behaviour. Specifically, it conflicted with local customs claiming that only men have the right to become a 'ratu' or chief.[15]

Table 6.2 Human Rights Conventions: Australia, New Zealand and Fiji

Accessions/ratifications 1999

	Social[a]	Civil[b]	Race[c]	Genocide[d]	Children[e]	Women[f]	Torture[g]
Australia	x	x	x[i r]	x	x[r]	x[r]	x[j]
New Zealand[k]	x	x[h]	x	x	x[r]	x[r]	x[i r]
Fiji			x[r]	x	x[r]		

a International Covenant on Economic, Social and Cultural Rights, 1966.
b International Covenant on Civil and Political Rights, 1996.
c International Convention on Elimination of All Forms of Racial Discrimination, 1969.
d Convention on the Prevention of the Crime and Punishment of Genocide, 1948.

e Convention on the Rights of the Child, 1989.
f Convention on Elimination of All forms of Racial Discrimination Against Women, 1979.
g Convention Against Torture and Other Cruel, Inhuman or Degrading Treatment, 1984.

State acceptance:
h Declaration Regarding Competence of Covenant Human Rights Committee.
i Declaration Regarding Competence of Convention Committee on Elimination of Racial Discrimination.
j Declaration Regarding Competence of Convention Committee on Torture.
k New Zealand ratification subjecting Cook Islands, Niue and Tokelau to these instruments.
x Ratification or accession.
r Reservations entered.

Source: UN Treaty data base

Institutions

Institutions at intergovernmental and transnational levels influencing indigenous rights questions include UN human rights bodies, advisory systems, and special purpose commissions. These have witnessed disputes about the standing of non-governmental indigenous bodies, frictions over insufficient resourcing, and the politics of theatre, rhetoric and symbolism that includes publicity-generating walk-outs from conference proceedings. Fallout from these events has filtered down to domestic institutional levels.

In Australia, previous state government dominance of Aboriginal affairs altered following a 1967 referendum whose outcome gave the Federal government conjoint jurisdiction. This facilitated institutional innovations that gathered pace under the Whitlam government. They included the National Aboriginal Consultative Committee (NACC), a Commonwealth Department of Aboriginal Affairs to fund the delivery of services and, in 1975, passage of the Racial Discrimination Act. This incorporated the ICERD into Australian domestic law. Under the Fraser administration, the NACC was slightly altered to emerge as the National Aboriginal Conference (NAC), a body that criticised the succeeding Hawke government for its abortive attempt to nationally unify indigenous land rights recognition. A statutory national commission entitled the Aboriginal and Torres Strait Islander Commission (ATSIC) replaced the NAC in 1989. This incorporated elected regional councils, assumed administrative functions for the Department of Aboriginal Affairs, gained indigenous representation, and acquired some executive authority over spending (Petersen and Sanders, 1998: 21). These functions fell broadly under the generics of programme delivery, advocacy, and advice to the Executive.

The formation of ATSIC was attacked by the government's opponents, a factor influencing formation of a Council of Aboriginal Reconciliation in 1991. With a balance of indigenous and non-indigenous representation, this has attempted to chart improved national unity in the decade preceding centenary of the federation (Petersen and Sanders, 1998: 21). Meanwhile, ATSIC has proved uncompromising in its willingness to criticise the government at home and abroad for perceived policy shortcomings and inconsistencies over indigenous rights. Its representatives viewed the ICERD outcome previously identified as a reprimand, and regrettable vindication of an unabated need to pursue domestic grievances by international means. However, ATSIC's dual role as advocate and administrator has led to potential conflicts of interest.[16]

Domestic/international linkages affecting institutional developments, emerged as Australian governments grew increasingly alert to the role expected of them within a post-imperial, post-Menzies Commonwealth. Following a controversial South African rugby football tour to Australia in 1971, governments successively headed by Whitlam, Fraser and Hawke distanced themselves from previous contacts with *apartheid* South Africa. That necessitated tangible measures to reduce external censure for poor domestic race relations. At the UN, Australia was active over human rights, environmental protection, and attempts to negotiate the cessation of nuclear weapons testing – global issues all directly affecting the Aboriginal experience.

Australian governments may have hoped that participation by Aboriginals in negotiation, representation, and reconciliation processes would lessen external simplification of complex internal questions. This has partly occurred: for example, the ATSIC Commissioner has told the UN that 'issues of concern to indigenous people are interrelated and inseparable and cannot be addressed under an agenda item of a body dealing with a wide range of human rights matters'.[17] In other respects, however, Aboriginal representatives have pursued domestic politics by international means including use of material designed to embarrass the government before international audiences. Contributing has been a domestic policy climate of administrative flux, legislative amendment, unsettled institutionalisation, and uneasy relations between federal, state, and indigenous representatives.

At times, Australian governments have attracted international publicity to themselves over aboriginal affairs. This occurred in August 1999 when Prime Minister Howard avoided making a formal apology over the 'stolen generations'.[18] (For a period of fifty years until the 1960s, up to 100,000 aboriginal children were removed from their parents and placed in white foster homes in the interests of 'assimilation'. The practice was subject of a damning 1997 report from an inquiry headed by Sir Ronald Wilson, then president of the Australian Human Rights Commission.) Although conceding mistreatment of aboriginals represented a blemished chapter in Australia's history, Howard's refusal to apologise further risked the country's international exposure through domestic indigenous protest at the Sydney Olympics in 2000, an event activists called 'The Games of Shame'.

In New Zealand, the institutional importance of the Treaty of Waitangi and the Waitangi Tribunal is discernible at different levels. First, the Tribunal's scope, powers and functions have been strengthened. Originally restricted to investigating current breaches with a view to their future avoidance, retrospective expansion of the Tribunal's jurisdiction by Parliament in 1985 to things done or omitted by the Crown since 1840 represented a major step. The Treaty of Waitangi (State Enterprises) Act (1988) authorised the Tribunal to make binding recommendations for the return to Maori ownership of land, or interests in land transferred to State owned enterprises. Under the Crown Forest Assets Act (1989), the Tribunal gained powers to recommend a return of Crown forest land to Maori ownership. The Treaty of Waitangi (Fisheries Claim) Settlement Act of 1992 gave effect to the Deed of Settlement signed by the Crown and Maori to settle commercial fisheries claims. Problems of delay and cost to litigants aside, the Tribunal is now a relatively advanced mechanism for settlement of indigenous grievances. It probes the historical significance of claims, respects their diversity, operates along culturally sensitive lines, and reports substantively. Like its parent, the Treaty, the Waitangi Tribunal has attracted international interest (Kingsbury, 1989: 121).

New Zealand governments and Maori representatives regard Waitangi Tribunal remedy processes as having greater specificity and relevance to local needs than the Draft Declaration's principled generalities. The Draft Declaration's role is viewed as stimulating needed domestic dialogue beyond existing preoccupations over fiscal limits and final settlement terms for outstanding claims before the Waitangi Tribunal. This dialogue requires a conscious effort by the dominant Pakeha culture to appreciate that, for Maori, cultural survival is inseparable from self-determination.

Currently lacking are coherent national structures that articulate and represent Maori opinion. Despite expectations generated by the Treaty settlement processes, and enhanced parliamentary representation realised under the 1996 introduced national mixed member proportional representational system, Maori politics is complicated by contrasting tribal, economic, residency and personal affiliations. Accordingly, New Zealand officials resent the tactics of some self-appointed 'representatives' claiming to speak abroad for all Maoridom before international conferences, but without authority, mandate, or accountability to discernible Maori institutions. However, that problem does not exonerate the shortcomings of some government agencies in failing to establish and maintain effective working relations with Maori.

This highlights a paradox of cultural politics also evident in Australia. Indigenous groups mobilise local and international support designed to protect lands, resources and culture. But it is the appeal for distributive justice and special attention due to existing difficulties that accounts for these results, more than convincing governments or non-indigenous majorities about the validity and significance of indigenous cultures (Coates, 1998: 72).

Fiji's demands for indigenous primacy were subject to modification by institutional means. The Constitutional Review Commission (1993-5) headed by a Maori, Sir Paul Reeves, former Governor General of New Zealand, remained mindful that its deliberations involved domestic and international considerations.[19] Although a substantial level of communal representation was maintained in Fiji's revised constitution (1997), this was more equitably distributed between different ethnic groups. Other important advances included appointment by merit to the Public Service, commitment to establish a Human Rights Commission (appointed 1999), and equal status for women, many of whom found the 'rhetoric of indigenous rights pretty hollow' (Bain cited by Robertson, 1998: 189). Human rights provisions in the 1997 Constitution drew heavily on the ICCPR, although Fiji has not ratified that Convention. However the Constitution states that in interpreting its human rights chapter, the courts must, where relevant, pay regard to the public international law applicable to the protection of rights identified.

Fiji's 1997 return to the Commonwealth after a decade of absence helped place local indigenous demands in perspective through domestic/international linkages unmatched by either the UN or the South Pacific Forum. They include sporting, educational, legal, professional and developmental associations, services, and advisory functions. Links to the Queen as head of the Commonwealth matter to Fijians.

Transformative Aspects

Some indigenous rights aspects assume constitutive dimensions, others less so. Assisting clarification are pertinent contributions from McHugh and Coates (1998), the former an academic lawyer, the latter a historian based in Canada with extensive experience in working among indigenous peoples. McHugh sees indigenous questions shaped by historical, still powerful, stucturalist approaches. This constructs identities through fixed, hierarchical systems including the nation, state, tribe or family. Membership is located accordingly, and relations between these identities are at their most comprehensible when posed dialectically, as when tribal interests contest with the state over resource access and restitution claims. These structures help familiarise the past, and impart coherence to existing social reality. Identity is defined through reference to these structures that envelop and implicate individuals.

Post-structural conditions, by contrast, envisage identities that are open, negotiated, many-layered and variable. Contingency operates with closure and exit options not available because contrasting identities remain perpetually interactive. McHugh (1998: 120) characterises this as a 'relational approach' to indigenous rights issues, where governments and indigenous peoples manage change through mechanisms acceptable to both. It is constructivist in that identity interests and feasible objectives emerge following persuasion and joint exploration. Problems are less solved than reduced, redefined, and revisited: activities necessarily placing a high premium upon the calibre and resilience of mediating processes.

Coates also favours more open, less adversarial processes of inter-cultural relations. He envisages systems of 'inter-cultural relations', where the vital consideration is cultural survival. This means relevant groups must avoid talking past one another, develop lasting accommodations, and sustain continuing co-operation. To function effectively, these principles need to imbue society by assuming an everyday reality in the lives of all citizens (Coates, 1998: 91). That is essential, because resolving legal and constitutional problems within restricted timetables may leave few immediately tangible outcomes as well as test the acquiescence of non-indigenous populations.

The approaches to self-determination previously identified contrast constructivist and more structured, instrumental appraisals of indigenous issues. The contructivism favoured by McHugh assumes that sufficient 'civic space' exists to allow an emergence of pluralist forms and commitment to ongoing relational approaches. Here, identities evolve in relation to other groups and form multiple associations. That is less likely to occur when the available civic space is cramped by substantial programmes of restructuring, deregulation, and state withdrawal. This is manifest in New Zealand through a 'transfer of responsibility for economic and social well-being of the community from elected representatives, especially those who form the government, to the individual citizen' (Wilson, 1998: 250).

Constructivism is evident where indigenous groups wish to keep the debate open-ended, as over self-determination. Aroha Mead believes the right to self- determination by Pacific indigenous peoples must respect the different divisions of indigenous peoples; acknowledge differences; identify commonalities; and work towards agreements that do not pre-determine how indigenous peoples might realise their right to self-determination. While the shared experience of colonisation is fundamental, decolonisation paths differ according to the needs and aspirations of respective indigenous peoples, and their view of future relations with colonising governments (Mead cited by Solomon, 1998: 62-3). In similar vein, a former Aboriginal and Torres Strait Islander Social Justice Commissioner has claimed that, correctly understood, every issue he represented 'is implicated in the concept of self-determination. The reason for this lies in the fact that self-determination is a process ... a right to make decisions'.[20]

For claims, entitlements, and restitution processes, the structured approach assumes salience, although that, too, requires qualification, Primary units of identity are legitimised for legal purposes. As the state retracts, devolves, and deregulates, it institutionalises dependency and perpetuate conditions of unemployment disproportionately afflicting indigenous peoples. The international link of significance is globalisation, which rewards opportunism and stylises indigenous formations as material artefacts. Under these conditions, cultural survival thrives by bidding up differences. This is not just about exploitation for tourism - a major industry in Australia, New Zealand and Fiji - but the notion that worth is gauged according to performance under competition and contestability, not co-existence. It is of interest that indigenous mentors of high standing in all three countries identified are highly paid sports internationals.

Advancement rewards the niche marketing of distinctive advantages admitted as legitimate by the dominant culture. This gives an entrée to policy, commercial, and knowledge environments. Indigenous symbolism that is convincingly 'authentic' is deployed to justify and consolidate entrance to these worlds. Tribal capitalism may emerge, although at the expense of traditional kin-based social supports considered inconsistent with orthodox economic growth prescriptions (Slatter, 1994: 24). Tension between those interests is longstanding in Fiji. Survival of indigenous economic interests under globalisation is about the marketing and promotion of structured differences. It is a conscious deployment of 'identity' as a rational calculation of expected gains.

In all three countries considered, wealth disparities within each indigenous community have widened, litigation over resource entitlements intensified, and ambivalence towards modernity magnified. Transformations activated by international factors are pervasive yet shallow – commonly enhanced by physical, social, and job mobility. Evident recourse to tribal atavism to justify material recompense is overlain by plural affiliations stemming from urban life-styles, acquired religious loyalties, and social and physical distancing from extended family linkages. This adds to difficulties when formulating valid generalisations about 'Aboriginal', 'Maori' or 'Fijian' identity.

Conclusions

Domestic and international interactivity affecting indigenous rights in Australia, New Zealand and Fiji is disparate, unsettled and pervasive. In Australia and New Zealand, Aboriginal and Maori interests have looked to international arenas for support when building shared interests for a post-colonial restitution of land, status and resource access. Although incomplete, and problematic for governments, the Draft Declaration is a project used to promote domestic indigenous agendas.

Reluctance by governments to endorse the Draft Declaration without clarification and negotiation, means several years will elapse before formal promulgation. That prospect has not blunted indigenous rights assertions in

Australia and New Zealand, although governments in both countries will sustain reservations towards the Draft Declaration's wording on self-determination.

Fiji emerged as a country where 'indigenous rights' has been the rallying call not of the subjugated, but of a chiefly-dominated paramountcy. Having 'self-determined' through decolonisation from the British in 1970, Fiji found little need to nail indigenous rights to the banner of furthering enhanced self-government. Although unique, Fiji's situation revealed a tension evident elsewhere between assertions of collective and individual human rights. As a companion chapter has suggested regarding the status of women in New Caledonia, gender rights in Fiji have co-existed uneasily with male-dominated agendas of indigenous rights.[21] Conservatism, insularity, and gradualism provided identifiable features of Fiji's cautious return to constitutional legitimacy during the decade that followed the 1987 military coups. External linkages played a role in that process, although this return's timing was essentially domestically driven.

Constructivist prescriptions, allowing the development of ongoing, contingent, and multi-layered inter-cultural relations, function best where domestic/international interactions foster win/win situations. These have partly emerged in New Zealand, but less evidently in Australia and Fiji. Although not pre-determining outcomes, globalisation facilitates a structured approach where binary indigenous/dominant cultural relations polarise through politics, in public, and before the courts. Another effect is the diminution of access to a public sphere already contracting through de-politicisation of the market. Until that changes, allowing poverty to end its retreat into stigmatism and collectivism's return to respectability, then indigenous and non-indigenous in poverty at the margins of these societies stand to make scant political headway.

Meanwhile, indigenous identity factors are consciously deployed to maximise quantifiable outcomes of resource return. This process is most advanced in New Zealand where, under Waitangi Tribunal procedures, the Crown has assumed complex fiduciary obligations towards Maori. In all societies considered, official commitments to improved race relations and inter-cultural cooperation are seriously engaged. Indigenous rights demands view such commitments as essential, but inadequate.

Finally, self-determination emerged as an essential connection linking domestic/international interactivity over indigenous rights. A formula originally conceived to achieve international status and sovereign statehood has been co-opted to serve domestic ends. Notwithstanding the authenticity of supporting aspirations, self-determination's emergence in the service of indigenous representation has been utilised primarily to extract material resource transfers. This has left self-determination in need of a conceptual, as well as a results based audit. Resource extraction from the state in the name of indigenous self-determination has generated legal, equity, and political problems not quickly resolved in Australia, New Zealand or Fiji. Nor will attempts to restrict the management of these problems within national borders succeed.

Notes

1   UN doc. E/CN.4/Sub.2/AC.4/1995/3.
2   ILO Convention 169, Article 8:1.
3   ICJ Reports (1975), *Western Sahara (Advisory Opinion)*, 12.
4   On the Hanson factor in Australia's politics, see Simon Jackman, 'Pauline Hanson, the Mainstream, and Political Elites: the Place of Race in Australian Political Ideology', *Australian Journal of Political Science*, 33, 2, 1998, pp. 167-86.
5   NFIP news media release, South Pacific Forum, Koro, Palau, 3 October 1999.
6   Preamble, *Fiji Constitution Amendment Act of 1997*, Suva: Government Print.
7   UN doc. A/51/493, para 41.
8   The Draft Declaration is contained in UN doc. E/CN.4/Sub.2/1994/2/Add.1. For evaluations see Anaya (1996); Kingsbury (1998); and Pritchard (1998).
9   UN doc. E/CN.4/1995/WG.15/2/Add.2, 30 November 1995.
10 AAP, Canberra, 21 August 1998.
11 *Fourth NGO Parallel Forum Communiqué*, Pohnpei, FSM, 14-17 August 1998.
12 The Mataatua Declaration is reprinted in *Indigenous Peoples and Sustainability: Cases and Actions*, Utrecht: IUCN Inter-Commission Task Force on Indigenous Peoples, 1997, Annex 7, pp. 191-94.
13 *Tavita v Minister of Immigration* (1994), NZLR, 257 at 266.
14 UN General Assembly Third Committee, Press Release GA/SHC/3488, 28 October 1998.
15 Edmund Toka, 'Women's rights come up against Pacific Island Cultures', *Asia Times*, 23 July 1999.
16 Justice Evatt's 1995-96 review of Heritage Protection Legislation reported a potential conflict of interest through ATSIC advising the Government, but assisting indigenous parties when applying for protection of sacred sites and objects. Justice Evatt criticised subsequent changes diluting the Federal Government's role in sacred site protection.
17 Ibid., para 124.
18 *The Economist*, 11 September 1999, p. 30.
19 For details of the Report and subsequent constitutional developments in Fiji, see Robert T. Robertson, *Multicultualism and Reconciliation in an Indulgent Republic. Fiji After the Coups: 1987–1998*, Suva: Fiji Institute of Applied Studies, 1998.

20 Aboriginal and Torres Strait Islander Social Justice Commissioner, First Report 1993, AGPS 93, p.41.
21 See supra p. 143.

References

Anaya, James S. (1996), *Indigenous Peoples in International Law*, Oxford: Oxford University Press.

Basawaiya, Nehla (1997), 'The Status of Indigenous Rights in Fiji', *St. Thomas Law Review*, 10, 1, pp. 197-209.

Bush, Joseph E. (1999), 'Defining Group Rights and Delineating Sovereignty: A Case from the Republic of Fiji', *American University International Law Review*, 14, 3, pp. 735-59.

Coates, Ken (1998), 'International Perspectives on Relations with Indigenous Peoples', in Ken Coates and P.G. McHugh, *Living Relationships: The Treaty of Waitangi in the New Millennium*, Wellington: Victoria University Press, pp. 19-102

Cobo, J.R. Martinez (1986), *Study of the Problem of Discrimination Against Indigenous Populations*, UN Sub-Commission on Prevention of Discrimination and the Protection of Minorities, E/CN.4/ Sub.2/1986/7/Add.4.

Dakavula, Jone (1992), 'Chiefs and Commoners: The Indigenous Dilemma', in David Robie (ed), *Tu Galala: Social Change in the Pacific*, Wellington: Bridget Williams Press, pp. 70-79.

Durie, E.T. (1995), 'United Nations or United Peoples?', address to the Australasian Law Teachers Association 50th Anniversary Conference, La Trobe University, 29 September 1995, pp. 1-3.

Durie, E.T. (1997), 'Aboriginal Autonomy', address at Treaty of Waitangi: Maori Political Representation Conference, Pipitea Marae, Wellington, 1 May, p. 1.

Fletcher, Christine (1997), 'Federalism and Indigenous Peoples in Australia', in Michael E. Brown and Sumit Ganguly (eds), *Government Policies and Ethnic Relations in Asia and the Pacific*, Cambridge: MIT Press, pp. 397-420.

Gobbi, Mark (1998), 'Enhancing Public Participation in the Treaty-Making Process: An Assessment of New Zealand's Constitutional Response', *Tulane Journal of International and Comparative Law*, 6, pp. 57-112.

Graham, Douglas (1998), 'The New Zealand Government's Policy', in Alison Quentin-Baxter (ed), *Recognising the Rights of Indigenous Peoples*, Wellington: VUW Institute of Policy Studies, pp. 3-21.

Grose, Peter (1997), 'Developments in the Recognition of Indigenous Rights in Canada: Implications for Australia', *James Cook University Law Review*, 4, 1997, pp. 68-88.

Havemann, Paul (1999) (ed), *Indigenous Peoples' Rights in Australia, Canada, and New Zealand*, Auckland: Oxford University Press.

Hayward, Janine (1999), 'Local Government and Maori: Talking Treaty?', *Political Science*, 50, 2, pp. 182-94.

Horowitz, Donald (1993), 'Democracy in Divided Societies', *Journal of Democracy*, 4, 4, pp.18-38.

Iorns Magallanes, Catherine J. (1999), 'International Human Rights and their Impact on Domestic Law on Indigenous Peoples' Rights in Australia, Canada and New Zealand', in Paul Havemann (ed), op. cit., pp. 235-76.

Kingsbury, Benedict (1989), 'The Treaty of Waitangi: Some International Law Aspects', in I. H. Kawharu (ed), *Waitangi: Maori and Pakeha Perspectives of the Treaty of Waitangi*, Auckland: Oxford University Press, pp. 121-57.

Kingsbury, Benedict (1998), ' "Indigenous Peoples" in International Law: A Constructivist Approach to the Asian Controversy', *American Journal of International Law*, 92, 3, pp. 414-57.

Kirby, Michael (1995), 'The Role of International Standards in Australian Courts', in Philip Alston and Madelaine Chiam (eds), *Treaty-Making and Australia. Globalisation versus Sovereignty*, Leichhardt: Federation Press and Centre for International and Public Law, ANU, pp. 81-92.

Kymlicka, Will (1995), *Multicultural Citizenship. A Liberal Theory of Minority Rights*, Oxford: Clarendon Press.

McAllister, Ian (1999), 'Tax Reform not Race Debate: The October 1998 Australian Federal Election', *Government and Opposition*, 34, 1, pp. 44-58.

McHugh, P. G. (1998), 'Aboriginal identity and Relations in North America and Australia', in Ken Coates and P. G. McHugh op. cit., pp. 107-86.

McHugh, P. G. (1999), 'From Sovereignty Talk to Settlement Time', in Paul Havemann (ed), op. cit., pp. 447-67.

Mason, Anthony (1997), 'The Rights of Indigenous Peoples in Lands once Parts of the Old Dominions of the Crown', *International and Comparative Law Quarterly*, 46, 4, pp. 812-30.

Maybury-Lewis, David (1997), *Indigenous Peoples, Ethnic Groups and the State*, Boston: Allyn and Bacon.

Mead, Aroha (1997), 'Cultural and Intellectual Property Rights of Indigenous Peoples of the Pacific', in *Cultural and Intellectual Property Rights*, II, Auckland: International Research Institute for Maori and Indigenous Education, pp. 22-31.

Mulgan, Richard (1998), 'Citizenship and Legitimacy in Post-colonial Australia', in Nicholas Petersen and Will Sanders (eds), *Citizenship and Indigenous Australians*, Cambridge: Cambridge University Press, 179-95.

Nettheim, Garth (1998), 'The International Law Context', in Nicholas Petersen and Will Sanders, (eds), *Citizenship and Indigenous Australians: Changing Conceptions and Possibilities*, Cambridge: Cambridge University Press.

New Zealand Law Commission (1996), *A New Zealand Guide to International Law and its Sources*, 34.

Palmer, Matthew S. R. (1998), 'The International Practice', in Alison Quentin-Baxter (ed), op. cit., pp. 22-53.

Patel, Surendra (1996), 'Can the Intellectual Property Rights System Serve the Interests of Indigenous Knowledge?', In Stephen Brush and Doreen Stabinsky (eds), *Valuing Local Knowledge. Indigenous People and Property Rights*. Washington DC: Island Press, pp. 305-22.

Perry, Richard J. (1996), *From Time Immemorial. Indigenous Peoples and State Systems*, Austin: University of Texas Press.

Petersen, Nicholas and Sanders, Will (1998), 'Introduction', in Nicholas Petersen and Will Sanders (eds), op. cit., pp. 1-32.

Pritchard, Sarah (ed) (1998), *Indigenous Peoples, The United Nations and Human Rights*, New York: St Martin's Press.

Quane, Helen (1998), 'The UN and the Evolving Right to Self-Determination', *International and Comparative Law Quarterly*, 47, 3, pp. 537-72.

Quentin-Baxter, Alison (1998), 'The International and Constitutional Law Contexts', in Alison Quentin-Baxter op. cit., pp. 22-53.

Robertson, Robert T. (1998), *Multiculturalism & Reconciliation in an Indulgent Republic. Fiji After the Coups: 1987-1998*, Suva: Fiji Institute of Applied Studies, 1998.

Rosen, Lawrence (1997), 'The Right to be Different Indigenous Peoples and the Quest for a Unified Theory', *The Yale Law Journal*, 107, pp. 227-59.

Rudland, Gina (1998), 'The Muddied Waters of Crown/Maori Relationship' in Ken Coates and P. G. McHugh, op. cit., pp. 232-46.

Sharp, Andrew (1997), 'Civil Rights, Amelioration, and Reparation in New Zealand', in Michael E. Brown and Sumit Ganguly, op. cit., pp. 421- 456.

Slatter, Claire (1994), 'Banking on the Growth Model? The World Bank and market policies in the Pacific', in Atu Emberson-Bain (ed), *Sustainable Development or Malignant Growth? Perspectives on Island Women*, Suva: Marama Publications, pp. 17-36.

Smith, Roy H. (1997), *The Nuclear Free and Independent Pacific Movement*, London: Tauris.

Solomon, Maui (1998), 'The Context for Maori (II)', in Alison Quentin-Baxter op. cit., pp. 60-84.

Stamatopoulou, Elsa (1994), 'Indigenous Peoples and the United Nations: Human Rights as a Developing Dynamic', *Human Rights Quarterly*, 16, pp. 58-81.

Stavenhagen, Rodolfo (1996), *Ethnic Conflicts and the Nation-State*, London: Macmillan/ New York: St. Martin's Press.

Taiaroa, Te Atawhai (1998), 'The Context for Maori (I)', in Alison Quentin-Baxter (ed), *Recognising the Rights of Indigenous Peoples*, Wellington: VUW Institute of Policy Studies, pp. 54-9.

Tatz, Colin (1994), 'A Question of Rights and Wrongs', in Oliver Mendelsohn and Uprendra Baxi (eds), *The Rights of Subordinated Peoples*, Oxford: Oxford University Press, pp. 159-77.

Te Puni Kokiri (1996), *Sites of Significance Process. A Step-by-Step Guide to Protecting Sites of Significance by Cultural, Spiritual and Historical Significance to Maori*, Wellington: Ministry of Maori Development.

White Paper (1997), *In the National Interest: Australia's Foreign and Trade Policy*, Canberra: DFAT.

Williams, Joe (1998), 'A Summing Up', in Alison Quentin-Baxter op. cit., pp. 187-97.

Wilson, Margaret (1998), 'A Path to Constitutional Change', commentary in Ken Coates and P. G. McHugh, op. cit., pp. 247-59.

7 Public Management in the South Pacific

Introduction

How Pacific Island countries (PICs) develop into the new century will depend significantly upon how they are administered. Effective utilisation of slender resources will require systems of governance able to maximise limited human and social capital. Often viewed as no more than bit players on the world stage, PICs offer insights of international relevance regarding the calibration of development and public management. A balance that helps reduce vulnerability is worth emulating in other small island locations. An imbalance that buckles state integrity or causes social dislocation, furnishes lessons about what to avoid. Whatever path emerges, interactivity between domestic and international factors will assume a prominent role. This chapter investigates that interaction and the purpose is to ascertain PIC public sector *capacity* to *formulate* and *sustain* services meeting the needs of all citizens.

Like other developing countries, PICs are currently undergoing public sector reform under a prescriptive rubric of 'good governance'. This seemingly neutral terminology has provoked unresolved debate about the appropriateness of applying external models to innately domestic questions. This extends beyond argument about how best to reorganise state functions. It encompasses societal, equity, trade liberalisation, conflict management, and sustainable resource management considerations. Under debate is whether a 'one size fits all' good governance formulation is applicable to contrasting local political and cultural circumstances. PIC responses to that question warrant consideration, but so does caution about the interests of those providing them.

How does public sector reform in the South Pacific relate to this study's central theme of interactivity between domestic and external political and social forces? The impact of exogenous good governance formulations has increased with the South Pacific's growing internationalisation. This has strained local political systems by the intrusion of interests and demands that, by expanding opportunities, have engendered abuse of public office. These conditions have justified external calls by interested parties for enhanced standards of governance. This chapter questions how international/domestic interactivity affects internal responses to external prescription. Domestic responses to external pressures for change in governance arrangements can assume diplomatic significance. How leaders govern at home affects their standing among peers abroad, a consideration that affects intergovernmental relations in the South Pacific.

As a narrative, this chapter's signposts include:
- The colonial legacy of the PIC public sector inheritance, and its reluctance to reform;
- Delineation of current administrative and political problems;
- The formulae for change;
- Responses to such change.

Countries discussed for this, and a following chapter, are identifiable on the Pacific Islands map at page 16. Most countries mentioned are members of the South Pacific Forum (SPF) listed in Table 7.1.

The PIC Setting

Discussion of PIC governance functions cannot ignore an abiding theme – that of continuing economic and physical vulnerability. Although size, population, and resource contrasts are readily evident between entities such as Papua New Guinea and Tuvalu, an evolved orthodoxy of relevant vulnerabilities includes:
- Small, undiversified economies heavily reliant upon slow growth agriculture for subsistence and limited cash income;[1]
- A narrow commodity base and cost penalties through distance from markets and prospective regional trade partners;
- Few opportunities to operate efficiencies of scale and restricted focus of concentration to a limited number of market outlets;
- Development constraints of poor soil fertility, lack of resources, and diseconomies of scale adversely afflicted by export commodity price

declines and costly import substitution;
- Erratic annual Gross Domestic Product (GDP) growth rates, persistent budget deficits, poor fiscal management, and continued dependence on foreign assistance;
- High density populations with high rates of growth (exceeding 2.45 percent per annum in Melanesia), indicating a doubling of the region's current 6.7 million by 2030 and aggravating existing land shortages;
- Contrasting hierarchies of land ownership rights, where attempted regulation for sustainability may challenge social status and complicate legal implementation;
- Continuing rural under-employment, growing urban unemployment, and inadequate vocational training;
- Outward population migration, associated skill loss, and dependency upon foreign earned remittances;
- High ratios of exclusive economic zones (EEZs) to land resources, and incidence of natural disasters such as tropical cyclones (Henderson-Sellers, 1996: 352);
- Critical shortages of local professional, technical, and managerial staff; weak public administrative capacity giving rise to corruption, fraud, and personalism; consequential erosion of impartiality, independent advice and merit-based promotion;
- Exiguous public management capacities stretched to meet international requirements that, in turn, may complicate core domestic task requirements.

This listing deserves brief comment. First, under some headings domestic/international interactivity has a potential to aggravate vulnerability, but in others help in its mitigation. Second, while all PICs encounter development constraints, some face significantly greater problems than others. Smaller islands battle poor soil fertility, lack of resources, proneness to natural disasters, diseconomies of scale, and distance from markets. Third, vulnerability is compounded by remoteness from major global centres, regional distances, and immense maritime spaces within countries. Fourth, some vulnerability factors generate synergies of difficulty, seen where physical disasters magnify their impact within small, remote, far flung PIC locations.[2]

Finally, the analysis of vulnerability has become subject to intergovernmental co-operation through the formulation of an index.

Relevant indicators include export diversification, capital openness, and vulnerability to natural disasters. A 1997 Commonwealth Study was seminal, while South Pacific regional bodies have provided environmental applications.[3]

Offsetting some of these disadvantages, customary social systems display resilience and may offer rudimentary welfare supports although their presence is not assured. Although educational facilities are undeveloped, most PICs outside Melanesia have relatively high standards of basic literacy. Constitutional authority is established, governmental succession normally peaceful, and access to external labour markets and educational facilities available. Over many generations, an accumulation of local knowledge has helped mitigate the impacts of recurring natural disasters. Vulnerability has some diplomatic advantages: deploying their frailty, PICs assert that already developed countries carry a moral obligation to furnish special trade and aid dispensations.

Public Policy System Problems

Compared to some other developing country situations, PIC public sector management is not grossly deficient. Nevertheless, its exposure to a wider spectrum of domestic and international demands has revealed weaknesses of magnitude. These demands have outstripped traditional modes of social accountability, ill-equipped to check chiefs with computers or holding offshore bank accounts. Imported consumption and lifestyle expectations have leapfrogged the means by which their pursuit by office-holders is constrained or rectified.

Structural deficiencies include incoherent planning, budgetary, and resource allocation functions. Requisite data gathering, statistical evaluation, internal audit, and forecast systems are either weak or non-existent. Indifferently managed public enterprises, including marketing and commodity boards, deliver inadequate return on capital because of relatively high wage costs, overstaffing, and political interference (Lim, 1993: 49). Scarce professional personnel frequently join international public or private sector agencies for placements abroad. A thin local private sector restricts opportunities to develop management skills beyond experience gained in cumbersome, unreformed local bureaucracies.

Public service professionalism emphasising teamwork is lacking, and policy advice systems often deficient or ineffectual. This has damaged confidence, which in turn has hampered performance. Judicial independence and official support for the rule of the law is uncertain. Cultural demands obstruct legal determinations, something evident in land disputes. Small state intimacy renders 'arms length' relationships between public officials and politicians difficult hampering the frank advice and critical evaluation required for effective policy advice. It also impedes merit-based appointment or promotion. Office-holders merge public functions with private rewards, reciprocity rationalised by perceived obligations to family and group affiliations. Imported bureaucratic idioms get translated into what is local, primordial, and familiar.

The absorptive and transformational capacity needed to maximise advantages from external assistance is often lacking. Haphazard accountability may accompany receipt of development assistance tied to procurement from donor sources. Confronting adverse economic circumstances, Pacific Islands governments may enforce local funding cuts to recurrent costs of overly ambitious, aid-assisted capital projects. Local skill acquisition measures are postponed leaving international agencies to 'backstop' completed projects with expatriate personnel. Governments also accept assistance packages for reasons unrelated to current priorities. According to the United Nations Development Programme (UNDP) 1994 Pacific Human Development Report, an excessive concentration on securing additional resources at aggregate levels has eroded needed investment in human development.[4] That shortcoming occurs as political processes fail to formulate a local consensus about development objectives, something evident in Papua New Guinea. This is a vacuum only partly filled by religious, non-governmental, and community service organisations.

Political Embroilment

Public service functions ostensibly organised to provide territorial legal control, sovereign supervision of the revenue, provision and maintenance of infrastructure functions, and delivery of essential services often encounter political intrusion. In PIC locations, this may distort resource allocations intended for public sector purposes, ignore technical and skill shortages, maintain indifferent relations with local communities, and inflict neglect upon those living in rural areas or outer islands.

More complex distortions result when demands nurtured through kin and electorate loyalties, confront public bureaucracies ostensibly adhering to principles of law and probity. Manifest strains include nepotism and public service employment distributed as 'fair shares' allocations between competing districts or islands. In some instances, for example the Cook Islands, personal dynasties have colonised bureaucratic systems. In others, self-serving entrenchment has provoked political responses alien to this setting's innate social conservatism and pragmatic consensus seeking. They include strikes, land occupations, sporadic riots, and overt inter-district civil conflict evident throughout Melanesia. Conversely, complicit acquiescence towards élite entrenchment is pervasive. It engenders cultures of compliance where people 'go along with the system' to promote and protect their wider networks of family welfare. This conduct is evident in Samoa.

While constitutional rule has been maintained – Fiji's 1987 military coups aside – secular civil society formations have not easily penetrated the inner sanctums of public policy determination. Roots of local government are often shallow, rendering decentralisation objectives problematic. This matters because durable agency performance at these levels can offset distant, under-performing central state agencies, or non-governmental community-based projects that may prove ephemeral.

Gaining access to public revenue has seen political activity exact concessions and subsidies for urban land incorporations (Vanuatu); maintain government spending significantly outpacing revenue, or retaining 'slush fund' schemes used for discretionary spending in electorates (Papua New Guinea); deny central bank warnings about needed price adjustments in the face of a weakening currency, declining reserves, and excessive demands for credit (the Solomon Islands); run unacceptable debt levels (Samoa); exploit lax fiduciary supervision of government owned banking and credit facilities (Fiji); or connive in tax fraud (the Cook Islands).

Corruption mars public life throughout the Pacific. This has been facilitated by rent seeking and rent creation, conduct seeking commercial advantage from public institutions through distorted formulation or application of economic policies, allocation of public money, and provision of access to services. Rent seeking is reduced by cutting price controls, but retained through arbitrary interference in revenue collection, state purchasing, and regulatory promulgation. In Melanesia, this conduct will often outrank service delivery as a function of governance. State withdrawal from service delivery functions may actually broaden regulatory discretion and its possible abuse for rent seeking. Some evidence of these problems among the PICs has surfaced through technical assistance surveys conducted preparatory to possible World Trade Organisation (WTO) membership.[5] These difficulties magnify where the rule of law does not operate, vitiating any benefits accrued through privatisation.

An antidote to corruption is the public resentment that it engenders. The corrective action that this may galvanise is obstructed when governments harass relevant news media investigation. This interference has occurred in Samoa, Tonga, the Solomon Islands and Vanuatu, and allowed governments to avoid domestic public accountability. Transparency International, through its chapters in Fiji and Papua New Guinea (PNG) has conducted limited external surveillance of PIC corruption. It identified PNG's Public Finance Management Act, and regulations intended to govern public supplies and tendering, as subject to frequent and conspicuous violation by senior officials and politicians.[6] That abuse compounds law and order problems identified as the most important constraint to PNG's development (Yala and Levantis, 1999: 11).

Misgivings have accumulated about the presumed advantages of tax havens currently operating in the Cook Islands, Samoa, Vanuatu and Nauru. These operations engender suspicion by pursuing money laundering and 'no questions asked' policies towards criminal interests utilising off-shore banks and front companies. In 1999, the Paris-based Financial Action Task Force claimed Nauru's tax haven was an outlet for Russian organised crime operating through American middlemen.[7] Other malign commercial penetrations include suspect dealings over land, sale of passports, and bogus schemes where PIC governments 'guarantee' letters of credit traded for commissions (Larmour, 1997 a: 10-11). Greatly increased financial flows, using electronic commerce to evade surveillance for transactional legitimacy, facilitate these practices.

Orthodox characterisations of PIC governance problems note the disjunction between outwardly 'representative' electoral systems, and a lack of popular control over formation of the executive, its policies, or proclivities to realign without warning or restraint. Lax party discipline within legislatures contributes to weak coalition formations and executive instability. Allocating the spoils of office overshadows policy promotion as the *leitmotiv* of political groupings. Lacking organisational depth, these formations are vulnerable to capture by dominant personalities and their key backers.

In Melanesia, parliamentary turnover following elections can run higher than forty per cent, outcomes constricting an accumulation of legislative experience needed to enhance ministerial performance. Much political representation is preoccupied with gratifying local, village, clan or extended family demands and 'as unbounded politics fosters political instability' (Steeves, 1996: 133). A vacuum in public life of national constituency interests emerges. Key policy needs like child care go unrepresented and unattended. Coherent policy formation is impeded by continuing Cabinet reshuffles, leadership challenges or defeats, and changes of government. This volatility results from machinations between politicians rather than outright electoral reversals. Weak party alignment makes it harder for voters to ensure that corrupt politicians are kept out of office.

In some locations (e.g. the Solomon Islands and the Federated States of Micronesia (FSM)) prior chiefly backing is essential to win nomination for electoral contest. Patronage is used to lever extended family connections into positions of influence, the few women entering public life often reliant upon such connections. Controlling status allocation retains political potency, particularly for land holding, resources use, and citizenship. Indigenous cultural norms are compromised through the sale of advantages now offering within a more interdependent, commercially driven external environment.

Notwithstanding dispersal of traditional supports through migration and urbanisation, the prerogatives of public appointment based on traditional cultural criteria are jealously guarded. This authority was recognised by the 1996 Fiji Constitutional Review Commission's recommendations regarding retention of important powers by the Council of Chiefs. Historically, such responsibilities have entailed reciprocities of stewardship to commoners, obligations subsequently eroded by mobility, individualisation of interest through the cash economy, or political rewards unrelated to needs traditionally conceived as group entitlements. Respect for chiefly authority continues, although it risks decline without commitment to tackling widening social and economic disparities.

Overall, the profile of PIC public sector competence is unsatisfactory. In urban and rural locations, services range from the barely adequate to the frequently non-existent. Such service reliability as exists depends upon private sector connections, personal access, and family connections to sources of bureaucratic decision. As a rule, public sector outcomes favour those with relative wealth, status, town occupancy, male gender, adulthood and identification within a dominant cultural identity. Correspondingly disadvantaged is a majority comprising those who are young, poor, marginalised, rural dwelling, or minority ethnic affiliation.

Diagnosis of PIC Public Sectors

External grant and funding agencies have sought enhanced PIC public sector effectiveness, economy and resilience. World Bank prescriptions and Organisation for Economic Cooperation and Development (OECD) directives have urged aid donors to seek greater public sector efficiency. Investors seek assurances of financial probity, effective pricing regimes, and transparency in public accounting systems. Evident have been 'more market' notions of public management. These allow senior operatives autonomy to control performance standards, output controls, service tendering, and restructuring of existing entities into corporatised units. The international discourse about good governance has influenced PIC public sector reform through prescriptions emphasising:
- Reinforcement of democratic public institutions;
- Transparency, accountability and scope for public participation in governing processes;
- Effective management of economic policies that further development;
- The rule of law and respect for human rights.

These calls gathered strength during the late 1980s as World Bank assistance criteria expanded to embrace key macroeconomic factors affecting loan recipients – particularly debt management and foreign exchange policies. Better office-holding accountability was urged so as to free bottlenecks impeding market and investment incentives and local entrepreneurship. An objective was to move beyond rent-seeking into wealth creation. Public accountability, furthermore, required the vigilance of a vibrant civil society exercising its civil and political rights.

Diagnosis of PIC public sector shortcomings emerged as a regional political question. In a widely foreshadowed June 1994 statement, Australian Minister for Pacific Island Affairs Bilney warned PIC governments about having to reform the public sector, develop the private sector, and change old social and economic attitudes. Hence it was 'only reasonable to assume that the preparedness of investors and aid partners alike to continue to play a role in the South Pacific will depend on how well individual countries formulate and implement the economic and structural reforms necessary for sustainable economic development'.[8] This message was reiterated a year later, when Canberra emphasised the need to institute rigorous national curbs against an unsustainable exploitation of natural resources. Unless that occurred, the impact of development assistance would remain cosmetic.[9]

In the event, Canberra's bark was worse than its bite; it claimed that 'those Pacific countries that adopt sound policies – as many are – will maximise their chances of development'.[10] The conditionality glimpsed in the 1997 Simons Report on Australian Overseas Aid was more warning than threat. This recommended Australia not hesitate to reduce aid funds to those PICs reluctant to commit to good governance, essential economic and resource management reform, or appropriate capacity enhancement.[11]

This measured advice contrasted with the tasteless tone of a 93 page document marked 'Australian Eyes Only', and left in a Cairns hotel foyer during the July 1997 South Pacific Forum Economic Ministers' meeting. A joint in-house concoction prepared by Treasury and Foreign Ministry officials for conference briefing purposes, this berated the poorest performing PICs for corruption, incompetent management, flirtation with quick-fix easy money schemes, and over-exploitation of natural resources. Individual PIC politicians were condescendingly vilified. Some comments were valid, including an opening claim that poor governance and economic mismanagement had degraded PIC fiscal positions and external balances. Nevertheless, the report's hostile reception embarrassed Australian standing in the region.[12]

Previous, and less inflammatory characterisations of PIC public management difficulties carried greater weight. A 1995 World Bank official claimed the PICs could not emerge as change agents while burdened with costly, inefficient bureaucratic structures inherited from a colonial past when public administration was viewed a development solution.[13] In March 1995, the World Bank encouraged PIC representatives to establish development strategies concentrating less on direct interventions or transactions, and more upon facilitating productivity and delivery of service.[14] External consultants regularly identified public sector reform as a necessary inducement for foreign investment.

The South Pacific Forum

This approach is reflected in current attempts by South Pacific Forum Economic Ministers (FEMM) to strengthen national and regional economic and public management. The 1997 Forum Economic Action Plan's section on agreed principles of best practice public accountability, drew from the International Monetary Fund (IMF) Code of Principles and Good Practices on Fiscal Transparency. Other endorsed principles emphasised independent scrutiny, oversight, and disclosure rights for legislative bodies; transparency in competitive tendering; prompt disciplining in respect of contravention of financial regulations; appropriate resourcing of Auditors General and Ombudsmen; and statutory recognition of independent advice and reporting by Central Banks. Reviewed a year later, governments recognised different capacities to implement comprehensive reforms, 'while accepting that public accountability and political commitment are of overriding importance'.[15]

Table 7.1 The South Pacific Forum[a]

Country	Area sq.km.	EEZ 000 sq. km.	Population 000 1998 est.	Independence year
Australia	7,682,300	8,600	18,898	1901
Cook Islands	240	1,830	16.5	1965[b]
FSM	700	2,978	114	1986
Fiji	18,272	1,290	797.8	1970
Kiribati	817	3,550	85.1	1979
Marshall Islands	170	2,131	61	1986
Nauru	21	320	12	1968
New Zealand	268,700	2,222	3,763	1907
Niue	258	390	2	1974[b]
Palau	488	629	19	1994
PNG	462,840	3120	4,412	1975
Samoa	2,935	120	175	1962
Solomon Islands	28,370	1,340	418	1978
Tonga	747	700	98	Uncolonised
Tuvalu	26	900	11	1978
Vanuatu	12190	680	182	1980

a   Renamed the Pacific Islands Forum in 1999 when New Caledonia was granted observer status.
b   Achieved current status of full internal self government in free association with New Zealand.

Although a foreign transplant, the Forum Action Plan's best practice accountability package was deemed suitable grafting stock for local conditions. Some functions assumed to exist were not evident, including a separation of executive and legislative functions, and standards of fiduciary independence. Nevertheless getting PIC governments committed to these principles was an advance. They did so against a backdrop of declining aid flows, altering trade patterns, and a worsening Asian economic downturn. A mood of urgency prompted the contemplation of hard choices – unless confronted now, the region risked further marginalisation.

Table 7.2 Pacific Island Countries: Selected Indicators

	GDP(US$) per capita	GDP growth pa	Ratio aid GDP %	Birth rate per 000	Life Expect. at birth	Adult literacy %
Cook Is.	4947	0.9	17.9	24.3	72	93
FSM	2070	1.9	...	31.0	65	71
Fiji	2684	1.6	2.3	24.3	66	93
Kiribati	702	1.9	25.7	31.0	61	92
Marshall Is.	1882	3.5	...	43.0	65	95
Nauru	3450	2.2	...	23.0	58	95
Niue	3714	0.5	121	15.0	74	97
Palau	8027	2.5	...	23.0	69	91
PNG	1196	2.2	6.7	32.1	54	28
Samoa	1060	0.5	30	26.7	66	95
Solomon Is.	926	3.2	16.2	35.9	64	30
Tonga	1868	-0.5	22	26.0	68	99
Tuvalu	1157	1.3	49*	28.0	67	95
Vanuatu	1231	2.5	22	32.6	65	33

* 1992

Source: UNDP 1999.

Public Sector Reform Processes

In 1995, the Asian Development Bank (ADB) identified good governance criteria that included: *accountability*, relating primarily to management of the public sector, its enterprises and staff; *participation*, including non-governmental organisations (NGOs), the private sector, and decentralisation to local levels; *predictability*, referring to legal frameworks and operable rule of law; and *transparency* over information disclosure enabling effectiveness in governing systems overall.

With twelve PIC members in its Pacific Developing Member countries group (Table 7.4), the ADB 'has emerged as the leading proponent of a comprehensive approach to public sector and economic restructuring. Reforms are time-bound, with access to programme loan components for consultancies, redundancies, and re-capitalising of failed institutions tied to completion of relevant restructuring tasks' (Hughes, 1998: 122). The objective is stricter financial discipline and spending priorities that emphasise human development and essential infrastructure.

PIC programmes of fiscal, economic and public sector management faced mounting pressures for reform. The catalyst was often a fiscal or currency crisis, though underlying causes ran deeper (Ray, 1998: 9). As a lead agency, the ADB played an increasingly significant role in the region via its national consultative group processes. The ADB has graded the PICs using social and economic indicators that determine recipient eligibility for concessional loan finance. Shared programme goals include public sector reform linkage to sought fiscal and public debt management improvements, enhanced co-ordination among central state agencies, and a broadening of the tax base. The extent of some macroeconomic imbalances concerned is evident from Table 7.3.

Table 7.3 PIC Economic Indicators: 1990 and 1995

	Total Revenue % of GDP		Government Expenditure % of GDP		Surplus/Deficit* % of GDP	
	1990	*1995*	*1990*	*1995*	*1990*	*1995*
Cook Islands	48.6	46.8	116.9	58.2	-68.3	-11.4
Fiji	26.6	28.7	28.2	34.2	-2.3	-6.5
Kiribati	114.6	112.7	115.7	128.0	-62.2	-51.5
Marshall Is.	109.2	90.0	109.2	90.0	-74.1	-57.2
FSM	104.7	73.6	102.6	77.9	2.1	-4.2
PNG	25.3	26.3	34.7	26.3	-10.7	-3.0
Samoa	48.5	60.0	70.1	51.0	-21.5	-29.8
Solomon Is.	31.8	29.6 (1994)	47.7	37.4 (1994)	-16.0	-6.0
Tonga	26.6	26.8	45.9	45.0	-19.4	-18.7
Tuvalu	74.7	41.8	76.5	69.7	-2.0	-35.7
Vanuatu	27.6	27.2	46.0	69.7	-18.4	-7.6

* Overall Budget Surplus/Deficit of Central Government.
Source: Asian Development Outlook (1998).

Commencing in 1996, and performed under joint ADB/New Zealand auspices, the *Cook Islands* underwent easily its most drastic public sector reorganisation since self-government in 1965. An ambitious economic restructuring programme cut public service staffing by 60 per cent, reduced salaries by 15 per cent, halved total government ministries and agencies, and introduced fiscal responsibility through New Zealand model-accrual accounting. By 1997, informal subsistence production and exports had increased following inception of the comprehensive economic restructuring programme (Mellor, 1997: 18-19).

In *Vanuatu*, the ADB was instrumental in a comprehensive public sector reform programme extending from 1997 to 2002, and including civil service downsizing, improved access to social services, and enactment of a supportive legal framework through good governance legislation. Funding was released on a step by step basis according to programme achievement.

The ADB has assisted *Tonga* with establishment of programme budgeting due for inception in 1999, and a rationalisation of public service functions designed to broaden the tax base.

The Solomon Islands and *Papua New Guinea* governments announced public service staff cuts in 1998. These initiatives proceeded in the Solomon Islands through a US$ 4.2 million ADB loan for downsizing the public service, relocation of staff, and redundancy payments. Difficult for the reform programme in both countries was clearing government debt arrears. Relevant ADB initiatives in the *Marshall Islands* encountered unmet deadlines, lack of government direction, and indifferent employee productivity gains. Some of those difficulties had eased by 1999.

In the *FSM*, significant public workforce reductions comprised a component of an ADB loan package (Peter and Samo, 1999: 188). This resulted in 20 per cent cuts in personnel and salaries, early retirements, and privatisation of utilities. Economic and public sector reform were seen as inseparable. To Jacob Nena, President of the FSM, 'the catalytic role of government will come from creating a competitive private sector environment ... good governance ... is required to ensure that investors will invest and that economic growth will proceed'.[16]

Viewed collectively, public sector restructuring has sought staff and expenditure downsizing; new sources of revenue and improved revenue administration; institutional reform in public finance, the judiciary, police and customs; corporatisation and privatisation; and stronger central government and planning functions.[17] Under meetings entitled the PIC/Partners consultations, regional governments have been joined by World Bank, Commonwealth Secretariat, the UN's Economic and Social Commission for Asia and the Pacific, IMF, European Union (EU), and UNDP representatives.[18] These meetings have reviewed current development assistance practices, in particular the impact of public sector aid flows upon economic performance. Although public sector restructuring and privatisation have begun to assist the South Pacific's trade liberalisation, and generated opportunities for foreign investment, related needs have made less progress. They include land reform, property rights, contractual obligations, and labour productivity (Jayaraman, 1998: 43).

Good governance principles are viewed as integral to open, liberal, and transparent investment policies professed in APEC non-binding principles. Through its 1996 Manila Framework for strengthening economic cooperation, APEC identified relevant modalities for the PICs. They are economic infrastructure; environmentally sustainable growth; small and medium business enterprises; human resources development; harnessing technologies for the future; and developing capital markets. The SPF responded positively to the suggestion that PIC economies benchmark their economic liberalisation against APEC best practice (Scollay, 1998: 119). Also relevant has been the use of public sector reforms to assist alignment with WTO procedures. This relates to adjustments needed following post-2000 retirements of special aid and trade concessions provided under African Caribbean Pacific (ACP) Lomé Convention arrangements. Eight PICs benefited from these access advantages now deemed incompatible under WTO rules.[19] Determinants affecting post-2000 Lomé arrangements for the PICs include poverty alleviation as a core criteria for receipt of development assistance, small state vulnerability as grounds for possible WTO rule waiver, and margin of trade preferences for canned tuna exports.[20]

Longer term, the EU seeks a regional economic partnership arrangement for the South Pacific based on a local free trade area. This could provide a template applicable to EU relations with African and Caribbean countries. Economic restructuring, good governance, and multilateral trade and tariff policies are meant to align the South Pacific to standards and target dates set by WTO and APEC, although though most PICs belong to neither. Such alignment would encourage foreign investment and relieve aid dependency. The intention is for good governance prescriptions to facilitate a transition where trade replaces aid as the key PIC development dynamic. This would arrive via the emerging WTO regime, and a refocused Africa/Caribbean/Pacific (ACP) relationship with the EU in a post-2000 period. These assumptions are far from secure and subject to critical opposition. Briguglio (1995) for example, has noted that for small island countries generally, the larger their trade dependence, reliance on exports, and dependence on imported energy, then the more acute their sensitivity to external shocks.

Table 7.4 The South Pacific: Regional and Intergovernmental Affiliations

Country	SPF	SPC	ADB	UN	MSG	C'wealth	WTO	APEC
Am. Samoa		x						
Australia	x	x	x	x		x	x	x
CNMI		x						
Cook Islands	x	x	x			x		
FSM	x	x	x	x				
Fiji	x	x	x	x	x	x	x	
Fr. Polynesia		x						
Guam		x						
Kiribati	x	x	x	x		x		
Marshall Islands	x	x	x	x				
New Caledonia	x[a]	x			x[b]			
Nauru	x	x	x	x		x		
New Zealand	x	x	x	x		x	x	x
Norfolk Island		x						
Niue	x	x						
Palau	x	x		x				
PNG	x	x	x	x	x	x	x	x
Pitcairn		x						
Samoa	x	x	x	x		x	(ap)	
Solomon Islands	x	x	x	x	x	x		
Tokelau		x						
Tonga	x	x	x	x		x	(ap)	
Tuvalu	x	x	x			x		
Vanuatu	x	x	x	x	x	x	(ap)	
Wallis & Futuna		x						

a New Caledonia granted observer status 1999.
b New Caledonia's FLNKS pro-independence movement attends MSG meetings

SPF South Pacific Forum
SPC South Pacific Community (formerly South Pacific Commission)
ADB Asian Development Bank
UN   United Nations

MSG	Melanesian Spearhead Group (sub-regional body)
C'wealth	Commonwealth
CNMI	Commonwealth of the North Mariana Islands
WTO	World Trade Organisation member; (ap): applicant
APEC	Asia Pacific Economic Cooperation

Source: UN, South Pacific Forum; Commonwealth

Good Governance Change Impacts

A combination of bilateral development assistance donor pressure, Forum Economic Minister proposals, and ADB prescriptions have resulted in significant, often painful changes to PIC public sectors. Results include years of previously unaudited treasury accounts submitted to Parliament by the Samoan government in 1998. The following year, Fiji passed legislated to improve public sector financial management through the inception of accrual accounting and enhanced budgetary reporting and procedures. Influenced by New Zealand practice (also followed in the Cook Islands), accrual accounting objectives entail moving beyond cash budgeting, and having the government act as purchaser of agency deliverables at an agreed price within a preset envelope (Peters, 1998: 383).

External factors encouraging PIC adoption of good governance prescriptions have varied according to location. Towards Melanesian states, donor disquiet at the rapid depletion of native timber resources strengthened calls to incorporate good governance prescriptions within future assistance arrangements. Yet given the dominance of foreign consultants, and potential crowding out of domestic responsibility for instigated changes, caution about reform 'ownership' has emerged from PIC representatives. Regarding the ADB's role in his country, Marshall Islands Finance Minister DeBrum has asked: 'Just because someone comes in from outside and tells us to jump, we don't have to respond "how high?" '.[21] More diplomatically 'over specification of the reform process can hamper intellectual participation by the national managers in shaping, timing and driving the reforms: participation that is essential to its durability' (Hughes, 1998: 123).

This claim mirrors broader, unresolved questions about whether the good governance criteria propounded by external agencies is suitable transplant material. If these prescriptions are to take root, it has been argued, they will grow not from external grafting, but through the domestic politics and state activity needed to generate and sustain them (Leftwich, 1994: 365). Another view maintains that the World Bank may have turned to the good governance agenda to avert concerns that 'poor development performance might be caused by fundamental flaws in the economic policies advocated by the Bank itself' (Macdonald, 1998: 25). Others believe disappointed results from years of development assistance have moved donor governments to reduce aid budgets, and to retreat behind the banners of accountability, participation, and responsibilities of civil society (Smillie and Helmich, 1993: 14).

A local critic believes undeveloped civil society institutions face further weakening by 'the new economic orthodoxy that requires everyone to co-operate in the strengthening of the private sector' (Helu, 1997: 4). Without commitment to the explicit recognition of social justice, good governance prescriptions are inadequate for current South Pacific needs (Helu, 1997: 3). However, the UNDP's 1994 Pacific Human Development Report has linked governance reform to social advancement, rural, subsistence sector improvement, and poverty reduction.[22] Key PIC human resource development needs arise from population growth, access to basic education, skills development, appropriate higher education, and greater gender equality of opportunity (Rofeta, 1993: 229). Whether these opportunities arrive may depend upon the impact of interests next considered.

Comparing Interests

State Bureaucratic

To one PIC analyst, bureaucratic designs have reinforced dependency and submissiveness. The long term impact of bureaucratic work has resulted in a collective conditioning towards dependency and passivity, created by government bureaucratic structures in the Pacific for over a century.[23] In the mid 1980s, the notion of smaller Polynesian and Micronesian island states as 'MIRAB' systems entered the public discourse. The term encompassed interlocking migration, remittances, aid, and bureaucracy factors. Involved was a 'transnational corporation of kin' utilising the regional labour market for inter-family remittances as a limited form of rational comparative advantage. Rent income eclipses traditional tradable activities, increasing development assistance needs. These effects offer enhanced living standards, but intensify dependency (Bertram and Watters, 1985). Nevertheless, it 'is a pareto-efficient, welfare-maximizing strategy to export labour services and geostrategic services when this is in line with the comparative advantage of a given country' (Poirine, 1998: 91).

Although the bureaucracy component of the model was not fully developed, it is a key site for resource transfers and non-tradable economic activity.[24] Stable remuneration from public sector employment replaces riskier cash returns realised through traditional subsistence and uncertain exports. In the meantime, imports expand. The pattern is less evident in Melanesia, where public revenues have fluctuated according to natural resource returns from timber, fishing, and minerals, or, as in Fiji, sugar production. Despite downsizing, it is unlikely the MIRAB phenomenon is something public sector reform can replace overnight.

Resistance to the reform agenda occurs elsewhere and relates to individual national circumstances. For example, without appropriate family connections, career advancement in the Samoan public service is problematic; lacking public service contacts, benefit to private sector development from that quarter is equally constrained. Samoan attempts to advance externally promoted, 'rational' public sector reforms have collided with the dominance of family structure (*aiga*) and collective ties and controls of traditional ways (*fa'a Samoa*) permeating that society.[25]

In Fiji, the now replaced 1990 Constitution stipulated that all grades of the public service comprise no less than fifty per cent indigenous Fijian and Rotuman personnel, a measure that degraded merit-based performance (Vallance, 1996: 96).[26] In 1999, newly elected Prime Minister Chaudhry claimed that during this period 'many people were promoted to positions of authority based on criteria other than merit and qualification. As a result, our public services have been reduced to a level of incompetency and inefficiency unheard of before'.[27] Although now rescinded, Fiji's attempted 'affirmative action' has resulted in lasting skill and technical shortages.

Elsewhere, employment reduction in the state sector and subsidy cutting have engendered societal strains (Larmour, 1998: 85). Downsizing has been politically contentious, exemplified by Papua New Guinea opposition leader Narakobi's inflammatory imagery when accusing the government of 'ethnic cleansing' the civil service by removing personnel originating from the Sepik region.[28] During 1999, it was a factor in serious inter-community strife in the Solomon Islands, nor discounted as a motive behind the assassination of a prominent Samoan Cabinet Minister. A confidential report by a New Zealand official on this episode, that involved complicity by prominent figures, found one of the conspirators 'a man increasingly out of control as his empire of corruption in the public sector headed for extinction'.[29]

Development Assistance Donors

The South Pacific receives more development assistance per head than other developing country regions. Although levels have declined, 1997 net receipts totalled US $1559 millions for a population of approximately seven million, or some US$ 223 per head. Comparable 1997 allocations for Sub-Saharan Africa, Latin America, and South and Central Asia stood at twenty five, ten, and four US dollars per head respectively. [30] Assistance per head in former US territories of the Marshall Islands, FSM and Palau combined was US $1042 in 1997. With those locations excluded, Oceania's 1997 figure reduced to US $197 net overseas development assistance per head.[31]

Some donor interests seeking PIC public sector reform have linked good governance to sustainability, poverty alleviation and community need. This is to ensure 'that political, social and economic priorities are based on a broad consensus in society and the voices of the poorest and the most vulnerable are heard in decision making over the allocation of development resources'.[32]

Wider shared objectives are threefold. A first aim is to ensure that the development assistance provided helps public sector systems to invigorate local economic activity. Behind this is a frequently asserted, but unproven linkage made by the donor community linking economic liberalisation to democratisation (Macdonald, 1997: 26). A second goal is satisfying donor country taxpayers that development assistance provides value for money. A third is to ensure complementarity and consistency of recommendations from donors concerning PIC public sector reform. This helps to signal a united policy front by enunciating principles considered indivisible and unexceptionable. Realisation of this aim has occurred through policy networks developed by regularising consultation among South Pacific Forum Economic Ministers.

Table 7.5 Oceania: Net ODA Receipts and Selected Indicators[a]

	ODA[b] 1994	ODA 1997	GNP/CAP 1996	Population 1998: 000s	GNP 1996	ODA/GNP 1996
CNMI	2	0	...	260	...	...
Cook Islands	14	10	...	17	...	...
FSM	104	96	2060	114	227	49.74
Fiji	40	44	2470	797	1986	2.28
French Polynesia	368	367	...	228	...	...
Kiribati	15	16	920	85	77	16.91
Marshall Islands	49	63	1890	61	114	64.09
New Caledonia	408	339	...	200	...	...
Nauru	2	3	...	12	...	...
Niue	7	5	...	2	...	...
Palau	202	39	...	19	...	...
PNG	326	349	1170	4412	4890	7.82
Samoa	48	28	1160	175	176	18.38
Solomon Islands	47	42	910	418	156	11.86
Tokelau	3	4	...	1.6	...	...
Tonga	35	28	1780	98	181	17.70
Tuvalu	7	10	...	11	...	...
Vanuatu	42	27	1290	182	227	13.67
Wallis & Futuna	0	1	...	10	...	...
Unallocated	68	90				
Total	**1790**	**1559**				

a Includes ODA flows from DAC/OECD counties and multilateral organisations.
b $US million.
CNMI Commonwealth of the North Mariana Islands

Source: Development Assistance Committee of the OECD (online, www.oecd.org/dac).

Powerholders

To PIC governments, the public sector is part employer, welfare provider, aid distributor, and status distributor. To those directing public sectors heavily centralised during the colonial order, resistance to reform was not difficult – at least until 1990s style donor conditionality began its watch. Calculations then began among politicians about which bits of the public sector to jettison. Sacrificing some of it was considered necessary to maintain sufficient patronage, and gratify public expectations about the capacity of office-holding politicians to generate and deliver wealth. A perceived need to retain control of these processes existed. Hence 'the single most salutary lesson from these sponsored reform measures is that if governments do not implement contemporary economic, financial, and administrative practices, they will be forced to accept externally determined economic policies and benchmarks when assistance is sought from international agencies. In such circumstances reform measures are likely to be more painful than internally introduced measures' (Ray, 1998: 9).

There was awareness that a shrinkage in real aid would continue. Without credible and serious public sector reform initiatives, heavier cuts loomed as a distinct possibility. While vulnerability has been a moral 'asset' to deploy from positions of weakness within these frameworks, most PIC governments appreciated that harsher international conditions determined public sector reform 'went with the territory' of global market liberalisation. However Fiji could test this generalisation: its Labour-led coalition gaining office in 1999 was headed by a leader from a strong public sector union background unsympathetic to public sector downsizing.

Institutional Aspects

When they were designed, South Pacific constitutional systems sought to accommodate domestic values within the legal and organisational frameworks provided by external models (Ghai, 1990; 1996: 173-99). These systems allowed for diversity and pragmatism, but assumed most public figures, most of the time, would play within the rules of the game. As that assumption came under pressure, introduced accountability mechanisms faced increasingly serious challenges.

The office of Ombudsman, established in PIC jurisdictions to advance standards of public administration and protect the rights of citizens in their dealings with governments, exists in Fiji, Vanuatu, Samoa, the Cook Islands, Papua New Guinea, and the Solomon Islands. Longer term, its possible establishment is under consideration in Niue, Tonga and Tuvalu. In 1999, the Commonwealth of North Marianas established a post of Labour Ombudsman, reporting to the United States Office of Insular Affairs, Department of the Interior.

In most instances, the institution has encountered impediments through resource constraints. This is evident in Papua New Guinea, notwithstanding resource stipulation provisions within this office's constitutional authorisation. Resource constraints have not prevented active investigation to ensure government bodies are responsive to public needs, including attempts to eliminate unfairness or discrimination. Powers available under the Leadership Code allowed investigation of military commander General Singarok's March 1997 conduct, when the armed forces defied civil authority during the Sandline mercenary incident.[33]

Easily the most spirited exercise of independent Ombudsman functions has occurred in Vanuatu. Appointed Ombudsman in 1994, Marie-Noelle Ferrieux-Patterson identified corruption in the Vanuatu public service; filed abuse of office allegations against former Prime Ministers Maxime Carlot Korman, Serge Vohor and their senior ministerial colleagues; and reported illegal dealings in land, passports, and letters of credit. The office ran radio campaigns highlighting problems of domestic violence against women; investigated the board of Air Vanuatu for irregularities; and took action to recover US $100 million in illegal bank guarantees.[34] Sometimes the Ombudsman's findings have opened with Biblical quotations, underlining to Vanuatu's devout the errant conduct of those subject to censure.

In July 1997, the Vanuatu government retaliated by threatening to abolish the office of Ombudsman. Moves to formulate fresh authorising legislation remained in abeyance and left the office operating under broadly defined constitutional, but inadequate statutory guidance. A further report, implicating senior politicians in the misuse of National Provident Fund moneys, helped trigger brief, but serious rioting in Port Vila during January 1998. In 1999, the only moderately qualified Hanington Alatoa was appointed to the office of Ombudsman in Vanuatu.

In Fiji, the 1997 constitution prescribes freedom of information legislation; a Code of Conduct designed to ensure probity in the conduct of senior officials and politicians; enhanced scrutiny functions for parliamentary backbenchers through sector standing committees; and a strengthened office of the Ombudsman and a Human Rights Commission (established 1999).[35] The Ombudsman also serves on the National Human Rights Commission established following the

1996 Constitutional Review's recommendations. Given the advocacy role inherent in effective human rights promotion, combining these functions could entail potential conflicts of interest.

The Samoan office provides an avenue for citizen complaint and a mechanism to assist civil servants delineate their professional functions.[36] In 1994, Controller and Chief Auditor Ah Chong disclosed serious deficiencies in government accountability of public expenditure, dereliction of financial reporting to Parliament, and extra-legal conduct by Ministers and senior public officials.[37] These allegations were sufficiently serious for the Samoan Ombudsman to chair an official inquiry into the report's allegations. The outcome was not their vindication, but a June 1997 amendment to the Samoan constitution that authorised Auditor Ah Chong's suspension from office by simple majority of the legislature.

Some external agencies attempt to facilitate good governance by supporting the Ombudsman, local government bodies, and selected NGOs. There is an expectation that strengthening these bodies may lift the performance of weaker institutions in need of reform.[38] Technical assistance designed to improved public policy performance has sought to enhance PIC monitoring, data collection, and border management, particularly customs administration.

Elsewhere, an incongruity exists through expectations that PICs comply with transparency standards ignored by transnational corporates operating within their countries. For example, accountability and transparency principles go unpractised by telecommunications monopolies keen to corner the fledgling South Pacific market.[39] Disclosure difficulties of substance have also occurred over proposed multilateral investment codes and patent provisions for intellectual property.[40]

Rules and Norms

Accountability is not just a requirement, but a result reached through responsiveness to public need and citizen competence grounded in durable rights. Against such criteria, how robust is the accountability platform needed to underpin PIC public sector reforms? Have external/domestic interactive processes reciprocated to erode or strengthen those reforms? In some PIC settings, introduced accountability mechanisms have fortified citizen interest group confidence over confronting arbitrary and unreasonable official conduct (Larmour, 1998: 85). Power-holders have retaliated by under-resourcing, bypassing, and ignoring these functions, or else castigated them as alien intrusions.

External assistance in dealing with accountability violations originating abroad and abetted by domestic interests has occurred over tax haven abuse. Regionally PIC governments have moved slowly to fulfil obligations agreed to under the 1992 Honiara Agreement. This called for mutual assistance in criminal enforcement, extradition, and forfeiture of the proceeds of crime. Local law enforcement officials see the South Pacific confronting increased cross-border drug trafficking, financial fraud, and money laundering. Other negative globalisation effects include trade and documentation fraud, dumping of inferior products, importation of pornography via electronic means, and violations of intellectual property rights.[41] External scrutiny has seen Transparency International criticise Samoa's removal of Auditor General Sua Rimoni Ah Chong, deplore the Vanuatu government's attacks on its Ombudsman, and promote the OECD Convention on Combating Bribery of Foreign Public Officials in International Business Transactions. In force since 1999, this Convention aims to reduce corruption by governments when they sell assets for privatisation purposes. It is open to accession by non-OECD members willing to participate in the relevant OECD Working group.[42]

To use global capital and foreign direct investment, PICs need better organised local financial markets. Of the ten PIC Commonwealth members (Table 7.4), relevant guidelines for good practice in handling private capital flows were delineated through the 1997 Commonwealth Code. Operative principles include stable and transparent political institutions, tax codes, and property rights; good governance in management and accountability in policy-making; and robust financial and banking sectors.[43] Caribbean experience is relevant, including Jamaican calls to ensure shifts to privatisation and deregulation do not avoid rule coverage regarding integrity in public office.[44] These objectives are supported through the 1997 FEMM good practice principles previously identified.

Transformations

What messages have good governance prescriptions conveyed for the purposes of PIC public sector transformation? How do such prescriptions measure when weighing threat against opportunity? Is the process one of instrumental adjustment, or deeper-seated attitudinal change regarding responsibility in public conduct and organisation of management? First, although good governance prescriptions have provided a template for downsizing, it has not furnished retention priority criteria. Prescriptions envisage lean, efficient mechanisms, professionally conducted, and delivering a core range of services. Less clear is whether these changes mean central state structures have the capacity, skills, or authority needed to tackle long-standing asset redistribution challenges like land reform. The badly needed expansion of basic educational services is another. Prescribed PIC public sector profiles could conceivably maintain these outcomes *once achieved*, but lack the breadth to *inaugurate* substantive reforms.

Second, power holder accountability remains a value resonating across most PIC cultures. This goes compromised when group expectations for a delivery of material rewards from leaders engender complacency towards, or collusion with corrupt public conduct. Vanuatu is an example (Morgan, 1998: 293). Third, continuing centralisation of political authority amidst haphazard deconcentration of administrative functions has further blurred accountability.

What then of PIC public sector performance? Data collection and information holding deficiencies impede adhesion to recommended principles of transparency and accountability throughout PIC public management systems. A comparison between Fiji, Papua New Guinea, the Solomon Islands, Samoa and Vanuatu across the 1985-95 decade is relevant. Indicators chosen, and utilised for table 7.6 include reported levels of female adult literacy, infant mortality, education per cent public expenditure, population per physician, and telephones in use. Enough is conveyed to suggest that in discharging essential human needs functions, these governments have been under-performing.

In Melanesia, this has been less a shortage of money than of cumbersome administration (Larmour, 1998: 87). With assistance from church education, female adult literacy has improved but not relative spending on education for girls. Countries with strongest resource endowments, that is Papua New

Guinea and the Solomon Islands, have failed to maintain adequate standards of state health and educational service delivery. In Papua New Guinea, only 46 per cent of children of school age attend school regularly.[45] Across the region, children suffer Vitamin A deficiency, poor immunisation, and lack of oral rehydration therapy which, if in place, could save many young lives.[46] Estimates for Fiji suggest a constant level of approximately 25 per cent of households living in relative poverty (Chung, 1998: 138).

Table 7.6 Selected PIC Government Delivery Indicators: 1985–95

Indicator	1985	1990	1995
Female adult literacy			
Fiji	80.9	87.4	89.3
PNG	35.3	37.8	62.7
Solomons	...	...	62
Samoa	92	92	98
Vanuatu	53.3	67.3	67
Infant mortality[a]			
Fiji	28.6	24.6	18
PNG	61.4	56	65
Solomons	57.4	47.5	25
Samoa	...	46.3	33 (1994)
Vanuatu	82.6	69.2	43.1
Education[b]			
Fiji	29.6	27.0	27.5
PNG	17.2	21	17.6 (1994)
Solomons	18.6	...	15.4 (1997)
Samoa	22.8	...	...
Vanuatu	25.1	19.6	19.3 (1993)
Population per physician[c]			
Fiji	1708	2080	1764
PNG	12416	...	...
Solomons	8438	...	...
Samoa	3383	...	...
Vanuatu	4789	7365	14100

Radios[c]

Fiji	529	592	612
PNG	67	73	77
Solomons	100	119	122
Samoa	433	463	485
Vanuatu	269	285	296

a   per 1000 live births
b   percent of total government expenditure
c   per 1000 population

Source: United Nations: ESCAP, 1998; UNDP, 1999.

The ADB's 1999 report on the PNG economy indicated governance and public sector management difficulties as problems impeding development. Loans provided to basic needs had produced meagre results for rural health services, population planning, provincial road assistance, and urban water and sanitation projects. In some instances, ADB funds lay unutilised through lack of appropriate local uptake arrangements, or projects in place justifying release of loan funds.[47]

In the Solomon Islands, a highly regarded local development trust surveyed village responses regarding governance efficacy across criteria that included health, education, natural resources management, and availability of credit. Over a 1989 to 1997 period that covered four national administrations, successive governments consistently failed expectations, approval levels often below fifty per cent.[48] A subsequent survey, before the 1997 elections, revealed correspondents believed eighty per cent of sitting parliamentarians did not warrant re-election.[49]

PIC public sector reform is seminal to the future economic prospects of these countries. To one observer, 'the best way to help Pacific Island economies (and other similar developing countries) might not be to finance their capitalist private sector (or their central government budgets), but rather to subsidise their traditional sector through price subsidies to cash crop exports, or to encourage local development projects on the village level as well as traditional cultural activities, even when they do not appear profitable' (Poirine, 1993: 55).

Considerable ambivalence exists within the PICs towards public sector reform. In part, that derives from a dichotomy that emerged through the constitutional arrangements made under state formation. This was manifest through a concern to evolve 'home-grown' systems, but where a primary consequence was 'the legitimation of administrative structures which had been established by colonial powers for colonial ends' (Ghai, 1990: 2).

Discrimination against women in the South Pacific remains widespread, only a gradual abatement evident since the 1995 Beijing Fourth World Conference on Women. Areas of critical need identified by local representatives include health, political participation, employment and economic empowerment, and violence against women.[50] While governments sign up to international instruments committing them to gender advancement, implementation has been inadequate. On the Convention on the Rights of the Child to which it has acceded, Papua New Guinea has not developed implementation capacity through appropriate budget, policy, project development, or staff training capacity.

While good governance prescriptions emphasise human capacity building, this is inadequate for decisively diminishing poverty and inequality. Although it might play a catalytic role in enhancing social service delivery capacity, this normally follows rather than precedes bigger political initiatives needed to stake out poverty alleviation and equity promotion as national goals. To date, the South Pacific awaits its local Julius Nyerere – a 'convinced and persuasive "champion" of the co-operative solution' (Hughes, 1998: 34). This does not diminish the case for substantial PIC public sector reform. It is justified in the light of local capacity deficiencies, poor social service delivery, and lack of engagement by key state agencies in tackling evident problems for which they are responsible.

Conclusions

The PIC public sector reform process has faced conflicting customary, public management, local political and international pressures. Historically, colonialism's internationalisation contributed to several problems identified: once created, state bureaucracies assumed quasi-welfare functions up to, and beyond independence. Whatever colonialism's shortcomings in the Pacific, it did not stint in erecting the scaffolding, if not the substance of public bureaucracy. Expanded aid programmes through unreformed public sector systems sharpened donor interrogation as to their purpose. Good governance prescriptions received collective endorsement by PIC donors and multilateral agencies, most in tune with prevailing liberal trading orthodoxies.

Domestic/international interactivity in this instance has posed dilemmas. The exogenously shaped good governance package ('one size fits all') conveyed basics PIC powerholders could not ignore, yet paid scant heed to local sensitivities. To some concerned publics, or those not immediate beneficiaries of the state's payroll or rent seeking apparatus, hurting local sensitivities was a lesser evil. To them, 'cultural defence' against external prescriptive intrusion appeared increasingly threadbare as a cover designed to protect privilege among the powerful. The more immediate reality was one of poor public service delivery, an evident remoteness of state response, and hostility among non-beneficiaries towards the rent-seeking conduct of public officials.

Enhanced international surveillance of corruption, human rights violations, and the needs of women complemented demands for stronger public accountability in the South Pacific. Yet it was evident that external pressure for governance reform could proceed only so far – particularly where those at the centre of national political systems exhibit a lack of will to proceed. Failure here relates to globalisation impacts that intensify risks of state capture by a narrow range of local interests.

Constitutional and electoral arrangements in the PICs are sufficiently democratic to facilitate the defeat of governments by popular means. Evolved political systems however, have expanded their tolerance for continued incumbency by miscreant power-holders. Democratically elected executives have abused office to enhance personal power and undermine formal instruments of accountability. These leaders have fashioned pervasive clientele networks to ensure power flows through their hands rather than formal institutions offering restraints.

Good governance calls for greater accountability by power holders have registered, but the PIC social and cultural terrain renders its national realisation problematic. This will continue should national politics fail to utilise what clan, local, ethnic, and client-based affiliations might offer to mobilise enhanced life chances. An evident need to curb abuse of these social processes does not detract from their importance as a source of human capital. Internationalisation has underlined the need to use this domestic social capacity by highlighting the costs of its neglect. Vulnerability to external shocks has magnified as governments attempt to rule without heed to citizen compliance, public trust, or community vitality. Harnessing the social forces that exist in these countries is as important for improved PIC governance as developing appropriate institutional supports and technical enhancement.

Notes

1. Over 75 per cent of the total population of PNG, the Solomon Islands, Vanuatu and Fiji live in rural communities off marginal cash income.
2. On the problematic formulation of a small island state vulnerability index, see *Pacific Human Development Report 1999*, Suva: UNDP, pp. 26-34.
3. Commonwealth Advisory Group, (1997), *A Future for Small States – Overcoming Vulnerability*, London: Commonwealth Secretariat.
4. *Pacific Human Development Report* (1994), Suva: UNDP, p. 37.
5. Integrated Framework for Trade-Related Technical Assistance to Least developed Countries. Needs Assessment papers, WTO, 1998: Samoa; Vanuatu; Solomon Islands; (online, www.ldcs.org).
6. Comments of Richard Kassman, Transparency International, *Post-Courier*, Port Moresby, 12 April 1999.
7. Michael Field, 'Nauru Accused of Money Laundering, Reviewing Tax Operations', *AFP*, 2 March 1999.
8. Excerpts from an Address by the Hon. Gordon Bilney to the Foreign Correspondents' Association, Sydney, 15 June 1994.
9. *Pacific Report*, 21, 4, March 1995, p. 6.
10. *Global Change and Australia's Overseas Aid Programme*, Ministerial Paper and Report to Parliament, Hon. Gordon Bilney, November 1995, p. 14.
11. *Report of the Committee of Review on the Australia Overseas Aid Program* (Simons Report), (1997), Canberra: AusAid, Recommendation 6.7.
12. The episode is described by Karin von Strokirch, 'The Region in Review: International Issues and Events, 1997', *The Contemporary Pacific*, 10, 2, 1998, pp. 413-15.
13. Comments of World Bank Pacific Island Director Marianne Haug to the March 1995 Forum Economic Ministers Meeting, *Pacific Report*, 8, 3, 6 March 1995, p. 1.
14. Ibid.
15. Forum Economic Ministers Meeting, Nadi, Fiji, South Pacific Forum Secretariat Press Statement, July 8 1998.
16. Address to the 29th South Pacific Forum, Pohnpei, 24 August 1998, South Pacific Forum, Suva.
17. *Annual Report of the Resident Coordinator*, UNDP, Suva, 1998.
18. Most Pacific Island countries discussed are members of the Commonwealth, an institution with record of involvement over issues straddling borders including decolonisation, *apartheid,* sustainable development, the rule of law, human rights, and numerous forms of professional, educational, sporting, cultural, and functional interchange. The Commonwealth has developed a discourse about the needs of small states and how to appraise, compare, and measure their vulnerability and resilience.

19 They included Fiji, Kiribati, PNG, Samoa, Solomon Islands, Tonga, Tuvalu and Tonga.
20 Press Statements of South Pacific Forum Secretariat, 1 October 1998; 3 March 1999.
21 'Marshall Islands no Longer Jumping to Asian Development Bank Message', *AFP*, Majuro, 17 November 1998.
22 *Pacific Human Development Report*, Suva: UNDP, 1994, pp. 4-9.
23 Papalii Failautusi Avegalio, 'Traditional Culture and Bureaucracy: Management Challenges in the Pacific', presentation to the Pacific and Asian Affairs Council, Honolulu, Hawaii, 24 March 1998.
24 For more recent commentary, including a defence of MIRAB, see Bernard Poirine, 'Should We Hate or Love MIRAB?', *The Contemporary Pacific*, 10, 1, 1998, pp. 65-105.
25 Cluny and La'avasa Macpherson, 'Where Theory Meets Practice: the Limits of the Good Governance Programme'. Paper delivered to the December 1998 Pacific Islands Political Studies Association Conference, Christchurch, New Zealand.
26 Rotuman Islanders are culturally distinct Polynesians and comprise 1.3 per cent of Fiji's population.
27 *PACNEWS/Fiji Times*, 28 June 1999.
28 Comments reported by Richard Dinnen, *Australian Broadcasting Corporation*, 11 May 1999.
29 *Agence France Presse*, Auckland, 15 August 1999.
30 ODA Receipts data from the Development Assistance Committee of the OECD, (online, www.oecd.org/dac).
31 Ibid.
32 New Zealand Official Development Assistance. *Good Governance Programme Guidelines*, Wellington: New Zealand Ministry of Foreign Affairs and Trade, 1998. p.1.
33 On this episode, see Sinclair Dinnen, Ron May and Anthony Regan (eds), *Challenging the State: The Sandline Affair in Papua New Guinea*, Canberra: RSPAS/ANU, 1997.
34 Vanuatu Ombudsman (1997), Report, (online, www.undp.org).
35 In order of items identified, respectively sections 174; 156; 74 (3); 42. *Constitution of the Republic of the Fiji Islands*, (1997), Suva: Government Print.
36 UNDP, *Governance for Sustainable Development in the Pacific Islands*, Second Quarter Report, April-June 1997.
37 Samoa Parliamentary Paper, 1994/95, No. 21.
38 UNDP, Governance for Sustainable Human Development in the Pacific Islands, Project Justification, 1997, (online, www.unddp.org.fj/governance/Project/).
39 PICs have faced warnings that a major supplier could exert 'considerable market power, which is reflected in market share, access to resources, substantial expertise, relationships with suppliers and control of information and knowledge'. Action Plan of the South Pacific Forum, Communications Policy Ministerial Meeting, Suva, Fiji, 26 April 1999, section 2.3.
40 South Pacific Forum Non-Governmental consultation, Pohnpei, August 1998.
41 South Pacific Forum Secretariat, Suva, Press Statement, 8 October 1998.
42 *Radio Australia*, 21 May 1999.
43 Commonwealth Code on Good Governance, approved Edinburgh CHOGM, 1997.
44 K. O. Rattray, Solicitor General of Jamaica, Commonwealth Law Ministers' Meeting, Kuala Lumpur, 15-20 April 1996, Commonwealth Secretariat, LMM (96), p. 42.

45 Information of Papua New Guinea Department of Education provided to the 14th Senior Education Officers Conference, Kamaliki Vocation Centre. *The Nation*, Port Moresby, 17 June 1999.
46 *The Sate of Pacific Children 1995*, Suva: UNICEF, 1995, p. 15.
47 Tande Teman, 'ADB Blasts Poor Use of Funds', *The Nation*, Port Moresby, 5 June 1999.
48 *Link* magazine, 1987-97. Bi-monthly publication of the Solomon Islands Development Trust. Honiara. Cited by John Roughan, 'Pacific Islands Non Government Organisations: Civil Society's Political Activist'. Paper delivered to the December 1998 Pacific Islands Political Studies Association Conference, Christchurch New Zealand.
49 *Radio Australia*, Indian Pacific, Programme 691, 2 February 1997.
50 *Radio Australia*, report of Asia Pacific Women's Development and Law Conference, Port Vila, 4 June 1999.

References

Asian Development Bank (1998), *Asian Development Outlook*, 1996-1997, Manila: Asian Development Bank.
St. J. Barclay, Glen (1995), 'Problems in Australian Foreign Policy, July-December 1994', *Australian Journal of Politics and History*, 41, pp. 175-87.
Bertram, Geoff and Watters, Ray (1985), 'The MIRAB Economy in the South Pacific Microstates', *Pacific Viewpoint*, 26, pp. 497-519.
Braibant, Guy (1996), 'Public Administration and Development', *International Review of Administrative Sciences*, 62, 2, pp.162-76.
Briguglio, L. (1995), 'Small Island Developing States and their Economic Vulnerabilities', *World Development*, 23, 9, pp. 1615-32.
Chung, Margaret (1998), 'The Fiji Poverty Report', *Pacific Economic Bulletin*, 13, 2, pp. 133-36.
Economic and Social Commission for Asia and the Pacific (ESCAP) (1998), *Economic and Social Survey of Asia and the Pacific 1998*, Bangkok: ESCAP.
Ghai, Yash (1990), 'Constitutional Foundations of Public Administration', in Yash Ghai, (ed), *Public Administration and Management in Small States: Pacific Experiences*, London: Commonwealth Secretariat, pp. 1-25.
Ghai, Yash (1996), 'Self-determination in the South Pacific', in Donald Clark and Robert Williamson, *Self Determination: International Perspectives*, London: Macmillan, pp. 173-99.
Helu, I. Futa (1997), 'Tradition and Good Governance', in *State, Society and Governance in Melanesia*, Discussion Papers, Canberra: RSPAS/ANU, pp.1-6.
Henderson-Sellers, A. (1996), 'Adaptation to Climate Change: Its Future Role in Oceania', in W.J. Bourma, G.I. Pearman and M.R. Manning (eds), *Greenhouse: Coping with Climate Change*, CSIRO, Australia, pp. 349-76.
Hughes, A.V. (1998), *A Different Kind of Voyage: Development and Dependence in the Pacific Islands*, Office of Pacific Operations: Asian Development Bank.
Jayaraman, T. K. (1998), 'Foreign Direct Investment as an Alternative to Aid to the South Pacific Countries: Problems in the Past and Prospects in the Twenty-First Century', *Journal of the Pacific Society*, 21, 3-4, pp. 29-44.

Larmour, Peter (1997a), 'Corruption and Governance in the South Pacific', *Pacific Studies*, 20, 3, 1-17.
Larmour, Peter (1997b), 'Introduction', in Peter Larmour (ed), *Governance and Reform in the South Pacific,* Canberra: ANU, National Centre for Development Studies, pp.1-20.
Larmour, Peter (1998), 'Migdal in Melanesia', in Peter Dauvergne (ed), *Weak and Strong States in Asia-Pacific Societies*, Canberra: Allen and Unwin/ANU/RSPAS, pp. 77-92.
Leftwich, A. (1994), 'Governance, the State and the Politics of Development', *Development and Change*, 25, 2, pp. 363-86.
Lim, David (1993), 'Relevance of East Asian Experiences to the South Pacific', in Rodney Cole and Somasak Tambunlertchai (eds), *The Future of Asia-Pacific Economies: Pacific Islands at the Crossroads?* Canberra: ANU Asia Pacific Development Centre, pp. 33-55.
Macdonald, Barrie (1997), ' "Good" governance and Pacific Island states', in Peter Larmour (ed), *Governance and Reform in the South Pacific*, Canberra: National Centre for Development Studies, ANU, pp. 21-53.
Mellor, Colin S. (1997), 'Economic Restructuring in the Cook Islands: A Review', *Pacific Economic Bulletin*, 12, 2, pp. 17-24.
Morgan, Michael (1998), 'Political Chronicles. Vanuatu 1995-98', *The Journal of Pacific History*, 33, 3, pp. 287-93.
Nena, Jacob (1998), Address as President of the Federated States of Micronesia to the 29th South Pacific Forum, Pohnpei, 24 August, pp. 3-4.
Peter, Joakim and Samo, Marcus (1999), 'Micronesia in Review: Issues and Events, 1 July 1997 to 30 June 1998', *The Contemporary Pacific*, 11, 1, pp. 188-90.
Peters, Lucian (1998), 'Downsizing the Civil Service in Developing Countries: Golden Handshakes or Smiling Farewells?', *Public Administration and Development*, 18, pp. 381-86.
Poirine, Bernard (1993), 'Migration, Unemployment and Rent Income in Small Islands', in *Three Essays from Polynesia*, Pacific Studies Monograph, No. 9, Sydney: University of New South Wales, pp. 61-73.
Poirine, Bernard (1998), 'Should we Hate or Love MIRAB?' *The Contemporary Pacific*, 10, 1, pp. 65-105.
Ray, Binayak (1998), 'Good Governance, Administrative Reform and Socio-Economic Realities: A South Pacific Perspective', in *State, Society and Governance in Melanesia*. Discussion Papers, Canberra: RSPAS/ANU, pp. 1 11.
Rofeta, John (1993), 'Issues in the Development and Management of Human and Natural Resources in the South Pacific', in Rodney Cole and Somasak Tambunlertchai (eds), op. cit., pp. 218-33.
Schoeffel, Penelope (1997), 'Myths of Community Management: Sustainability, the State and Rural Development in Papua New Guinea, Solomon Islands and Vanuatu', in *State, Society and Governance in Melanesia*. Discussion Papers, Canberra: RSPAS/ANU, pp. 1-10.
Scollay, Robert (1998), 'APEC development Co-operation with non-members: the Forum island countries', *Pacific Economic Bulletin*, 13, 1, 1998, pp. 116-123.
Smillie, I. and Helmich, H. (eds) (1993), *Non-governmental Organisations and Governments: Stakeholders for Development*, Paris: OECD/Development Centre.
Steeves, J. (1996), 'Unbounded Politics in the Solomon Islands: Leadership and Party Alignments', *Pacific Studies*, 19, 1, pp. 115-38.
United Nations Development Programme (1994), *The Pacific Human Development Report*, Suva: UNDP.

United Nations Development Programme (1999), *Pacific Human Development Report 1999: Creating Opportunities,* Suva: UNDP.

Vallance, S. (1996), 'The Human Resources Crisis in Fiji's Public Sector. Trouble in Paradise?' *Public Administration and Development*, 16, 1, pp. 91-103.

Warrington, Edward (1994), 'A Capacity for Policy Management: Re-Appraising the Context in Micro-States', *Asian Journal of Public Administration*, 16, 1, pp. 109-33.

Yala, Charles and Levantis, Theodore (1999), 'Recent Economic Developments in Papua New Guinea: A Continuing Drought in Development', *Pacific Economic Bulletin*, 14, 1, pp. 1-16.

8 Environmental Prescription in the South Pacific

Introduction

Environmental understanding is about appreciating the elaborate symbiosis that exists between living organisms in dispersed locations. Mankind's relatively brief 350 year 'experiment' with sovereignty has neglected that reality, although the costs of doing so now force its belated recognition. However, the borderless world environmentalists take for granted arouses apprehension within arenas of intergovernmental decision. In part, that uncertainty stems from unresolved differences over what constitutes 'sustainable development', a prescription for integrating economic and environmental objectives. This terminology has broadened to encompass 'sustainable human development', advancing notions of participation, community engagement, human rights, gender emancipation, and accountable public conduct. The prescriptive infrastructure of sustainable human development is extensive. It is not surprising governments find meeting this challenge beyond their existing capacities.

This is the juncture where governmental hesitations and reservations over formal treaty commitment gather. To numerous power-holders 'sustainable human development' is a laudable long term objective, but not deserving immediate priority or commitment to specific implementation. There is a perception that, with implementation, come external conditionalities over development assistance, loans, debt relief, and public sector refurbishment. The gap between intentions declared internationally, and actual domestic implementation highlights a significant feature of the external/domestic divide. Governments may enunciate support for environmental sustainability, but effectively undermine it through various sins of omission or commission. Yet the authority structures responsible for poor environmental management are those from whom cooperation is essential for its alleviation. This dilemma constantly straddles intergovernmental problem solving, paralleled elsewhere – over human rights or disarmament for example. On environmental questions, compounding difficulties may include social inequity, injustice, population pressure, and unheeded calls for land reform.

Pacific Island countries (PICs) are not immune from these dilemmas. They jealously safeguard their sovereignty, but will berate the international community over perceived lack of response to problems directly affecting them. Impacts of nuclear weapons testing, and concerns about climate change have encouraged PICs to support international norms of environmental protection and sustainability. Both are high profile issues – one dating from Cold War legacies of nuclear war preparedness, the other viewing with alarm an advent of unchecked sea level rise inundating low lying Pacific atolls. Modest national diplomatic capabilities have joined regional intergovernmental mechanisms to further environmental protection and sustainability. International news media attention to sea level rise inundation of defenceless small island states has added political salience.[1]

This picture alters once PIC domestic compliance with internationally developed environmental norms enters the frame. A divergence is evident between international obligations undertaken and national implementation. The purpose of this chapter is to evaluate how domestic/international interactivity highlights that problem. It assesses the prospects for aligning national practices to internationally derived norms.

That alignment is not easy. Physical, social, historical and equity considerations interact to formulate systems of international environmental co-operation. Linkages built by negotiation, institutionalisation, and implementation shape what happens next. The latter two components – institutionalisation and implementation – pose particular challenges. This involves attempts to integrate environmental management within national economic decision-making. That task confronts contesting values where sustainability interests may conflict with economic growth, where public management faces answerability to competing political interests.

The societal and institutional depth needed to monitor and maintain environmental sustainability objectives within PIC environments is limited. Some convergence between domestic practice and evolving international rules and norms of environmental sustainability has occurred, but PIC administrators face conflicting pressures trying to accomplish that task. Indicative policy frameworks emanating from international deliberations, notably the so-called

Agenda 21 from the 1992 UN Conference on Environment and Development (UNCED), offer practical ideas for small island state environmental management. These have evolved through international deliberations conducted by the UN on the environment, global warming, and special needs of small island states. Developing philosophies of rule prescription and compliance offer scope for emulation by the PICs, but this may not extend to towards formal treaty adhesion.

National environmental management initiatives cannot avoid public sector difficulties evident throughout PIC legal, administrative, and service systems. Common are skill and personnel shortages, deficiencies in policy design, and incoherent inter-agency working arrangements. Economies display immediate dependency on natural resources, the subsistence economy, and traditional customary tenure over land and fishing. This necessitates conservation management approaches directly engaging local users (Hunt, 1998: 132). However the Pacific has few instances where practical, nationally applicable guidelines for environmental management have emerged (Thistlethwaite and Davis, 1996: 33).

A bigger problem concerns resource access by external users. In Melanesia, dual systems allow local customary, as well as state level authorities rights to negotiate resource access contracts with foreign commercial operators. Over logging and fishing, external interests have manipulated this duality to their advantage and compromised attempts to further national conservation and resource management standards. In some instances, political leaders bypass national administrative systems by dealing directly with foreign companies prepared to channel funds towards community projects, health and educational services, church construction, or land purchases. Overall, development, financial, and investment systems operate without reference to sustainable development objectives.

These difficulties are not new. A South Pacific evaluation prepared for the OECD Development Assistance Committee in 1991 identified a need for 'adjustment of inherited government administration processes to reflect an increased recognition of the importance to national well-being of a long-term perspective for economic development which is firmly grounded on the principles of ecologically sustainable development' (OECD/DAC, 1991: 32). At that time, the Papua New Guinea government acknowledged an inadequacy of policy guidelines, poor inter-agency coordination, scarce resources, and insufficient staff training. Other PIC representatives admitted to these shortcomings (Ferguson, 1991: 74). These difficulties are substantial and the costs of their neglect even greater. More positively though, a record of meeting local needs can enhance a national standing of responsible sovereign stewardship. This status goal provides a tangible incentive to comply with international norms that prescribe pathways towards accountable environmental management.

Environmental Vulnerabilities

Although they do not function in isolation, sources of PIC environmental vulnerability divide into three main categories. First, *innate factors* embrace small island size; low-lying locations; poor soil; restricted water storage; and proneness to natural disasters. Tropical cyclones are the commonest natural disaster, causing extensive infrastructure, agricultural and natural habitat damage (Fairburn, 1998: 55). Although complex, local ecosystem fragility renders it subject to disproportionate ecological disruption within small island locations. Second, *imposed aspects* comprise heavy dependence upon imported energy; disproportionate coastal concentrations of settler habitation and tourist development; well established mineral and resource extraction processes (as with phosphate in Nauru, or nickel in New Caledonia); global warming; and military activity, including previous nuclear weapons testing. Third, *local aggravations* include gross over-harvesting of Melanesian tropical hardwoods; neglect of essential water, sewage and waste disposal infrastructures and services; and failure to manage land reform in the face of palpable population pressures. Social climates of localism, apathy, and complacency further impede mitigation of vulnerability.

Key South Pacific Agencies

Despite their relatively recent emergence from colonial status, the PICs have furthered intergovernmental cooperation through regional organisations promoting environmental objectives. They include the following institutions.

The South Pacific Regional Environmental Programme (SPREP), is the intergovernmental body with an explicit mandate for enhancing environmental cooperation throughout the South Pacific. It is designed to pursue sustainable development, foster environmental education and awareness, manage pollution, encourage National Environmental Management Strategies, and coordinate South Pacific positions. This occurred prior to the 1992 UNCED meeting; the 1994 Barbados Global Conference on the Sustainable Development of Small Island States (GCSDSIS); and, in 1998, PIC protest at potential environmental damage threatened by proposed commercial satellite launching immediately beyond Kiribati's Exclusive Economic Zone (EEZ).

SPREP was focal in developing regional environmental agreements such as the 1986 Convention on the Protection of the Natural Resources and Environment of the South Pacific. In force since 1990, this pledges parties to prevent, reduce, and control pollution from any source; ensure sound environmental management; protect endangered species; exchange information; promote guidelines for conservation; and ban unwanted, environmentally damaging activities including nuclear testing. SPREP's 1997-2000 Action Plan sought enhanced national capacity to conserve biological diversity; cope with climate change; integrate coastal, waste, and environmental management; deal with pollution emergencies; plan institutional enhancement; and foster environmental education, information and training (SPREP, 1997). With enhanced funding and improved facilities in Samoa, SPREP has strengthened its institutional profile.

The South Pacific Forum (from 2000, *The Pacific Islands Forum*) as the leading political body of the region has reaffirmed commitments to sustainable development at heads of government level. The Forum has observer status at the UN General Assembly, Asia Pacific Economic Cooperation (APEC), and the UN Commission on Sustainable Development. A key Forum function has been trade development. It maintains liaison with SPREP over the South Pacific Sea Level and Climate Monitoring Project, and the 1995 Waigani Convention hazardous wastes agreement. The Forum also assists regional cooperation by convening meetings of South Pacific Organisations Coordinating Committee (SPOCC), where eight regional bodies meet to coordinate policy initiatives and development priorities. Although the Forum emphasises sovereign equality, consensus, and partnership as guiding values, perceptions exist among PIC nations that Australia and New Zealand effectively dominate by contributing approximately 75 per cent of the institution's budget. PIC governments lack the policy capacity needed to engage and challenge Australian and New Zealand initiatives.

As Law of the Sea negotiations proceeded, South Pacific Forum countries harmonised establishment of their EEZ arrangements. This resulted in massive expansions of potential fish and marines resource access areas (see Table 7.1). As a consequence, the *Forum Fisheries Agency* (FFA) was established in 1979. Based in Honiara, the Solomon Islands, the 16 member agency's responsibilities include the sustainable management of the region's fisheries; regulation of distant water fishing nation activity in the South Pacific (including maintenance of regional register of foreign fishing vessels); regional cooperation in fostering enhanced surveillance, data compilation, and technical assistance. While these data collecting and policy harmonising functions are vital, the FFA is not empowered to regulate catch levels.

Through FFA auspices, a multilateral treaty on fisheries was concluded with the United States in 1986. This provided a benchmark for further multilateral arrangements with distant water fishing nations. By 1999, the FFA was engaged in further negotiations with distant water fishing nations, Pacific territories, and other coastal states through attempts to develop a conservation and management Convention for the highly migratory fish stocks of the western and central Pacific. This sought a comprehensive fisheries arrangement by 2000, striking a balance between needed co-operation over highly migratory species and straddling stocks, and the sovereign rights of coastal states.

Under complex negotiations termed the Multilateral High Level Conference on the Conservation and Management of Highly Migratory Fish Stocks in the Western and Central Pacific, the proposed 28 nation regime is focused on territorial waters west of longitude 150° longitude. This ambitious fisheries management programme aims to cover almost a third of the globe to include most of Polynesia, Micronesia, and Melanesia. By September 1999, management boundaries along the eastern American littoral and 60° south had been agreed, but remained unsettled among east Pacific states. Other unresolved issues entering 2000 included the composition of a permanent Commission, setting total allowable catch limits, and Taiwan's participating status.

Table 8.1 South Pacific Environmental Conventions: Accessions and Ratifications

	Waigani	Apia	Noumea	SPREP
Australia	x	x	x	x
Cook Islands	x	x	x	x
FSM	x		x	x
Fiji	x	x	x	x
Kiribati				
Marshall Islands	x		x	x
Nauru	x		x	x
New Zealand	x		x	x
Niue			x	x
Palau	x		x	x
PNG	x		x	x
Samoa	x	x	x	x
Solomon Islands	x	x	x	x
Tonga	x			x
Tuvalu	x		x	x
Vanuatu				x

Waigani	1995 Waigani Convention prohibiting the importing of hazardous or radioactive wastes, and controlling movement of wastes generated by Pacific countries within the region (not yet in force).
Apia	1990 Convention on the Conservation of Nature in the South Pacific
Noumea	1990 Convention for the Protection of Natural Resources and Environment of the South Pacific.
SPREP	1995 Agreement Establishing the South Pacific Regional Environmental Programme

Source: UN Multilateral Treaty Database

Extra-regional Multilateral Involvement

The UN is the political arena where small island states advance shared interests (Alley, 1998). Proceedings before the 1994 UN-sponsored Barbados Conference on the Sustainable Development of Small Island States highlighted PIC concerns. They included national budgetary constraints; needed local and non-governmental involvement in decisions affecting local resource allocations; due recognition of traditional cultural practices; and rectification of deficient inter-ministerial government coordination adversely affecting resource use efficiencies. The Barbados Programme of Action's call for new and additional resource transfers from industrialised states helped realise limited new funding from the Global Environmental Facility (GEF).

The United Nations Development Programme (UNDP) has collaborated with SPREP in the South Pacific Biodiversity Programme (inaugurated 1993) funded by the GEF. The United Nations Environmental Programme (UNEP) has assisted SPREP in responding to PIC requests for assistance in environment impact assessment and marine pollution control. The Economic Commission for Asia and the Pacific, through its Port Vila, Vanuatu Pacific Operations Centre (ESCAP/POC), has cooperated with SPREP over climate change, waste awareness, pollution assessment, and sustainable development advisory services. The UNDP, EU, World Conservation Union, and Australian and New Zealand bilateral assistance programmes provide financial and technical assistance for national environment and legislative strategies. Since 1990, the Asian Development Bank has provided some regional technical assistance. Recipients include the Cook Islands, the Federated States of Micronesia, and the Solomon Islands.

This ground is covered to indicate that the PICs inhabit regional and international policy settings responsive to their environmental needs and concerns. South Pacific regional intergovernmental collaboration is now an established feature; opportunities beyond exist to amplify the small island state sustainable development agenda. This has been assisted by individual policy entrepreneurship, such as that provided by Robert van Lierop, Vanuatu's former Ambassador to the UN (Shibuya, 1996-97: 551-4). Neroni Slade of Samoa continued to perform that role. Access to development funding from the UN Commission on Sustainable Development and the GEF has been facilitated, while a platform of rule formation assisting the management of external access to local resource use provided. This has occurred through fishing treaty renewal negotiations, rented access by distant water fishing interests traded for enhanced technical assistance.

From a professional perspective, intergovernmental conduct has assisted PIC governments with personnel exchanges, expert advice, and accumulation of applied local knowledge potentially advantageous to national environmental policy formation. This has developed though the FFA, and partly via the South Pacific Applied Geoscience Commission. A weak local science and technology base is a persisting handicap.

In totality, these activities encourage governments to support sustainability as a public good. Prescriptive *Agenda 21* formulae promulgated at UNCED in 1992 have provided policy frameworks. Through these avenues, small island states can address problems of coastal area management, sustainable tourism, local energy resource development, telecommunications; and transport (United Nations, 1996 a). Enhanced methods of electronic access to UN, and international agency documents provide national officials an opportunity to elicit and sift policy material that helps inform and promote national environmental management.

The PICs have joined electronic list serving arrangements developed through small island state sustainable development networks. Although the UN cannot enforce compliance with international accords, its Commission on Sustainable Development has established reporting methodologies to assist implementation of *Agenda 21* guidelines. PICs have often found some of these functions onerous, duplicative and redundant, indicating a needed rationalisation of UN reporting and environmental conference sequencing. (Lack of resources to implement environmental Conventions is a problem faced by many developing countries. This difficulty is magnified for very small states with scanty resources and tiny government bureaucracies. Even governments prepared to give environment and resource management protection policy priority, find qualified personnel difficult to obtain. These constraints hamper multilateral participation and attendance at meetings of parties to environmental Conventions. Travel costs are usually high and servicing needs often unmet. These concerns are regularly expressed by PIC representatives).

Table 8.2 South Pacific Forum Accessions and Ratifications to Global Environmental Conventions

	FCCC	Montreal	Biodiversity	CITES	London
Australia	x	x^{ab}	x	x	x
Cook Islands	x		x		
FSM	x	x	x		
Fiji	x	x^a	x	x	
Kiribati	x	x	x		x
Marshall Islands	x	x^{ab}	x		
Nauru	x		x		x
New Zealand	x	x^{ab}	x	x	x
Niue	x		x		
Palau					
PNG	x	x^a	x	x	x
Samoa	x	x	x		
Solomon Islands	x	x	x		x
Tonga		x	x		
Tuvalu	x	x			
Vanuatu	x	x^{ab}	x	x	x

Source: UN Multilateral Treaty Database

FCCC	1992 Framework Convention on Climate Change
Montreal	1987 Montreal Protocol on Substances that Deplete the Ozone Layer
Biodiversity	1992 Convention on Biological Diversity
CITES	1973 Convention on International Trade in Endangered Species, Wild Fauna and Flora
London	1978 Convention on the Prevention of Marine Pollution by Dumping of Wastes and Other Matter

a   ratified 1992 amendment
b   ratified 1994 amendment

Key Challenges

Climate Change

Pacific sea levels and temperatures are rising more quickly than global averages. Temperatures in the region have been increasing by 0.1° C each decade and sea levels by 2mm each year. Overall, air surface temperatures throughout the Pacific rose during the twentieth century by 0.3° – 0.8 C°, higher than average global warming. These changes are not short term anomalies. A South Pacific tidal monitoring facility, established with Australian funding in 1989, has recorded accelerated Pacific sea level rise. Weather pattern fluctuations triggered by alternation between El Niño and La Niña effects, have altered migration of lucrative tuna and lowered catch volumes.[2] The region has sustained unprecedented droughts that have devastated primary production outputs and aggravated existing freshwater shortages. Sea level rise has altered subsistence crop patterns through saline penetration of the fresh water lens, harming staple taro and yam crops. Warm weather mosquito-borne diseases, such as dengue fever and malaria, have spread throughout the South Pacific. In sum, a key point about climate change and sea level rise is the *additional* stress placed on systems already under heavy pressure.

At diplomatic levels, the PICs have joined other small island states through the Alliance of Small Island States (AOSIS), a grouping substantially assisted by the London-based Foundation for International Environmental Law. To publicise the dilemmas posed by climate change and sea level rise, 'a crisis element was needed to increase the visibility of the issue. The disappearance of the low-lying islands was a powerful motivating factor for organisation as well as an effective image to use in the debate over the problem' (Shibuya, 1996-97: 554). The PICs have sought to advance a proposal for an insurance pool to give some cover against sea-level rise impacts, and associated salt water penetration and storm surge damage (Grubb, 1995: 476).

Regarding the 1997 Kyoto conference outcomes, PIC representatives expressed disquiet over the failure of developed countries (the Annex I category) to reduce greenhouse gas emission levels.[3] Kyoto Protocol arrangements permitting 'flexibility' through emissions trading, a clean development mechanism, and joint implementation, were described as devices designed to smudge rich country emission reduction obligations. Prime Minister Paeniu of Tuvalu conveyed that message at the November 1998 Fourth

Session of conference parties to the UN Framework Convention on Climate Change. He did so on behalf of a group of small island countries comprising Nauru, the Marshall Islands, Niue, and the Cook Islands.[4] At the same meeting, SPREP on behalf of the PICs maintained that they do not have the luxury of time to respond to climate change, warned against 'undue influence on the integrity of IPCC processes', and believed agreement over 'sinks' was premature.[5] Shortly after, New Zealand and Australia flatly rejected the EU's 1999 position allowing industrialised countries no more than 50 per cent greenhouse gas reduction offsets through the previously mentioned 'flexibility' arrangements.

To the PICs, these developments conveyed little comfort. In the unlikely event of all countries meeting their Kyoto commitments, and an improbable application of technologies ceasing all emissions by 2020, small island states, some only 1.5 metres above sea level, will face sea level rises of between 14 and 32 cm, peaking in about 2050.[6] For them, the damage has already occurred and will probably worsen. Nevertheless a Pacific Island country – Fiji – was the first state to ratify the 1997 Kyoto Protocol.[7]

Fisheries Resource Management

For several PICs, tuna is a major source of income and sole exploitable natural resource of magnitude. Nearly half of the canned tuna, and almost half of fresh supplies, come from the region's EEZs. As a common property resource, tuna stocks face growing, although not immediately calamitous depletion through unregulated fishing and open access. Of most concern are stocks of the four main tuna species (skipjack, yellowfin, bigeye and albacore) that together constitute the world's largest tuna fishery. Bigeye and albacore present special management problems, being highly migratory species. Current arrangements are not meeting those needs, nor ensuring appropriate cooperation with distant water fishing nations (Aqorau and Bergin, 1998: 36). Steps taken to meet precautionary management criteria, stipulated by the 1995 straddling and highly migratory fish stocks agreement, are inadequate (Aqorau and Bergin, 1998: 21-2). Some preliminary cooperation has developed between the FFA and the Inter-American Tropical Tuna Commission exercising responsibility for delimiting tuna catch limits in the Eastern Pacific.

Estimates place the value of South Pacific commercial fishing at $US 2 billion annually, tuna comprising some 75 per cent share of total market share.

A good deal of local fishing is conducted for subsistence or barter, these values unrecorded in national accounts. Commercial extraction is dominated by distant water fishing operations, particularly those based in the United States, Japan, South Korea and Taiwan. Returns to PICs range between four and five per cent of total market value, realised through license arrangements with distant water fishing states (Hughes, 1998: 58). Bilateral technical assistance accompanies these deals, Japan using it to resist inclusion in multilateral arrangements. Illegal fishing and under-reporting of catch is prevalent, these practices in Papua New Guinea's EEZ costing it upwards of \$US 140 million annually.[8]

A 24 per cent margin of preference in EU markets has helped overcome PIC distance and cost structure disadvantages, although these concessions are under review. Good returns have generated problems for the sustainable management of the lucrative West Pacific tuna resource, since sovereign, coastal state authority over resource exploitation inside individual EEZs is strongly upheld. Nevertheless, limits to exploitation are required in the interests of conservation and sustainable management. In 1999, Australia and New Zealand successfully took a case against Japan before the Law of the Sea International Tribunal. This claim alleged Japan was using so-called 'scientific research' to hide its over exploitation of Southern bluefin tuna in Pacific waters.

Distant water vessels now encounter scrutiny through global satellite vessel monitoring systems, although Japanese operators have resisted its installation. Other control attempts include regional vessel registration, setting minimum terms and conditions of access, and stipulating the statistical reporting needed to monitor tuna fisheries sustainability. These initiatives are a necessary but inadequate advance given the huge maritime expanses entailed.

Coastal Area Management

In small island states, coastal zones assume major social and economic prominence for human settlement, subsistence agriculture, fisheries, and tourism. Combined pressure from these demands has jeopardised South Pacific resource viability. Manifestations include mangrove swamp destruction, coral reef degradation, and coastal erosion that aggravates tidal and storm surge impacts. Although inundation does not threaten higher island locations, saline penetration of the fresh water lens under stress from population increases and intensified coastal settlement, poses serious difficulties. Chapter 17 principles of UNCED's Agenda 21, calling for integrated management and sustainable development of coastal and marine areas (reiterated in the 1994 Barbados Small Island States Programme) remain inadequately addressed by PIC governments. National sector agencies have not appraised these problems from a holistic perspective.

Although not industrialised, most PICs face coastal pollution problems. Human settlement land use planning is often defective, with regulatory and institutional mechanisms to reduce, prevent, control, and monitor coastal waters pollution and waste management undeveloped. Over-fishing of vulnerable local species have strained the coastal resource base. This has deprived those most vulnerable needed access to traditional food sources and income.[9] Existing PIC coastal area surveillance functions are incomplete. They need monitoring, extending beyond information gathering to include standards-based assessments, and investigations explicitly aimed at rectifying deficiencies. Lacking are appropriate laboratory facilities and trained sampling or analytical staff. This capacity is needed to deal with growing problems of toxic and hazardous wastes, point source pollution, and industrial sewage contributing to marine pollution and coastal degradation.[10]

Forestry

Of all countries with less than five per cent land area under forest cover, half are small islands (Bass and Dalal-Clayton, 1995: 5). While bigger South Pacific nations such as Papua New Guinea and the Solomon Islands are well endowed, their current rates of depletion are disturbing. Excessive logging of Melanesian hardwoods has assumed notoriety, drawing condemnation from conservation lobbies within and beyond the Pacific. Once established, foreign logging operatives in Melanesia have harvested local resources rapidly, cheaply and unsustainably. Their activities have strained state environmental capacity, maximised corporate profits, and reduced accountability, taxation and royalty payments (Dauvergne, 1998-99: 524-25).

The UNDP's Pacific Human Development Report identified environmental regeneration as a key strategy (1994: 35). It criticised the Solomon Islands for its deforestation practices as an example of failure to accord sufficient attention to environmental costs, adding that significant under-reporting of volumes and values has cost the Solomon Islands in royalties and export taxes. Some critics see exploitation as part of a wider problem - where agriculture and mining export industries exert a predatory impact and have 'siphoned off land and labour resources, destroyed or contaminated food grounds, and lowered health and nutritional standards' (Emberson-Bain, 1994: 42).

In PNG, the forestry industry has been enmeshed in widespread corruption, resource plunder, and fraud against traditional landowners. Support for large-scale commercial production has handicapped smaller, locally based operations and a traditional forest food role for rural communities (Holzknecht and Kalit, 1995: 99).

The South Pacific Forum's Voluntary Code of Conduct on Logging Practice embodies precautionary principles of sustainability designed for member states with significant forestry assets (Australia, Fiji, New Zealand, Papua New Guinea, Solomon Islands, and Vanuatu). This arrangement has exerted some 'peer pressure' upon governments to join, as did the Solomon Islands in 1997. Of greater immediate impact has been the 1998 export downturn following deterioration of East Asian market conditions. Overall, forestry has provided the most spectacular case of gross resource exploitation in the South Pacific. More than any other issue, it has highlighted free riding, rapid returns, and blatant doublespeak by leaders professing goals of sustainability.[11]

Biodiversity

The South Pacific is noted for its high levels of species diversity and endemism – a species lost on one island may mean it has gone forever. Retention is threatened by logging and loss of tree cover, consequential soil erosion and loss of watershed, mining, and inadequate reforestation following clearance for commercial plantation and farming. Biodiversity is under further pressure from tourism, economic development, and imported pests. Rates of animal and plant extinction remain low, although the total of species threatened is considerable. Economic risk factors include unemployment, growth of relative poverty, and heavy reliance on high-cost imported fuels resulting in further depletion of local wood resources from inefficient, environmentally hostile energy use. This loads added burdens upon rural women who provide the core of village fuel supply labour.

Resettlement and demographic change resulting from urbanisation and emigration, have weakened biodiversity by eroding stocks of conservation knowledge. Protecting the intellectual property of traditional collective knowledge through establishing equitable permit systems, based on Convention on Biological Diversity (CBD) principles, has been an important PIC objective (SPREP, 1997: 13). Most PICs are signatories to the CBD (see Table 8.2). However, compliance remains hesitant; a 1998 regional workshop indicated only four countries had filed national reports to the CBD Secretariat as required, although eight had established inter-agency committees.[12]

South Pacific indigenous people's organisations have collaborated to advance shared interests at CBD conferences of parties. Non-governmental organisations have used local expert knowledge to assist customary interests negotiate bio-prospecting access agreements with foreign firms. At just less than seven million people, but with a wide array of species diversity, Pacific Islanders carry a disproportionate burden of international responsibility for biodiversity retention. Since 1990, 17 conservation areas in 12 PICs have been designated with support from local communities. This programme risks weakening by possible GEF funding retirement from 2001.

Regional objectives include calls for enhanced national collaboration with local communities on rules regarding access to local resources, database development, biotechnology controls, training, and expanded technical assistance.[13] Indigenous groups have taken a close interest in biodiversity related intellectual property issues, collaborating to advance shared interests at CBD conferences of parties. Externally, a global, liberal-trading order is as much a threat as a promise to the preservation of indigenous intellectual property given the polarisation now evident over relevant norm formation.[14]

National Performance

Effective domestic implementation of international and regional environmental agreements requires appropriate commitment of funding, legislative enactment, regulation, and the public promotion of objectives by informational or educational means. These functions are vital in that the performance of domestic institutions is often a core variable determining global environmental cooperation outcomes (Raustiala, 1997: 483).

PIC governments have conveyed support for national environmental guidelines by signing into 1986 SPREP Convention provisions that include:

- The desirability of national implementation of international agreements already in existence concerning the marine and coastal environment (Convention perambular)
- Establishing and adopting recommended practices, procedures, and measures to prevent, reduce and control pollution from all sources and to promote sustained resource management (Article 5.4)
- Undertaking environmental impact assessments of major projects affecting the marine environment (Article 16); transmitting to SPREP information regarding implementation of the SPREP Convention and its protocols (e.g. measures for combating pollution emergencies) (Article 19)
- Jointly considering information submitted under Article 19.

In response, PICs have developed national environmental units. At times, these have coexisted uneasily within units of natural resource management. In most instances, the environmental agencies established have been modest and lacked the resources, political impetus, or ministerial seniority needed to build constituencies for sustainability. Compared to sectoral agencies furthering development objectives, PIC environment departments lack political weight (Hunt, 1998: 137-38).

With funding and project design assistance from the ADB, the UNDP, and some donor governments, National Environmental Management Strategies (NEMs) have been established.[15] Their stated objective is to link economic development and environmental management. Other program indicators include establishment of national frameworks for sustainable development, incorporation of sustainable development objectives into national development bank lending practices, and improved capacity of land and sea management resource systems. SPREP has provided guidelines for personnel training and 'establishment of a comprehensive legal framework that meets national needs and is consistent with international environmental agreements' (SPREP, 1997: 20). It has also supplied performance indicators for waste handling, coastal environmental management, environmental education, information and training.

By 1997, 13 PICs had adopted NEMs by designating national parks and conservation areas, promoting conservation through educational and community activities, and establishing marine management areas. In Samoa waste management, population issues, water supply, and land use are NEM priorities, although implementation has faced serious resource constraints.

Prescribed monitoring functions attempt to incorporate traditional landholding, and non-governmental activities. These objectives have been assessed by agency staff interviews, reports from workshop or training seminars, and national legislative reviews. Although United Nations Environmental Progamme (UNEP) funding has assisted Kiribati, Tuvalu and Vanuatu in legislative drafting, PIC environment law requires reform. Links with UNEP's Global Program of Action for the Protection of the Marine Environment from Land-based activities have been initiated. This scheme is potentially useful for its data clearing-house, and information delivery functions regarding sources of land-based pollutants contaminating marine environments.

The NEMs foster official liaison with local landowners, non-governmental interests, and sources of expert advice. In Samoa, villages have collaborated to manage local fishing resources and conserve marine resources, functions assisted by Fisheries Division extension staff. Local participation for biodiversity project implementation has evolved at provincial council levels in Fiji. By contrast, other initiatives have engendered local tensions, as in Vanuatu where local level customary authorities have refused cooperation over conservation projects. They view them as 'externally' imposed initiatives that may inflame unresolved land disputes, or introduce unfamiliar modes of non-governmental activity.

Comparing Discontinuities

Discontinuity between South Pacific acceptance of international prescriptive guidelines for environmental management and national practice suggests the following. A first set of difficulties is absence or inadequacy of the legislative and regulatory systems needed to authorise and implement objectives, or to accumulate the data needed for compliance monitoring. Attempts to monitor and control land-based pollution are vitiated by lack of implementation guidelines for the sustainable management of solid and liquid wastes. This has resulted in reliance upon poorly run, inadequately maintained, and inefficient methods of incineration (United Nations, 1998). More elementary is the absence of essential infrastructure. This neutralises implementation attempts, as with ship-borne waste left unchecked because of absent port facilities.

In Fiji, public health and local government legislation meant to control the collection and disposal of waste and sewage fails to provide for sanitary landfills. This problem's rectification stays delayed pending a proposed Sustainable Development Bill. Comprehensive in scope, providing for environmental impact assessments, and designed to chart Fiji towards a future of effectively administered sustainable management, this initiative risks inoperability while current implementation retains its modest capacity

Second, the PICs have no environmental counterpart to the South Pacific Forum Economic Ministers Action Plan of 1997 discussed in the previous chapter.[16] Briefly that seeks enhanced public accountability through legislative oversight; transparency of loan agreements and contracts; and internal audit of public enterprises in conjunction with independent advice, review, and monitoring functions. Administrators serving PIC governments lack guidance when asked to balance economic and environmental needs. Looking elsewhere has limited utility; assessed effectiveness of attempts to integrate environmental considerations within small island state national economic decision making is poorly researched.

Third, PIC governments have not resolved internal policy differences about the modalities of extractive resource utilisation. This includes safeguarding the rights and interests of different groups and individuals, in particular customary land users. It entails appropriate licensing access or 'gatekeeping' responsibilities at different levels of government and within public agencies. Workable methods of arbitrating settlement of competing resources claims are required. So, too, is sensitivity about the implications of extractive practices for social development, sustainability, land ownership, and national sovereignty (Henningham and May, 1992: 2). Weakness of central state institutions has meant that nationally prescribed rules and values over 'a matter as sensitive, as culturally loaded, and as variable as land tenure will not be uniformly accepted or observed by claimants to customary land' (Ward, 1997: 20).

This is not hospitable policy territory for conservation regimes based on national regulation. Some local groups keen to conserve traditional areas for conservation purposes have encountered indifference, even hostility from their national governments. In 1998, the Papua New Guinea Department of Forestry attempted to merge a major rainforest tract designated for conservation purposes (the Hunstein Ranges) to an adjoining sector for logging extraction. This resulted in legal challenges against the government's forestry management agency for punitive damages. The basis of claim was that officials had misled community representatives into signing a merger agreement (Thompson, 1998:

19-21). This suggests needed prior agreement about, and participation between, local and national interests over shared, readily comprehensible sustainable management principles.

Achieving these objectives is a major challenge since much political representation is preoccupied with village, clan, or extended family demands, rendering hazardous the careers of those committed to an impartial enforcement of national rules and standards. A 1996 observation claims that: 'Concern about the environment and its protection has often been entirely subjugated to the pursuit of economic development ... it is evident from their various public statements that many politicians still have scant regard for environmental values, despite official government protestations about sustainable development and the protection of the environment' (Thistlethwaite and Davis, 1996: 32). Under these conditions, administrators lack the firebreaks needed to shield them from pressures threatening professional standards. This has resulted in able staff turning elsewhere for career purposes.

Fourth, in numerous PICs, the reach of central government is either weak or inconsistent. Historically, the South Pacific's indigenous peoples and rural dwellers evolved attitudes towards administrative processes shaped by the minimalist nature of these functions. Among the bigger PICs, including Papua New Guinea, the Solomon Islands, Vanuatu and Fiji, three quarters of the population subsist in rural settings, on marginal cash incomes, and with limited access to health, educational, and communications services. Partnerships that institutionalise durable methods of sustainable resource use and conservation have not emerged; they require externally resourced supports to maintain a continuing commitment and presence. In some instances, these supports come via non-governmental means, as has occurred through World Wildlife Fund projects. Although neither comprehensive nor durable, supporting non-governmental activities perform educative and external linkage functions.

Towards Convergence?

A range of international prescriptions encouraging PIC conformity to environmental norms has been identified. At more modest levels, national practices indicate limited incorporation of international norms. To what extent, then, is enhanced convergence possible? Relevant questions consider the scope, incentives and possible management for improved convergence.

Extent of Convergence

Gaps between declared support for internationally derived norms, and commitments to national implementation emerge when assessing PIC performance against Agenda 21 guidelines on coastal management, Convention on Biodiversity prescriptions, the South Pacific Forum's voluntary logging code, and individual SPREP Convention specifications. In Melanesia, the convergence gap has widened through open violation of sustainability norms for logging. Increased convergence has occurred in some national sectors, where cooperative partnerships have operated locally, or in some small PIC entities where sustainability norms have been 'mainstreamed' as in Tokelau. This is intended to have environmental considerations incorporated at an early 'ground floor' stage of policy development. Coolness to this concept among the PICs has been attributed to a generic policy making weakness, indicating lack of weight accorded technical inputs at a political level (Hughes, 1998: 117). Fiji's ambitious, but domestically resisted Sustainable Development Bill, represented an attempt to foster convergence by aligning national standards with international prescriptions.

Convergence Incentives

PIC aspirations to perform as demonstrably responsible sovereign states, capable of discharging international obligations entered into, is a political incentive for convergence More negatively, compliance may involve the desire to avoid adverse publicity surrounding sustainable development assistance conditionalities. PICs do not seek to emulate the Solomon Islands, where the Australian government withdrew project assistance funding on grounds of the recipient's policies and administration impeding environmental sustainability. This step occurred against a background of widespread allegations regarding high level government corruption in the Solomon Islands logging industry (Kabutaulaka, 1998: 128).

Negative publicity also surrounded arrangements between the World Bank and Papua New Guinea, following a 1995 US $50 million loan agreement for the first phase of a government reform programme developed with the Bank's analytic assistance. This aimed to lower fiscal deficits, adjust relative prices, and improve fiscal management through structural reforms aimed at enhancing PNG's competitiveness, public service delivery, and project implementation.

A key objective was promotion of sustainable natural resource development through implementation of forestry conservation and revenue policies. These proposals generated tensions that resulted in postponement of loan instalments amidst government accusations about unwarranted Bank interference in the country's affairs (Kavanamur, 1998: 109).

Disjunction between environmental sustainability and resource utilisation practices need not remain a constant. The 1997 Commonwealth Advisory Group's report on small state vulnerability envisaged feasible strategies integrating environmental considerations into the earliest stages of economic policy making (Commonwealth, 1997: 96). Rather than traditional 'command and control' regulatory approaches, the report favoured market-based mechanisms permitting pricing policies that reflected true environmental costs, and incentives for sustainable resource use (Commonwealth, 1997: 100).

The region's potential for so-called 'eco-tourism' offers another incentive. It has hardened local resistance towards waste dumping proposals as under consideration in the Marshall Islands. Similar warnings have emerged regarding potential loss of tourist revenue through unregulated resource extraction; overcrowding and poor servicing of town, coastal settlement, and lagoon communities; and unrecoverable species loss from deforestation harming conservation sanctuary development.

Managing Convergence

Among PIC leaderships and officials, attitudes towards convergence are mixed. Collective action to sustain fisheries through mutual adjustments of sovereign interests has seen some national alignment to externally developed norms. This is less likely when local participation is absent from rule-creation, or where national policy is primarily shaped by perceived external pressures. Regional intergovernmental 'peer pressure', designed to secure compliance (for example the voluntary code on sustainable logging) assist convergence, but need supporting material incentives. They include technical assistance commitments, and enhanced funding from international agencies supporting environmental sustainability.

PIC governments now confront sustainability demands that carry heavier political backing. That has emerged from a variety of concerns: growing demographic pressures, declining levels of external assistance, downsizing of public sector staffing levels, and unchecked, unaccountable resource depletions. Although well established in the Solomon Islands, corporate logging practices have provoked local opposition and even sabotage of equipment (Dauvergne, 1998: 112). Belated legislative responses followed with a Solomon Islands 1998 enactment aimed at protecting dwindling forest stocks through cutting and pollution controls, environmental impact assessments, and monitoring procedures. This retrieved some of the ground that was lost in 1995 when the Mamaloni government lowered log export taxes, and dropped plans to monitor foreign logging operations (Dauvergne, 1998-99: 534). Post-1998 implementation has been impeded by the decline in internal security precipitated by worsening relations between Guadalcanal and Malaitan communities.

Where policy conduct by central state institutions has been weak, arbitrary, or incompetent, as over forestry policy in Papua New Guinea, the Solomon Islands and Vanuatu, professional administrative standards of conduct are openly flouted. Adaptations include enlistment of local or non-governmental support, and use of the Churches (as in the Solomon Islands) to promote sustainable management practices. Some governments have shown a commitment to improved forestry practices. Another tactic has been deliberate implementation delay by administrators aware their political masters are acting illegally. Publicity and public education supporting sustainable management practices has begun, but faces parochialism and apathy.

The South Pacific Forum recognises environmental issues as matters of regional importance raising rule enforcement concern that include waste dumping, driftnet fishing, wildlife smuggling, oil spills and other pollution emergencies.[17] Over oil spills, five PICs (the Cook Islands, Vanuatu, Fiji, Samoa, Tuvalu) anticipated a model plan and used draft SPREP guidelines to establish national contingency arrangements.[18] A crucial test remains implementation of the planned conservation and management Convention for highly migratory fish stocks of the western and central Pacific.

Towards the Future

Some domestic/international interactive processes are assisting PICs towards sustainable futures. They require social practices that permit a more inclusive role for non-governmental activity, an assured role for women, and stewardship values within increasingly urbanised, mobile, and consumption-oriented societies. Despite limited capacities, PICs have access to external advice, technical assistance, and framework guidelines to promote environmental sustainability. Edward Wolfers (May and Henningham, 1992: 245) has suggested an environmental advocate, performing ombudsman functions, independent of government and resource extractive interests, and acting as an officer mandated to investigate and press for redress of local grievances. SPREP's performance indicators furnish appropriate checklists to validate national progress on sustainability. Vanuatu's former ombudsman, Marie-Noelle Ferrieux-Patterson, incriminated senior politicians and officials over resource management corruption. Such willingness to face down misconduct at high levels has not found wider emulation in the region.

Neglect is significant in Melanesia where excessive rent seeking, associated corruption, and transnational exploitation of logging through defective legal controls has handicapped administrative efficacy. Environmental sustainability retains a secondary status in relation to economic and export growth imperatives, although these values need not prove incompatible. Harder to change are deeper-seated PIC attitudes towards the administrative apparatus of statehood, regarded as an introduced artifice tolerated more for what it might deliver as welfare and employment, than for what it might activate, facilitate, or reconcile. This has encouraged a passivity toward environmental management rationalised on grounds that this is an imposition by aid donors wanting enhanced economic performance. Those attitudes will not change until the international donor community adopts common principles on sustainability within their development assistance profiles.

Agenda 21 prescriptions for small island states, enunciated at the 1992 Rio UNCED conference, offer a comprehensive agenda for the UN's Commission on Sustainable Development small island state component.[19] Realisation of the *Agenda 21* blueprint requires political and social conditions where global and domestic sustainability responses reinforce, not contradict each other. Local constituencies may conceive sustainability not as policy, but as proprietary social custom – as something falling within the rubric of customary land tenure and established resource access methods. It is here that a linkage between environmental sustainability and indigenous rights demands may grow in significance.

Despite unresolved tensions between economic growth, environmental sustainability, and local ways, there is scope to overcome the constraints that hamper planning and implementation of sustainable development. Stronger national and administrative capacity can emerge through appropriate external financial and technical support for needed legal, investigative, audit, information management, statistical, and extension services. The collection of accurate data, replicable through standardised formats, is an essential prerequisite for the effective implementation of international environmental Conventions. Other PIC needs include overhaul of defective national environmental law, sustainable land management, and use of education and information to reduce the implementation gap. Currently developed along conventional line arrangements, PIC national environmental management could develop the flatter, multi-skilled team approaches needed to foster stronger local stakeholder participation. A 1998 proposal for non-governmental representation in government departments warrants consideration (PIANGO, 1998: 7).

Conclusions

While a good deal of this chapter has been descriptive, it has raised questions about what the PIC environmental management experience represents in totality. A previous chapter, dealing with Australia's climate change diplomacy, referred to the Antarctic 'ozone hole' as the 'smoking gun' needed to galvanise political momentum for the Montreal Protocol. The South Pacific has had not one such alarm signal but several: most conspicuously sea-level rise, deforestation and, longer term, fish stock depletion. Yet neither regionally nor globally, do regimes exist that provide effective and comprehensive management of these problems. As a goal and operational principle, environmental sustainability has shaped numerous, often modestly funded official development and non-governmental PIC projects. Some progress exists through partial rule formation and institutionalisation. International activity has helped keep environmental concerns and issues of sustainability before PIC governments.

Against that, non-sustainable resource exploitation emerged starkly. The extent of depredation and responses to halt it, gained local salience through international publicity. Threats of severe PIC resource exploitation engaged non-governmental and official responses that assisted treaty formation. That occurred over the 1989 driftnet fishing ban, easily the most conspicuous maritime initiative of its kind, but unmatched by any regional response on logging.

Sustainability is a touchstone to other significant domestic/international linkages affecting the PICs. They include good governance, regional political relations (notably over climate change), global promotion of small island state domestic predicaments, and the uneasy interface between customary tenure and corporate extractive activity. International and regional activity 'helps to keep environmental concerns and issues of sustainability to the fore in the consciousness of national governments' (Yabaki, 1997: 273).

Localism is a dynamic for sustainable management, although its participation among PICs is distinct and does not replicate elsewhere. Devolution of national administrative capacity for environmental management has been under-resourced, but does not preclude local PIC communities adhering to international environmental norms, irrespective of state positions on endorsement and compliance. This is already occurring, although it will normally need mediation through legitimised non-governmental or expert advice to operate effectively where outside interests are involved. Even where they fail to follow original design or lack progress, the NEMs activities identified have assisted local/international linkages.

PICs are gradually subscribing to international norms of sustainability, but disjunction with national practice raises convergence failure costs. Strains facing PIC national environmental management reveal unresolved contest over custody of local land and resource interests, customary ownership differences, and inconsistent demarcations between private interests and public functions. Contemplating a future of economic difficulty, the PICs face growing domestic and international pressures to improve national stewardship of finite resources. The South Pacific has an opportunity to calibrate national environmental management planning within frameworks of enhanced public sector management. That will facilitate consonance with internationally derived norms and guidelines.

Notes

1   As for example broadcast by the BBC: 'Two Pacific islands have disappeared beneath the waves, as climate change raises sea levels to new heights ...The news is reported by the Independent on Sunday, which says the predictions of the danger are coming true more quickly than anyone expected'. BBC, 14 June 1999, (online, http://news/bbc.co.uk).

2   Observations of Pacific Community oceanographer Lédet, to June 1999 World Tuna Conference, French Polynesia. *PINA Nius Online*, Pape'ete 21 June 1999.
3   On Kyoto outcomes, see supra pp. 71-74.
4   Address of Prime Minister Paeniu, COP4, UNFCCC, Buenos Aires, 12 November 1998.
5   Statement by SPREP to COP4, UNFCCC, Buenos Aires, November 1998. On relevant details, see supra p. 230.
6   Comments of Gerald Miles, head of SPREP Environmental and Planning Division, *Pacific Island Report*, 12, 4, 1 March 1999, p. 1.
7   For details of the Kyoto Protocol, see supra pp. 71-73.
8   *The National*, Port Moresby, 23 November 1998.
9   Second Pacific Community Fisheries Management Workshop, *Outputs of the Meeting*. Noumea: New Caledonia, 12-16 October 1998, p. 3.
10 South Pacific Environment Outlook, (unpublished Second Draft), SPREP/UNEP, 1998, 1.10.
11 See Vanessa Griffin, 'The Politics of Sustainable Development in the Pacific', in Atu Emberson Bain (ed), *Sustainable Development or Malignant Growth? Perspectives of Pacific Island Women*, Suva: Marama Publications, 1994, pp. 263-74. On international trading arrangements impacts on public goods, see Anne Orford, 'Locating the International: Military and Monetary Interventions after the Cold War', *Harvard International Law Journal*, 38, 2, 1997, pp. 453-85.
12 South Pacific Environment Outlook, (unpublished Second Draft), SPREP/UNEP, 1998, 3 (2a).
13 Report on the Pacific Workshop on the CBD (The Nadi Statement). SPREP in co-operation with the Foundation for International Environmental Law and World Wide Fund for Nature (South Pacific), 3 April 1998.
14 See supra pp. 165-67.
15 Other donors included the Australian Agency for International Development, with technical assistance from the Union for the Conservation of Nature.
16 See supra pp. 193-94.
17 South Pacific Forum Declaration on Law Enforcement Co-operation, 1997. Suva: Forum Secretariat.
18 SPREP Press Release, Apia, 1 October 1999.
19 For an initial matching of Agenda 21 chapters to the SPREP work programme, see Vili A. Fuavo, 'South Pacific Regional Environmental Programme: Implications of Agenda 21 for the Pacific', *Pacific Economic Bulletin*, 8, 2, 1993, pp. 22-31.

References

Alley, Roderic (1998), *The United Nations in Southeast Asia and the South Pacific*, London: Macmillan.
Aqorau, Transform and Bergin, Anthony (1998), 'The UN Fish Stocks Agreement - A New Era for International Cooperation to Conserve Tuna in the Central Western Pacific', *Ocean Development and International Law*, 29, pp. 21-42.

Bass, S. and Dalal-Clayton, B. (1995), *Small Island States and Sustainable Development: Strategic Issues and Experience*, London: International Institute for Environment and Development.

Bergin, A. and Haward, M. (1994), 'The Last Jewel in a Disintegrating Crown - the Case of Japanese Distant Water Tuna Fisheries', *Ocean Development and International Law*, 25, pp.187-215.

Bertram, G. (1993), 'Sustainability, Aid, and Material Welfare in small Pacific Island Economies, 1900-90', *World Development*, 21, 2, pp. 247-58.

Briguglio, L. (1995), 'Small Island Developing States and their Economic Vulnerability', *World Development*, 23, 9, pp. 1615-32.

Burt, Ben and Clerk, Christian (eds) (1997), *Environment and Development in the Pacific Islands*, Canberra: National Centre for Development Studies, ANU, and University of PNG Press.

Commonwealth Secretariat (1997), *A Future for Small States. Overcoming Vulnerability*, Report of Commonwealth Advisory Group, London: Commonwealth Secretariat.

Costello, M. (1995), 'Policy Priorities for the Department of Foreign Affairs and Trade in 1995', *Australian Journal of International Affairs*, 49,1, pp.135-43.

Cox, A. and Elmqvist, T. (1997), 'Ecocolonialism and Indigenous-controlled Rainforest Reserves in Western Samoa', *Ambio*, 26, 2, pp. 84-89.

Dauvergne, Peter (1998), 'Transforming Multinational loggers in Solomon Islands', *Pacific Economic Bulletin*, 13, 1, pp. 106-113.

Dauvergne, Peter (1998-99), 'Corporate Power in the Forests of the Solomon Islands', *Pacific Affairs*, 71, 4, pp. 524-46.

Emberson-Bain, Atu (ed) (1994), *Sustainable Development or Malignant Growth? Perspectives on Island Women*, Suva: Marama Publications.

Fairburn, Te'o I. J. (1998), 'Economic consequences of natural disasters among Pacific island countries', *Pacific Economic Bulletin*, 13, 2, pp. 54-63.

Ferguson, Roy (1991), 'Environmental Problems in the Pacific Island Region: Challenges and Responses', in R. Thakur (ed), *The South Pacific: Problems, Issues and Prospects*, Basingstoke: Macmillan and University of Otago Press, pp. 65-79.

Fuavao, V.A. (1993), 'South Pacific Regional Environmental Programme: Implications of Agenda 21 for The Pacific', *Pacific Economic Bulletin*, 8, 2, pp. 22-31.

Griffin, V. (1994), 'The Politics of Sustainable Development in the Pacific', in Emberson-Bain, A. (ed), op. cit., pp. 263-74.

Grubb, Michael (1995), 'Ethics, the Environment and Changing International Order', *International Affairs*, 71, 3, pp. 463- 96.

Henderson-Sellers, A. (1996), 'Adaptation to Climate Change: Its Future Role in Oceania', in W. J. Bourma, G. I. Pearman, and M. R. Manning (eds), *Greenhouse: Coping with Climate Change*, Australia: CSIRO, pp. 349-76.

Henningham, Stephen, and May, R. J. (1992), 'Introduction', in Stephen Henningham, and R. J. May (eds), *Resources, Development and Politics in the Pacific Islands*, Bathurst: Crawford House Press, pp. 1-10.

Herr, R. A. (1994), 'The United Nations, Regionalism, and the South Pacific', *The Pacific Review*, 7, 3, pp. 261-69.

Hewison, Grant (1993), 'The Convention for the Prohibition of Fishing with Long Driftnets in the South Pacific', *Case Western Reserve Journal of International Law*, 25, pp. 449-530.

Hughes, A. V. (1998), *A Different Kind of Voyage: Development and Dependence in the Pacific Islands*, Office of Pacific Operations: Asian Development Bank.
Holzknecht, H. and Kalit, K. N. (1995), 'Forest Resources: What hope for the Future?', *Pacific Economic Bulletin*, 10,1, pp. 95-100.
Hunt, Colin (1998), 'Public Policy for Pacific Environments and Resources', *Pacific Economic Bulletin*, 13, 1, pp. 132-37.
Kabutaulaka, Tarcisius Tara (1998), 'Deforestation and Politics in the Solomon Islands', in Peter Larmour (ed), *Governance and Reform in the South Pacific*, Canberra: National Centre for Development Studies, Australian National University, pp. 121-53.
Kavanamur, David (1998), 'The Politics of Structural Adjustment in Papua New Guinea', in Peter Larmour, op. cit., pp. 99-120.
Lawrence, P. (1994), 'Regional Strategies for the Implementation of Environmental Conventions: Lessons from the South Pacific?', *The Australian Yearbook of International Law*, 15, pp. 203-29.
Natural Disaster Reduction in Pacific Island Countries, (1994), Report to the World Conference on Natural Disaster Reduction, Yokohama, Japan. SPREP, UN Department Humanitarian Affairs, South Pacific, and Emergency Management, Australia.
Ogashiwa, Yoko S. (1990), 'Regional Protest Against Nuclear Waste Dumping in the Pacific', *Journal of Pacific Studies*, 15, pp. 51-66.
Organisation for Economic Cooperation and Development (1991), Development Assistance Committee, The Environment of the South Pacific: Issues for Sustainable Development. Unpublished OECD/DAC, 91 32.
Osborne, P. (1996), *Trade Issues and Development Prospects of Island Developing Countries of the Pacific*. UNCTAD, UN doc. E/CN.17/1996/IDC Misc. 2.
Pacific Human Development Report, (1994), Suva: UNDP.
Pacific Island Association of Non-Government Organisations (1998), *PIANGO Link*, February 1998.
Pacific Islands Report (1998), 28 April. Honolulu: Pacific Islands Development Program/ Center for Pacific Islands Studies.
Powell, Philip T. (1998), 'Traditional Production, communal land tenure, and policies for environmental preservation of the South Pacific', *Ecological Economics*, 14, pp. 89-101.
Raustiala, Kal (1997), 'Domestic Institutions and International Regulatory Cooperation. Comparative Responses to the Convention on Biological Diversity', *World Politics*, 49, 4, pp. 482-509.
Shibuya, Eric (1996-97), ' "Roaring Mice Against the Tide": The South Pacific Islands and Agenda-Building in Global Warming', *Pacific Affairs*, 69, 4, pp. 541-55.
Siwatibau, S. (1991), 'Some aspects of development in the South Pacific: An Insider's View', in P. Bauer, S. Siwatibau and W. Kasper, *Aid and Development in the South Pacific*, Auckland: Centre for Independent Studies, pp. 29-44.
South Pacific Forum Economic Ministers Meeting (1997), *Action Plan*, Cairns, 11 July.
South Pacific Forum, (1989; 1992; 1993), *Heads of Government Meeting Communiqués*, Suva: Forum Secretariat, South Pacific Regional Environmental Program (1992), *Submission to UNCED Conference*.
South Pacific Forum, (1986), *Convention for the Protection of the Natural Resources and Environment of the South Pacific Region*.
South Pacific Forum, (1997), *Regional Input to the UNGA Session*, AP 4/6/1, unpublished circular, 11 February.

South Pacific Forum (1997), *Action Plan for Managing the Environment of the South Pacific Region 1997-2000*.
South Pacific Forum (1998 a), News Release, 26 June 1998.
South Pacific Forum (1998 b), News Release, 6 July 1998.
Taplin, R. E. (1994), 'International Policy on the Greenhouse Effect and the Island South Pacific', *The Pacific Review*, 7, 2, pp. 271-81.
Thistlethwaite, Bob and Davis, Derrin (1996), *Pacific 2010 A Sustainable Future for Melanesia?* Canberra: National Centre for Development Studies.
Thompson, Liz (1998), 'The Struggle to Protect the Hunstein', *Pacific Islands Monthly*, March, pp.19-21.
United Nations (1993), *Report of the Preparatory Committee for the Global Conference on the Sustainable Development of Small Island Developing States*, 30 August-10 September, UN doc. A/ 48/36. Annex III.
United Nations Capacity 21, *Programme Summaries* (1994), South Pacific, 7, 2.
United Nations (1996 a), Commission on Sustainable Development. *Progress in Implementation of the Program of Actions for Small Island Developing States*, UN doc. E/CN. 17/1996/20.
United Nations (1996 b), Department for Policy Coordination and Sustainable Development, *Implementation Action for Sustainable Development of Small Island States*, A/51/354.
United Nations (1998), Commission on Sustainable Development. *The Management of Wastes*. UN doc. E/CN.17/1998/7/ Add.2.
United Nations Development Programme (1993), 'Regional Project for the Pacific Island countries'. Project Document Fiscal and Monetary Management Reform and Statistical Improvement (unpublished), Suva: UNDP.
United Nations Development Programme (1994), *Pacific Regional Programmes*, UNDP, Suva.
United Nations Multilateral Treaty Database (1999), (online, www.un.org).
Ward, R. Gerard (1997), 'Changing forms of communal tenure', in Peter Larmour (ed), *The Governance of Common Property in the Pacific Region*, Canberra: National Centre for Development Studies, ANU, pp.19-32.
Warrington, Edward, (1994), 'A Capacity for Policy Management: Re-Appraising the Context in Micro-States', *Asian Journal of Public Administration*, 16,1, pp. 109-33.
Weiskel, T. C. (1993), 'UNCED and After: Global Issues, Country Problems, and Regional Solutions in the Asia-Pacific Area, *Journal of Developing Areas*, 28, 1, pp.13-20.
Wolfers, Edward (1992), 'Politics, Development and Resources: Reflections on Constructs, Conflict and Consultants', in Stephen Henningham and R. J. May op. cit., pp. 238-57.
The World Bank (1995), *Pacific Island Economies: Building a Resilient Economic Base for the 21st Century*, Washington DC: World Bank, 13803-EAP.
World Commission on Environment and Development (WCED) (1987), *Our Common Future* (The Brundtland Report), Oxford: Oxford University Press.
Yabaki, Akuila (1997), 'International and Regional links for sustainable development', in Ben Burt and Christian Clerk (eds), *Environment and Development in the Pacific Islands*, Canberra: ANU, pp. 269-88.

9 Conclusions

What has this study revealed? How has it advanced the investigation of interactivity between domestic and international politics? What further enquiry is warranted, and how might it proceed? An introductory criticism concerned the limited cross fertilisation between international and comparative political studies. Two cases in this study indicated how representatives from the Pacific Islands, drew implications from the global warming problem markedly different to those of their Australian counterparts. Comparativists might explain that contrasts by considering the nature and dynamics of relevant domestic interests, national institutions, and policy formulation processes. Analysis from International Relations might view them as responses to external constraints, incentives and advantages. Both approaches are valid but, between them, something seemed missing warranting fuller investigation.

What kinds of questions, therefore, emerge? In reviewing the preceding chapters, domestic/international activity helped distinguish a number. The thesis advanced was not just that domestic and international factors influence one another, but that this is a process which, *of itself*, can generate outcomes. The study thus included enquiry about the politics of *a transnational project*; the international dimensions of *a defensive national strategy*; the international setting as framework for *political emancipation*, and *reaffirmation of identity*; domestic responses to internationally derived *prescriptive devices*; and challenges facing *domestic implementation* following international rule formulation.

Chapter Findings Compared

The New Zealand chapter saw domestic/international interactivity utilised to further the goals of a distinct project. Having the World Court deliver an advisory opinion on nuclear weapons was the immediate objective. This was part of a campaign designed to abolish nuclear weapons. As ideology, the abolitionist credo conveyed a blueprint (including a proposed international Convention), that attracted true believers, sought to proselytise and convert, comprised a coherent set of beliefs, and attracted hostility from those propounding doctrines of nuclear deterrence. Representatives of nuclear weapons states regarded the campaign to abolish nuclear weapons as misguided: while based on worthy ideals, the abolition cause was impractical and misleading of public opinion. As a form of domestic/international interactivity, the abolition campaign threatened nuclear deterrence on medical, moral, and legal grounds where it was vulnerable. By contrast, the World Court Project claimed that without abolition, nuclear weapons proliferation was inevitable. Moreover, the ethical dimension was unmistakable and unavoidable. The differences dividing the abolitionist position from nuclear deterrence gained amplification from public processes.

The World Court Project's supporters drove this exercise from grounds of strong conviction. While public opinion played a vital role, high motivation was required to sustain an array of public, propaganda, and international deliberative processes. The comprehension and utilisation of domestic and international processes was required. Information, contacts, and diplomatic intelligence enhanced the lobbying capacity of New Zealand activists operating at these levels. The case illustrated how non-governmental activity can harness and employ dual processes offered by domestic/international interactivity. Conviction extended beyond determination to utilise available modalities. It embraced a willingness to act as if international humanitarian law's existing normative principles were already operative, accepted, and legitimised. The project contained sufficient validity for those pursuing it to act as though its principles were already part realised, attitudes motivating the formulation and promotion of a model Convention for the elimination of nuclear weapons. A world without nuclear weapons was an imaginable project, sustained by a range of domestic/international interactivity. Here, sovereign security interest and nuclear deterrence would not vanish but recede in the face of more compelling forces. As true believers, the abolitionists believed that this not happen quickly, but happen it would.

In contrast, Australian policy on global warming and greenhouse gas limitations illustrated the pursuit of domestic interests by international means. It saw a government overtly deploy an assumed national vulnerability to justify a vigorous assertion of domestic interests. This was in response to external rule prescription perceived as unbalanced. The Australian government told its domestic audience that existing international arrangements contained serious distortions permitting non-participation by developing countries. The country's dominant ally, the United States, endorsed this position.

Preceding the seminal Kyoto conference, Deputy Prime Minister Fisher maintained: 'we make no apology for pushing our national interests because the Europeans, Americans, Japanese, indeed everybody is doing exactly the same ... simplistic solutions that pretend that economic costs don't matter – or which throw up new barriers to growth and trade – will not be in the interests of Australia, the region or the globe'.[1] The politician's hyperbole aside, this accurately reflected the Australian government's belief that, by promoting and preserving a distinct 'national interest', it was preserving jobs, competitiveness, export opportunities, and maintenance of local industries. Making that claim was not difficult. The government's representation of a world beyond putting 'growth' ahead of 'sustainability', fell on fertile domestic ground.

Domestic determinants served as a shield to withstand attack from domestic and international environmental lobbies, political opponents, and experts of standing. Common to critics was their view that Australia's fossil fuel abundance and dependency enhanced the power of strong national energy lobbies promoting interests impeding energy efficiency, and inflating greenhouse gas abatement rates. The diplomatic costs of pursuing a policy incurring palpable resentment from Australia's South Pacific Island state neighbours was deemed bearable. Overall, domestic/international interactivity was one dynamic used by power holders to consolidate a national position promoted with vigour at home and abroad.

The Bougainville case illustrated how a stalemated conflict unloosened to allow a peace process to take root. Restorative demands began asserting a greater impact. War weariness, a mutually hurting stalemate, and the BRA's fruitless pursuit of international recognition in search of legitimacy, generated opportunities for externally derived settlement formulation. They began to crystallise as the issue of self-determination question did not so much abate, as face reappraisal as a priority. At first unevenly, but then with growing impetus, a collective voice for settlement and peace began emerging. This demanded a self-determination of substance requiring major physical reconstruction, social healing, and public commitment to total community need. The Lincoln peace process provided the setting where these demands could begin to coagulate towards fruition.

Domestic/international interactivity aggravated the Bougainville conflict yet assisted the peace process. Negative impacts included the conflict's period of relative seclusion, and consequential vulnerability to distorted representation abroad by different interests and their agendas. Those interests comprised an uneven amalgam of supports within and beyond Bougainville.

External intervention for peace settlement only derived standing after gaining local consent. Local participation's first hand experience gauged impartiality and legitimacy of external intent. Bougainville's protracted isolation under conflict heightened the physical, group, and vivid experiences shared through the New Zealand meetings that galvanised the peace process. Belligerents literally went from the jungle to the peace table. Settlement space bought time to contemplate the advantages of longer term reconciliation and reconstruction. Aware of colonialism's legacies of discrimination, division, and dislocation, Bougainville's people saw the conflict concentrating local attitudes about how domestic/international interactivity might affect future choices. On that question, developments in East Timor and New Caledonia were identified as relevant factors in coming years.

The decolonisation discussion revealed unrequited emancipation demands. In each case considered a convoluted, often arbitrary internal/external dynamic was evident. It was arbitrary given the international community's tolerance of Indonesia's assertion of *uti possidetis* in East Timor, and acquiescence of Jakarta's dubious 1969 exercise of 'self determination' in Irian Jaya. In New Caledonia, France's final phase in the territory coincided with growing international scrutiny about appropriate sovereignty forms following self-determination. The option of a special form of autonomy, carrying advantages of economic association with a stronger entity, now emerged as less unpalatable than previously. The chapter further indicated that the Melanesian setting is one where primary social units incur difficulty in forming national identities – regardless of internationally recognised status. Internationalisation, moreover, has exposed local identity systems to disruptions that they have had to confront directly without intervening state mediation.

The discussion indicated how a belated reckoning of decolonisation could exacerbate internal divisions within subject territories. It can also foment ructions within the metropole. East Timor has indeed proved the nemesis of the Suharto order and its aftermath. The colonial experience fostered conditions of what were termed systematised cleavage (New Caledonia); severe social dislocation (East Timor), and sustained fragmentation (West Irian). To the international and relevant regional community of these territories, a challenge rests in trying to ensure decolonisation is managed so that it does not exacerbate such tensions. That is difficult given the sensitivities involved in ensuring that the governments most directly involved are discharging their international responsibilities. In 1999, this problem exploded with Indonesian military support for militias in East Timor violently opposing independence and the UN-sponsored referendum. For this discussion, domestic/international interactivity was crucial in mobilising a UN Security Council enforcement response. It was equally vital as a dynamic affecting Indonesia's relations with its ASEAN partners, Australia, and members of the South Pacific Forum.

Indigenous rights demands indicated that domestic/international interactivity highlighted the Draft UN Declaration's role as a mechanism through which to progress shared demands and strategies. Domestic/international interactivity has facilitated reciprocity strategies between indigenous peoples and governments of the countries that they inhabit. Governments ignoring indigenous rights demands at home, found that this response added incentive for their pursuit abroad. This saw officials following defensive international strategies, but granting some domestic concessions. The indigenous rights discussion indicated that, in Australia and New Zealand, internationalisation has magnified systems of binary indigenous/dominant cultural relations.

Fiji by contrast, has seen communal electoral representation reify indigenous rights demands, and reinforce chiefly hierarchies at the expense of autochthonous commoner social need. Ironically, that neglect has generated retaliation against ruling élites by proclaiming indigenous demands through electoral sloganeering and ethnic populism. Nevertheless, as with the other cases, indigenous rights developments in Fiji have forced national identity appraisals. This has seen indigenous rights interests test 'sovereignty' by harnessing its terminology to situational need. Rectification of past grievances justified relative usage: as alien sovereign rule once forced indigenous adjustment, indigenous demands now demanded sovereign accommodation. This chapter revealed domestic/international interactivity as a dynamic able to challenging established diplomatic and constitutional forms demarcating sovereign responsibility.

Decolonisation and indigenous rights demands relate to the historical legacies of prior external control and domination. 'Good governance' by contrast revealed contemporary, more complex forms of prescriptive intrusion. In the South Pacific environment, externally derived formulae designed to remedy serious public sector shortcomings, fell upon vacant ground. Little local initiative or consensus exists over the criteria needed to guide national public sector performance. Public sector downsizing clarified some realities previously obscured throughout the South Pacific. To those not immediate beneficiaries of the state payroll, or poorly served by government services, cultural defences raised to ward off external prescriptions of public sector reform rang hollow. Abuse of power by corrupt state executives tested fiduciary and accountability procedures under existing constitutional arrangements. Yet abuse of customary processes does not preclude their representing a force for future social cohesion and local self-management. How Pacific Island governments adapt to external trading and commercial environments will shape internal governance, but external factors need not deny local ownership of problem management.

Environmental management in the Pacific Islands illustrated domestic/international interaction as a challenge of implementation. Lack of convergence between external norms and local practice, revealed under-resourcing of appropriate national capacity. That has not prevented local communities developing *de facto* modes of compliance, irrespective of state adherence to international environmental norms. Sea level rise threatening atoll inundation provided the most graphic illustration of a Pacific Islands domestic problem's projection for international purposes. The Pacific Islands also face many local environmental problems where stronger domestic compliance to international norms offers material advantage. Realisation of UNCED's *Agenda 21* blueprint for small island states, it was claimed, will need political and social conditions that facilitate reinforcing, not contradictory national responses towards sustainability goals. Australia's self-interested strategy over greenhouse gas emissions jarred with its record of assistance to South Pacific regional sustainability goals. That dissonance helped explain why the Howard government's environmental posture emerged in a poor light throughout the South Pacific in 1997.

Findings in Review

When the Introduction's schema is revisited what findings emerge for comparative purposes? Regarding *preferences and interests*, conditions facilitating heightened domestic/international interactivity saw mixed outcomes. Domestic interests advancing preferences not favoured by governments have gained greater opportunities, but incurred heavier risks. Opportunities to advance causes within international settings offer scope for enhanced international publicity that may add pressure for official policy change. Although international initiatives may falter, lessons learned about system deliberation are stored as a potential asset for future use. Mobilisation of support is facilitated and there is scope to influence agenda formation and deliberation.

Risks include the failure by domestic non-governmental or unofficial coalitions to gain recognition, or make visible international headway with objectives. This leads to disappointed followings among constituencies. In some instances, this risk is unavoidable, some domestic groups warning supporters that international engagement entails persistence through a 'long-haul' strategy. Here, decolonisation and indigenous rights experiences are instructive.

Questions concerning *affiliations of identity* indicated that territorial restriction is not always a constraint. The contrast between East Timor, New Caledonia and West Irian, indicated that international projection of identity claims was possible in the first instance, to some extent in the second, but hardly at all in the third. Over Bougainville, a combination of the territory's innate social complexity, and the denied external recognition of abortive secession submerged identity claims. That did not nullify these claims as a force affecting future prospects for self-determination. However muffled or suppressed, identity claims retain consonance to general principles and international yardsticks. This gives those claims added local and international traction. Bleeding and battered though it emerged from its 1999 referendum, East Timor's aspirations for independence survived the cynicism of preceding American, Australian and Indonesian *realpolitik* by dogged adherence to international principles of self-determination.

Issue identity, by contrast, could survive on non-territorial space. Indigenous rights demands coalesced transnationally over loss of land and, in some instances, assumed an international standing denied at home. Nuclear abolition demands, and some environmental activism, treated local and international campaigns as reinforcing and occupying composite worlds through imperatives unrestrained by sovereign demarcation.

The role of domestic/international interactivity in reaffirming or strengthening *adherence to international norms* was evident in several instances. They included returning France and Indonesia to orderly decolonisation; the linkage of humanitarian law to total nuclear disarmament; the *Agenda 21* blueprint for small island states' environmental management; principles of public sector accountability; domestic obligation to comply with international instruments entered into; use of the International Court of Justice; International Labour Organisation codes regarding indigenous rights; and the Law of the Sea as central to future Pacific Islands maritime resource exploitation. The precautionary principle, and intergenerational equity extended beyond environmental debate to embrace nuclear disarmament. Normative prescription has expanded regardless of sovereign demarcation, its uses informing possibilities, and creating currently 'liveable' frameworks. These afford actuality to developing systems of rule governed international behaviour.

Institutional responses to domestic/international interactivity were identified. The Australian government utilised an inherited system of consultation and advice linking industrial, agricultural, and business interests to assist in its defence of the differential principle regarding greenhouse gas emissions reductions. This was promoted domestically and internationally and supported by fossil fuel interests. The UN's institutional devices for decolonisation were utilised partially for New Caledonia, not for West Irian, and only latterly for East Timor. International institutionalisation of indigenous rights is prospective yet uncertain. Domestic institutionalisation of international rule formation has evolved in Australia and New Zealand through significant court rulings and procedural innovation within legislatures.

Relevant *transformations*, as distinct from inchoate change, saw domestic/international interactions performing facilitating functions. Relative to immediately previous conditions, the Bougainville peace constituted an incipient transformation. The 1997 Kyoto Protocol constituted a limited, but important beginning towards emissions restraints, as did the previous year's World Court ruling enter a conditional censure of nuclear deterrence. Haphazardly, the collapse of the Suharto regime launched East Timor towards a fundamental reorientation, prospects for similar change in Irian Jaya made less remote.

In various respects the end of the Cold War as international system transformation affected cases considered. South Pacific donor conditionality shaping good governance demands would have been unlikely during the Cold War, while Pacific environmentalism looked beyond nuclear testing to claim international attention. Indonesia could no longer use the Cold War to shield its conduct over East Timor. Nuclear deterrence faced increasingly critical scrutiny, its obvious selectivity contradicting the universalism of democratisation, accountability, and rule of law favoured by some nuclear weapons states.

Developing Stronger Theory

Beyond empirical investigation, what kind of theorising is feasible about domestic/international interactivity? Where the question is issue determined, treatments employing bargaining, coalition formation, and Putnam's previously described dual game approach offer scope. That might suit analysis of Australia's conduct over Kyoto more than discussion of the international promotion of indigenous rights. Here identity formations and their supports utilised the institutions and procedures of intergovernmental conduct, but not as arenas for compromise. If these systems could not produce the status redistribution and compensation goals sought by indigenous rights representatives, then the resulting stalemate left them no worse off. Similarly, World Court Project adherents regarded the intergovernmental conduct that they observed within established disarmament systems as confirming, not compromising their nuclear weapons abolition goals.

From such contrasts, a schema capable of including ideological demands and ethical consistencies is required. As discernibly domestic identities look to the international setting to promote their objectives, their demands and methods may alter with fresh opportunities. However, emancipatory objectives will not readily alter, since the values at stake do not brook compromise. Rights issues are an example, and so are the wellsprings of self-determination. As projects, they enlist normative and institutional modes that challenge sovereignty. That does not deny the significant role of statehood and government in shaping outcomes and facilitating accommodations.

What might domestic/international interactivity models offer conflict settlement – particularly for the pervasive problem of internal war? Here there is a need to distinguish explanatory from prescriptive accounts. Regarding the latter, the Bougainville chapter noted the refusal of New Zealand officials to confide in international problem-solving expertise. One reason was that most of those interested lacked the necessary knowledge of either the conflict or its *dramatis personae*. This suggests that an internal conflict situation must write its own script for problem resolution. If it can't, then it won't. This does not diminish the essential, although inadequate role performed by methodologies enlisting a mix of domestic and international components. While internal conflict studies have expanded their theoretical base, the task of addressing the relevant impacts of causal economic asymmetries, or unequal resource distributions, has some distance to travel before furnishing valid generalisations.

Finally, there is no substitute for local knowledge that is more than information and intelligence. This encompasses a breadth of understanding that governments with their 'executive situation summaries' readily neglect. Domestic/international interactivity has taught external relations practitioners the value of historical, social and cultural perspectives, but it is a lesson only reluctantly heeded. The first chapter's discussion about nuclear disarmament cited de Madariaga's sage advice regarding the necessity of attending to the immediacy of local problems which, if left untended, may spiral beyond conflict into war. The departing century has ignored that advice, doubtless with a cost to the lives of those entering the new. That failure represents a breakdown of human responsibility whose effective remedy necessitates better knowledge about how to manage the many tensions occurring at the interface of domestic politics and international relations. Investigating this interface and its effects deserves recognition as an enduring endeavour of social and political enquiry.

Note

1   Statement of Deputy Prime Minister Fisher 19 August 1997, Canberra, p. 5.

Select Bibliography

Books

Alley, Roderic (1998), *The United Nations in Southeast Asia and the South Pacific*, Macmillan: London.

Anaya, James S. (1996), *Indigenous Peoples in International Law*, Oxford: Oxford University Press.

Bass, S. and Dalal-Clayton, B. (1995), *Small Island States and Sustainable Development: Strategic Issues and Experience*, London: International Institute for Environment and Development.

Bourma, W. J., Pearman, G.I. and Manning, M.R. (eds) (1996), *Coping with Climate Change*, Collingwood: CSIRO Publishing.

Camilleri, Joseph and Falk, Jim (1992), *The End of Sovereignty? The Politics of a Shrinking and Fragmenting World*, Aldershot: Edward Elgar.

Cassese, Antonio (1995), *Self Determination of Peoples. A Legal Reappraisal*, Cambridge: Cambridge University Press.

Clark, Donald and Williamson, Robert (1996), *Self Determination: International Perspectives*, London: Macmillan.

Clark, Roger and Sann, Madeleine (eds) (1996), *The Case Against the Bomb: Marshall Islands, Samoa, and the Solomon Islands before the International Court of Justice in Advisory Proceedings on the Legality of the Threat or Use of Nuclear Weapons*, Camden: Rutgers University School of Law.

Commonwealth Advisory Group, (1997), *A Future for Small States – Overcoming Vulnerability*, London: Commonwealth Secretariat.

Emberson-Bain, Atu (ed) (1994), *Sustainable Development or Malignant Growth? Perspectives on Island Women*, Suva: Marama Publications.

Finnemore, Martha (1996), *National Interests in International Society*, Ithaca: Cornell University Press.

Green, Robert D. (1998), *Fast Track to Zero Nuclear Weapons: The Middle Powers Initiative*, Cambridge Mass., Middle Powers Initiative.

Grief, Nicholas (1992), *The World Court Project on Nuclear Weapons and International Law*, Northampton Mass.: Aletheia Press.

Havemann, Paul (ed) (1999), *Indigenous Peoples' Rights in Australia, Canada, and New Zealand*, Auckland: Oxford University Press, pp. 235-76.

Henningham, Stephen and May, R.J. (eds) (1992), *Resources, Development and Politics in the Pacific Islands*, Bathurst: Crawford House Press.

Hughes, A.V. (1998), *A Different Kind of Voyage: Development and Dependence in the Pacific Islands*, Office of Pacific Operations: Asian Development Bank.

Kahler, Miles (1984), *Decolonisation in Britain and France*, Princeton: Princeton University Press.

Kymlicka, Will (1995), *Multicultural Citizenship. A Liberal Theory of Minority Rights*, Oxford: Clarendon Press.

Larmour, Peter (ed) (1997), *The Governance of Common Property in the Pacific Region*, Canberra: National Centre for Development Studies, ANU.

Larmour, Peter (ed) (1998), *Governance and Reform in the South Pacific*, Canberra: National Centre for Development Studies, ANU.

Maclellan, Nic and Chesneaux, Jean (1998), *After Moruroa. France in the South Pacific*, Melbourne, Ocean Press.

Maybury-Lewis, David (1997), *Indigenous Peoples, Ethnic Groups and the State*, Boston: Allyn & Bacon.

Mittelman, James H. (ed) (1996), *Globalization; Critical Reflections*, Boulder: Lynne Reinner.

Perry, Richard J. (1996), *From Time Immemorial. Indigenous Peoples and State Systems*, Austin: University of Texas Press.

Petersen, Nicholas and Sanders, Will (eds) (1998), *Citizenship and Indigenous Australians*, Cambridge: Cambridge University Press.

Robertson, Robert T. (1998), *Multiculturalism & Reconciliation in an Indulgent Republic. Fiji After the Coups: 1987-1998*, Suva: Fiji Institute of Applied Studies.

Skidmore, David (ed) (1997), *Contested Social Orders and International Politics*, Nashville: Vanderbilt University Press.

Strange, Susan (1996), *The Retreat of the State: The Diffusion of Power in the World Economy*, Cambridge: Cambridge University Press.

Victor, David G., Raustiala, Kal and Skolnikoff, Eugene. B. (eds) (1998), *The Implementation and Effectiveness of International Environmental Commitments: Theory and Practice*, Cambridge Mass.: MIT Press.

Articles

Aqorau, Transform and Bergin, Anthony (1998), 'The UN Fish Stocks Agreement - A New Era for International Cooperation to Conserve Tuna in the Central Western Pacific', *Ocean Development and International Law*, 29, pp. 21-42.

Barkin, Samuel and Cronin, Bruce (1994), 'The State and the Nation: Changing Norms and the Rules of Sovereignty in International Relations', *International Organization*, 48, 1, pp.107-30.

Bensa, Alban and Wittersheim, Eric (1998), 'National and Interdependence: the Political Thought of Jean-Marie Tjibaou', *The Contemporary Pacific*, 10, 2, pp. 369-90.

Berman, Alan (1998), '1998 and Beyond in New Caledonia: At Freedom's Gate?' *Pacific Rim Law and Policy Journal*, 7, pp.1-76.

Bertram, G. (1993), 'Sustainability, Aid, and Material Welfare in small Pacific Island Economies, 1900-90', *World Development,* 21, 2, pp. 247-58.

Bertram, Geoff and Watters, Ray (1985), 'The MIRAB Economy in the South Pacific Microstates', *Pacific Viewpoint*, 26, 497-519.

Briguglio, L. (1995), 'Small Island Developing States and their Economic Vulnerabilities', *World Development*, 23, 9, pp. 1615-32.

Dauvergne, Peter, (1998-99), 'Corporate Power in the Forests of the Solomon Islands', *Pacific Affairs*, 71, 4, pp. 524-46.

Dewes, Kate and Green, Robert (1995), 'The History of the World Court Project', *Pacifica Review*, 7, 2, pp. 17-37.

Falk, Richard (1994), 'The United Nations and the Rule of Law', *Transnational Law & Contemporary Problems*, 4, 2, pp. 611-42.

Grubb, Michael (1995), 'Ethics, the Environment and Changing International Order', *International Affairs*, 71, 3, pp. 463-96.

Held, David (1997), 'Democracy and Globalization', *Global Governance*, 3, 3, pp. 251-67.

Huntley, Wade (1996), 'The Kiwi That Roared: Nuclear Free New Zealand in a Nuclear Armed World', *The Nonproliferation Review*, 4, 1, pp. 1-16.

Kingsbury, Benedict (1998), ' "Indigenous Peoples" in International Law: A Constructivist Approach to the Asian Controversy', *American Journal of International Law*, 92, 3, pp. 414-57.

Leftwich, A. (1994), 'Governance, the State and the Politics of Development', *Development and Change*, 25, pp. 363-86.

Poirine, Bernard (1998), 'Should We Hate or Love MIRAB?', *The Contemporary Pacific*, 10, 1, pp. 65-105.

Putnam, Robert D. (1988), 'Diplomacy and Domestic Politics: the Logic of Two-Level Games', *International Organization*, 42, 3, pp. 427-60.

Quentin-Baxter, Alison (ed) (1998), *Recognising the Rights of Indigenous Peoples*, Wellington: VUW Institute of Policy Studies, pp. 22-53.

Regan, Anthony (1998), 'Causes and Course of the Bougainville Conflict', *The Journal of Pacific History*, 33, 3, 1998, pp. 269-85.

Ruggie, John Gerard (1993), 'Territoriality and Beyond: Problematising Modernity in International Relations', *International Organization*, 47, 1, pp. 139-74.

Shibuya, Eric (1996-97), '"Roaring Mice Against the Tide": The South Pacific Islands and Agenda-Building on Global Warming', *Pacific Affairs*, 69, 4, pp. 541- 555.

Skærseth, Jon Birger (1995), 'The Fruitfulness of Various Models in the Study of Environmental Politics', *Cooperation and Conflict*, 30, 2, pp. 155–78.

Taplin, R. E. (1994), 'International Policy on the Greenhouse Effect and the Island South Pacific', *The Pacific Review*, 7, 2, pp. 271-81.

Weiss, Peter, et al, (1994), 'Introduction' (Draft Memorial in support of the WHO Application to the ICJ), *Transnational Law & Contemporary Problems*, 4, 2, pp. 709-16.

Wendt, Alexander, (1992), 'Anarchy is What States Make of It: the Social Construction of Power Politics', *International Organization*, 46, (Spring), pp. 391-425.

Reports

Asian Development Outlook, 1996-1997 (1998), Manila: Asian Development Bank.

Cobo, J. R. Martinez (1986), *Study of the Problem of Discrimination Against Indigenous Populations*, UN ESCOR UN Sub-Commission on Prevention of Discrimination and the Protection of Minorities, E/CN.4/ Sub.2/1986/7/Add.4.

Office of Australian Ombudsman (1998), *Report of the Investigation into ABARE's External Funding of Climate Change Economic Modelling*, Commonwealth Ombudsman's Office, Canberra.

United Development Programme (1994), *The Pacific Human Development Report*, Suva: UNDP.

United Development Programme (1999), *Pacific Human Development Report 1999: Creating Opportunities*, Suva: UNDP.

The World Bank (1995), *Pacific Island Economies: Building a Resilient Economic Base for the 21st Century*, World Bank, Washington DC, 13803-EAP.

Index

References from Notes indicated by 'n' after page reference.

'Abolition 2000' 48n
Aboriginals:
    Aboriginal and Torres Strait Islanders 153, 154, 155, 157, 169, 172, 177
    Aboriginal and Torres Strait Islanders Commission 171, 172, 179n
    Council of Aboriginal Reconciliation 172
    Djerrkura, Gatjil 163
    Mirrar people 167
    National Consultative Committee 171
    Protection Act 167
    sacred sites 167-68
    'stolen generations' 173
accountability 2, 3, 5, 13, 32, 40, 112, 138, 174, 186, 187, 191, 193, 194, 195, 207, 213, 237, 254, 256
Aceh 126
AC Nielsen-McNair polling 64
Agenda 21 221, 227, 231-32, 241, 242, 254, 256
Ah Chong, Sua Rimoni 207, 208
Aitarak militia 125
Akoitai, Samuel 93, 113n
Alatas, A. 125
Alatoa, H. 206
Albright, Madeleine 73
Algeria 116, 117
Alliance of Small Island States 58, 66, 68, 229
American Samoa 119
Amnesty International 113n, 147n
Anderton, Jim 30
Antarctica 'ozone hole' 65
Anyaoku, Chief Emeka 96
ANZUS 29, 30, 37
apartheid 41, 118, 172
Apia Convention 225

Arawa 41
Arrhenius, S. 52
Asian Development Bank 195, 196, 199, 200, 211, 226, 235
    Pacific Developing Members 195
Asia Pacific Economic Cooperation 62, 198, 122, 223
    Auckland Summit 126
    Manila Framework 197
    Vancouver Summit 69
Association of Southeast Asian Nations (ASEAN) 124, 129, 132, 139, 141
Atlantic alliance 117
Atomic Energy Commission 25
Australia 15, 44, 50n, 118, 144, 150, 166, 176, 177, 178
    Aboriginal rights 154-57, 166, 171, 179, 193
    aid to Bougainville 94, 95, 103, 105, 110, 125
    aid to the Pacific 80, 191, 192, 223, 239, 254
    Ambassadors 76, 124, 27
    Bougainville conflict 87, 93, 95, 96, 97, 100, 101, 102, 103, 107
    climate change 54-56, 58, 67-72, 75, 250
    Commonwealth Scientific and Industrial Research Organisation 70
    Department of Aboriginal Affairs 171
    Develop Australia Bonds 66
    differentiation energy policy 60-61, 72, 78
    Downer, Alexander 101, 164
    energy interests 55, 61, 63, 67
    Energy Research and Development Corporation (ERDC) 69
    energy use 59, 62, 71, 77

environmental convention membership 225, 228
Evans, Senator Gareth 49n, 107, 164
extinguishment of native title 155, 156
federal system 65, 66, 70, 78, 179n
Fisher, Tim 251
Fraser, Malcolm 172
Goods and Services Tax (GST) 74
Green Party 66
Hawke, Robert 32, 67, 171, 172
Hayden, Bill 131
Heritage Bureau 167
High Court 70, 87, 156, 168,
Howard, John 44, 66, 67, 69, 70, 72, 75, 77, 79, 95, 101, 254
Human Rights Equal Opportunity Commission 169, 176
and International Conventions 70, 155, 168, 170, 171, 172
Institute of 63
Jabiluka mine site 167, 168
Kakadu National Park 167, 168
Lucas Heights 69
Mabo case 155, 168
military aid to PNG 94, 95, 103
National Farmers' representation 79
National Greenhouse Response Strategy 77
Native Title Act (1993) 155
1998 amendments 168, 169
nuclear weapons 33
Ombudsman 63
and Pacific islands 68-69, 192
parliamentary delegation to Bougainville 113n
public opinion in 64
and 'Sandline' episode 95-96
Simons Report 192
Sustainable Energy Industries Council 73
Sydney Olympics 173
Teoh case 168, 169
terra nullius doctrine 166
and 'umbrella group' 77
Victoria, state of 65, 66
Whitlam government 171, 172
Wik Peoples v. Queensland case 156, 164
Australian Bureau for Agriculture and Resource Economics (ABARE) 59, 63, 78
Australian Coal Association 63
Australian Conservation Foundation 60
Australian Democrats 66, 74
Australian Greenhouse Response Strategy 77
Australian Greens 66, 69
Australian Institute of Company Directors 64
Australian Labour Party 66, 67
Australian Papuan Association 129
autonomy forms 152
Indian movement 163
options of 164
Axworthy, Lloyd 45

Barbados Conference on small island states 223, 226
Barkin, Samuel 7, 110
Bavadra, Timothy 159
Belgium 68
Belo, Bishop Carlos 124
Besah Merah Putih militia 125
Bilney, Gordon 191
Bjerregaard, Ritt 72
Blair, Tony 2
Bolger, James 33, 93
Boseto, Leslie 100
Bosnia 97
Bougainville 135, 139, 251, 252, 255, 258
Akoitai, Samuel 93, 113n
and Amnesty International 113n
assistance needs 105, 106, 107, 110
and Australia 87, 93, 94, 97, 110, 113n
Buka island 86, 91
Cairns meeting 100
'care' centres 91
Catholic Church 86
colonial background 86
conflict 47, 88-89
conflict death toll 85
constitutional development 106, 108, 109, 110
Endeavour Accord 89, 97
entities in conflict 92, 103
Havini, Moses 87, 99, 113n
Lincoln agreement 100-02, 105, 109, 110, 251
location 86, 89

misrepresentation of conflict 94-95
and New Zealand 93, 97-103, 109, 252, 258
Nissan island 86
peace process 100-02, 109, 251
provincial government 87
reconstruction 96, 101, 105, 108, 112
resistance forces 92, 93
rule of law problems 107, 110, 112
and the UN 87, 91, 97,101, 104, 111
Bougainville Copper Limited (BCL) 87, 104
contract terms 87-88
Bougainville Interim Government (BIG) 88, 92, 98
Bougainville Reconciliation Government 92
Bougainville Revolutionary Army (BRA) 89, 91, 92, 93, 98, 104, 110, 111
Bougainville Transitional Government 92, 108, 110
Boutros-Ghali, Boutros 8, 107
Brazil 44
Briguglio, L. 198
Broken Hill Proprietary 63
Brundtland Report 57
Bugis people 127
Buka island 86, 109
Burnham Truce 100, 110
Butler, Lee 43

Caetano dictatorship 116
Cambodia 25, 108
Canada 50n, 58, 62, 71, 77
    Ambassador Mason 49n
    carbon dioxide emissions 57
    Nanuvut 150
Canberra Commission 43-44
carbon emissions 52, 53, 57, 68
    Australia 55, 59, 60, 61, 62, 65, 66, 68
    international comparisons 62
Carlsnaes, Walter 6
Carribean public sector 208
Chan, Sir Julius 95, 96, 97, 103
Chemical Weapons Convention 41
Chernobyl accident 30
China 3, 57, 62, 72, 74
    nuclear testing 24, 42
Chirac, J. 2, 121, 122

Christian Evangelical Church 129
Clark, Helen 30
clean development mechanism 71, 72, 229,
climate change impacts 52-54, 220, 231
Clinton Administration 1, 2, 126
Clodumur, Kinza 69
'CNN factor' 93
Coates, Ken 175
Cobo, J. R. Martinez 152
Cold War 24, 28, 31, 37, 131, 144, 146, 257
Colonialism 153, 154
    and Bougainville 86
    legacies of 150, 154, 176
    and the Pacific 117, 212
Commonwealth 97, 102, 118, 174, 175, 197, 199, 208, 214n
    Advisory Group on small states 186, 240
    Anyaoku, Chief Emeka 96
Comprehensive Test Ban Treaty 24, 31, 41, 42
conditionality 54, 192, 205
Conference on Disarmament 45, 47, 50n
constructivist approach 12, 14, 176, 178
Convention on Biological Diversity 166, 228, 234, 239,
    Nadi Statement on 245n
Convention to Eliminate Discrimination Against Women 170
Convention against Genocide 170
Convention Rights of the Child 168, 170, 212
Convention against Torture 212
Conzinc Riotinto 87
Cook Islands 68, 69, 117, 136, 171, 189, 193, 194, 196, 199, 204, 205, 225, 226, 228, 241
    location of 16
    public sector changes 196, 200
Cronin, Bruce 7, 110

Daes, Erica-Irene 152, 162
DeBrum, Tony 200
de Castro, Judge 29
Decade of International Law 26
Decolonisation 176, 258
    and domestic politics 116-17, 136, 150
    and Britain 117-18

266 *The Domestic Politics of International Relations*

and France 116, 117, 118, 121, 137
  UN resolutions on 117
  options regarding 134-37
de Madariaga, Salvador 40, 258
Denmark 162
dependent territories 119
Dewes, Kate 26, 27, 28, 32, 34, 38, 43
differentiation energy policy 60-61, 72, 78
Dili 126, 131
Djerrkura, Gatjil 163
domestic implementation 3, 219, 220
Dowiyogo, Bernard 134,
Downer, Alexander 101, 164
Doyle, M. 14
Draft Declaration on Indigenous Rights 161, 162, 163, 164, 167, 170, 173, 177, 253

East Timor 93, 105, 108, 118, 123-27, 133, 134, 135, 138, 140, 143, 146
  Action Network 132
  Asia-Pacific Coalition on 132
  Belo, Bishop Carlos 124
  British Parliamentarians for 132
  demography of 119, 123
  diaspora 132, 146n
  Dili massacre 131
  Gusmao, Xanana 125, 131, 140
  Horta, Ramos 126, 131, 140
  and Indonesia 123, 125, 132, 144
  International Platform of Jurists for 132
  location of 124
  referendum of 1999 125, 126, 132, 255
  social dislocation 123
  and UN 116, 125-26, 146
Egypt 44
El Niño effects 53, 229
emissions trading 53, 68, 71, 72, 78
Endeavour Accord 89, 97
European Parliament 132
European Union (EU) 57, 58, 60, 67, 72, 75, 80, 230
  'bubble' 68
  and Lomé Convention 198
  margins of preference 198, 231
  and Pacific 145, 197, 226
Evans, Gareth 107, 164
Evans, Harold 26, 32, 38

Evatt, Justice 179n
Executive Outcomes 95
Exxon 63

Faleomavaega, Eni 130
Falk, Richard 9, 26, 32, 40
Federated States of Micronesia 190, 193, 194, 196, 199, 203, 204, 225, 226, 228
  public sector changes 197
Ferrieux-Patterson, Marie-Noelle 206, 242
Fiji 96, 100, 134, 176, 178, 179, 188, 189, 193, 194, 196, 199, 205, 209, 210-11, 225, 228, 233, 238
  Bavadra, Timothy 159
  Chiefs 170, 159, 190, 253
  and Commonwealth 174, 175
  Constitution of 1970 159
  Constitution of 1990 202
  Constitution of 1997 161, 174, 178, 206
  Constitutional Review Commission 174, 190, 207
  environmental management 236-37, 239, 241
  government delivery indicators 210
  Human Rights Commission 170, 174, 206
  indigenous issues 150, 153, 154, 159-61, 253
  and International Conventions 170, 171, 174, 225, 228
  Kyoto Protocol 230
  Labour-led coalition 159, 205
  Labour Party 159
  location of 16
  Mara, Ratu Sir Kamisese 159
  military coups 131, 160, 188
  Prime Minister Chaudhry 202
  public sector changes 200
  Rabuka, Sitiveni 160, 165
  reservations to international conventions 170
  Rotumans 202, 215n
Financial Action Task Force 189
Fisher, Tim 251
fisheries 224, 227, 230-31, 243
foreign relations 27, 28, 29-30, 37, 57, 68, 76, 77, 107, 117, 124, 126, 138, 164

analysis of 6-8, 10-12,
   and democracy 3, 13, 14, 18
   and executive functions 5-6,
Forster, Mike 91
Forum Fisheries Agency 224, 230
Foundation for International Environmental Law 229, 245n
Framework Convention on Climate Change 55, 72, 75, 76, 228, 230
   Annex I party commitments 229
   Berlin conference 57, 68, 75
   'Berlin Mandate' 57, 77-78
   Buenos Aires conference 74
   Protocols 57
France 32, 117, 118, 120, 123, 165
   and Atlantic alliance 117
   Chirac, J. 2, 121, 122
   domestic politics 116, 117
   Le Pen, M. 121
   National Assembly 118
   nuclear testing 24, 28, 29, 33, 42, 47, 135, 137, 141
   state functions 137
   and UN 121, 138, 141, 143
Fraser, Malcolm 172
Freeport McMoRan 128
French Pacific Territories 16, 28, 33, 110, 116, 119, 120, 133, 134, 135 143, 178, 194, 199, 252, 255, 256
   Futuna 119, 121, 199
   Wallis 119, 121, 142, 199
French Polynesia 16, 28, 33, 119, 199
Frieden, Jeffrey A. 1

Geiringer, Eric 34, 38
Geneva Conventions 48n, 49n,
Germany 50n, 62, 68,
   colonial role 86
Ghai, Yash 110-11
Gillespie, Rosemary 94, 95
Global Environmental Facility 76, 226, 234
globalisation 3, 6, 7, 8, 9, 109, 145, 150, 176, 177, 178
global warming 52-54, 75, 76, 222
Goldman Prize 168
good governance criteria 183, 191, 192, 195, 200, 203, 205, 207, 212, 213

Gorbachev, Mikhail 29
Greece 50n, 68
Green, Robert 27, 34, 35, 49n
greenhouse gases 71
   emissions 52, 56, 58, 63, 229
Greenpeace Australia 64, 74, 75
Greenpeace International 4, 30, 64, 65
Grief, Nicholas 27
'Group of 77' (G77) 58
Guam 16, 119, 199
Gusmao, Xanana 125, 131, 140

Habibie, B. J. 125, 126, 130
Hagan, Joe 11
Hague Convention 27
Hague Declaration 26
Hannett, Leo 88
Hanrieder, W. 6
Hanson, Pauline 156
Haug, Marianne 214n
Havini, Moses 87, 99, 113n
Hawai'i 16, 160, 165
Hawke, Robert 32, 67, 171, 172
Hawkins Holmes, Genta 67
Hayden, Bill 131
Hayes, John 98
Helms, J. 2
Helsinki Final Act, 1975 136
Henry, Geoffrey 69
Hill, Robert 79, 81n
Holy Loch nuclear base 146n
Honiara Agreement 208
Honiara Declaration 96
Horta, Ramos 126, 131, 139
Howard, John 66, 67, 69, 70, 72, 75, 77, 79, 95, 101, 156, 164, 173, 254
human rights 3, 7, 8, 13, 14, 27, 32, 37, 40, 102, 104, 111, 138, 157, 173, 178, 191, 257
Human Rights Watch 132, 139

Iceland 71
India, 62, 166
   climate change 57
   nuclear testing 44, 45, 46
indigenous rights 150, 151, 153, 154, 161,

268 *The Domestic Politics of International Relations*

162, 163, 175, 177, 242
constructivist approach 176, 178
definitions 152, 153
demands 151, 152, 153, 161, 162, 163, 164, 176
and globalisation 150, 176-77, 178
grievances 150, 151, 157
Indo-China 116, 117
Indonesia 4, 62
  Aceh 126
  Ambon 128
  Bugis people 127
  East Timor 116, 117, 125, 131, 132, 133, 142, 144, 252, 255, 257
  human rights 138
  Kopassus 126, 147n
  military 125, 126, 142
  and UN 34, 126, 138
  West Irian 93, 127-30, 133, 252
intellectual property 165-67
  Mataatu Declaration on 166, 179n
Interactivity, domestic/foreign 2, 6, 42, 252
  analytical aspects 2, 3, 4, 7, 9, 11, 249
  Bougainville 85, 109, 111, 112, 251-52
  climate change 55
  decolonisation 116, 118, 135, 141, 144
  foreign relations 6-8, 11
  indigenous rights, 150, 153, 161, 168
  and norms 12-14, 36-37, 41-42, 47, 137-39, 207-08, 250, 256
  Pacific islands' environmental issues 220, 241-44, 254
  Pacific islands' public sectors 184, 186, 213
Inter-American Tropical Tuna Commission 230
intergenerational equity 54, 256
Intergovernmental Panel on Climate Change 52, 61, 64
Intermediate Range Nuclear Force treaty 29
internal conflict 7, 90-91, 258
International Association of Lawyers Against Nuclear Arms 26
International Committee of the Red Cross 49n, 129
International Convention on Eliminating Racial Discrimination 156, 168, 169, 170, 172

and Australia 169, 172
International Court of Justice 28, 29, 32, 33, 48, 256
  Advisory Opinion Nuclear Weapons 15, 19, 23, 34, 35, 36, 41, 43, 249
  Advisory Opinion *West Sahara* 155
  Trail Smelter case 28
International Covenant Civil and Political Rights 155, 168, 169, 170, 174
  First Optional Protocol to 168
  Human Rights Committee of 168
International Covenant Economic, Social, Cultural Rights 170
International Criminal Court 8
International Energy Agency 61
international humanitarian law 27, 28, 36, 49n
International Labour Organiation (ILO) 256
  Convention 107 (1957) 152
  Convention 169 (1989) 152, 153, 170
  Convention ratifications 170
International Law 13, 54, 70, 147n, 153, 155, 168
  Lotus case 33
  Trail Smelter case 28
International Law Commission 27
International Monetary Fund 193
International Peace Bureau 26
International Physicians for the Prevention of Nuclear War 26
Iran 62
Ireland 44
Israel 46
Italy 50n, 6

Jaba river 94
Jabiluka mine site 167, 168
Japan 77, 80, 125, 166
  and fishing 231
  and Kyoto conference 67, 71
joint implementation 56, 71, 72, 78, 229

Kabui, Joseph 88, 97, 101, 106, 108, 113n, 114n
Kahler, Miles 116
Kakadu National Park 167, 168
Kanaks (see New Caledonia)

Kaouna, Sam 85, 96
Karembeu, Christian 120
Katzenstein, P. 11
Keating, Paul 43, 67
Keith, Kenneth 42
Kelly, Paul 67
Keohane, R. 4, 5
Kiribati 16, 193, 194, 196, 199, 204, 223, 225, 228, 236
Komite Solidaritas Rakyat Irian Kosorairi 129
Kopassus 126, 147n
Korman, Maxime Carlot 206
Kosovar Albanians 1
Krieger, David 46
Kyoto conference 55, 57, 58, 65, 67, 70, 80
    preparatory stages 63, 70
    Protocol outcome 71-73, 74, 76, 78, 79, 229, 256, 257

Lange, David 30, 131
La Niña effects 53, 229
Law of the Sea 185, 224, 256
    International Tribunal 231
Lawyers' Committee on Nuclear Policy 43
Leadership Code 206
League of Nations 40, 86
Lebanon 86
Leite, Pedro 138
Le Pen, M. 121
Lepu, Bernard 123
Lester, Lord 169
Leung, Graham 170
Libya 131
Lincoln agreement 100-02, 105, 109, 110
Lomé Convention 198
London Nuclear Warfare Tribunal 26
Lotus case 33
Luxembourg 68

Mabo case 155, 168
MacBride, Sean 26, 27
Machoro, Eloi 122
McHugh, P. G. 175, 176
McKinnon, Don 31, 37, 44, 97, 105, 109, 110

McNamara, Robert 43
Mahidi militia 125
Mamaloni, Solomon 241
Mandela, Nelson 131
Manus Island 108
Maori 97, 152, 154, 157-59, 164, 166, 173, 174, 177
    electoral representation 154
    land entitlements 41
    politics 174
    tribal affiliations 174
Mara, Ratu Sir Kamisese 159
Mariana Islands 16
Marshall Islands, Republic of 16, 193, 194, 196, 197, 199, 200, 203, 204, 225, 228, 240
    public sector changes 197
Martens clause 27, 33, 49n
Masai 163
Mason, Ambassador 49n
Mataatu Declaration 166, 179n
Matignon Accords 122, 123, 134, 140, 142, 145
Mead, Aroha 176
Médecins Sans Frontières 105
Melanesia 86, 118, 119, 133, 134, 186, 188, 190, 200, 209, 221, 232, 239, 242
    social structure 86, 144, 190, 252
Melanesian Alliance 88
Melanesian Spearhead Group 199
Mexico 44, 62
Middle Powers Initiative 45
Minority Groups International 129
'MIRAB' economies 201, 202
    Bernard Poirine 215n
Miriori, Martin 98
Miriung, Theodore 92
Mirrar people 167
Mitterand, Danielle 141
Mitterrand, Francois 118, 122
Mobil Oil 63
Momis, Father J. 87, 106, 108
money laundering 189
Montreal Protocol 65, 228, 243
Moore, Mike 33
Mothersson, Keith 27, 39

Nanaro, Marcel 122

Narakobi, B. 202
national environmental strategies 220, 235, 240
Native Title Act (1993) 155
  1998 amendments 156
NATO 32, 45
Nauru 16, 69, 134, 189, 193, 194, 196, 199, 204, 222, 225, 228
N'Diaye, Bacre Waly 104
Nduga tribe 129
Netherlands 127
New Agenda Coalition 44, 45
New Caledonia 33, 110, 116, 120, 133, 134, 135 143, 178, 194, 199, 252, 255, 256
  civil conflict 122
  demography 119, 121
  identity issues 121, 131
  Kanak culture 120, 121, 122, 131, 142
  Kanak Liberation Front (FLNKS) 120, 135, 141, 199
  land 131
  location of 16
  map of 120
  Matignon Accords 122, 123, 134, 140, 142, 145
  nickel industry 143, 222
  Noumea 131
  Noumea Accords 123, 133, 139
  Ouvea outrage 122
  referenda 121, 123
  Rocard government 122
  settler interests 120, 123, 137
  social cleavages 143, 145, 146
New South Wales 66
New York 23
New Zealand 15, 16, 78, 117, 118, 119, 125, 136, 144, 150, 160, 176, 177, 178, 179, 193, 223
  accrual accounting 196
  Anderton, Jim 30
  anti-nuclear law 30, 31, 32, 46
  anti-nuclear policy 15, 29, 30, 44
  and Bougainville 93, 97-103, 109, 252, 258
  Clark, Helen 30
  Court of Appeal 158
  development assistance 196, 215n, 223
  dispute with the US 29-30, 37
  electoral system 47
  environmental convention membership 225, 228
  and ICJ 28, 34, 41, 47
  indigenous rights 166, 168, 253
  and International Conventions 167, 170, 171
  Law Commission 169
  local disarmament activity 24, 37, 28, 32, 41, 47, 250
  Maori 41, 97, 152, 154, 157-59, 164, 166, 168, 173, 174, 177, 197
  Minerals and Energy Council 73
  Moore, Mike 33
  nuclear weapons 24, 28-29
  Pakeha 174
  Prime Minister Lange 30
  public advisory committee on disarmament 32
  public opinion 31, 41
  State Enterprises Act 173
  Tavita case 169
  Treaty of Waitangi 98, 157-58, 164, 168, 173, 178
  Waitangi Tribunal 158, 173, 178
Nissan island 86
Niue 136, 193, 194, 199, 204, 206, 225, 228
Nobel Peace Prize 25, 26, 124
non-aligned movement 34, 138
  Cairo meeting of 1994 34
Non-governmental organisations 12, 25, 45, 48, 77, 111, 125, 165, 171, 195, 234, 241, 243
Norfolk Island 118, 199
norm creation 12-15, 41, 168-70, 207-08, 241-43
North Marianas, Commonwealth of 199, 200
North Solomons
  Province 88
  Republic of 87
North/South differences 53, 54, 57, 76
Norway 50n, 71
Noumea Accords 123, 133, 139
Noumea Convention 225
nuclear deterrence 25-26, 40, 43, 47, 250, 257
Nuclear Free and Independent Pacific Movement 160

Nuclear Non-Proliferation Treaty 23, 24, 44, 46
  Article 6 provisions 23, 24, 46
  indefinite extension of 23, 24
nuclear weapons 35, 37, 172, 250
  draft Convention to eliminate 41, 43, 250
Nuremberg principles 27
Nyerere, Julius 212

Ona, Francis 88, 94, 99
One Nation Party 156
'Open Letters' 32
Operasi Papua Merdeka 129, 143
Organisation for Economic Co-operation and Development 55, 59, 191, 204, 208, 221
  Convention Combating Bribery 208
Organisation for Security and Co-operation in Europe 136
Ottawa Process 45

Pacific Human Development Report 187, 201, 232
Pacific Island countries 15, 16, 18, 183,
  aid receipts 203, 204
  biodiversity 233-34
  civil society formations 190, 201
  coastal area management 231-32
  Commonwealth members 199
  conservation areas 235-36
  corruption in 188, 189, 202, 206, 213, 233, 239, 242
  economic indicators 196
  'eco-touism' 240
  electoral turnover 189
  environmental convention membership 225, 228
  environmental stress 53, 185, 200, 221, 229, 242
  exclusive economic zones 185
  executive instability 189, 190, 213
  fiscal difficulties 195
  health issues 210
  map of 16
  national environmental management strategies 220, 235, 240
  non-governmental activity 234, 241, 243

Ombudsman, offices of 193, 205, 207, 242
  population growth 187, 222
  public sector changes 18, 183, 197
  rural subsistence 184, 190, 238
  sea level rise 220, 229
  tax havens 189, 208
  telecommunications 207, 215n
  tuna fishing 224, 230
  vulnerabilities 184-85, 186, 198, 202, 222
  waste disposal 222, 240
Paeniu, B. 69, 229
Pakistan 44, 45, 46
Palau 16, 193, 194, 196, 199, 203, 204, 225, 228
Panguna Landowners Association 88
Panguna mine 87, 88, 95, 96, 99, 109
Papua Association 129
Papua New Guinea (PNG) 134, 184, 187, 188, 189, 193, 194, 196, 199, 205, 209, 225, 228, 233, 238
  and Bougainville 85, 93, 95, 102, 105, 107, 110, 112
  Chan, Sir Julius 95, 96, 97, 103
  Council of Churches 130, 147n
  educational conditions 107, 210, 212
  forest depletion 232, 233
  Forestry Department 237
  government delivery indicators 210
  Hunstein Ranges 237
  Leadership Code 206
  location of 16
  outer islands of 108, 114n
  Prime Ministers 95, 96, 97, 103
  provincial government 88, 106
  public sector changes 105, 197, 239
  rule of law 107
  Sepik region 202
  Skate, William 96, 113n
  and World Bank 239, 240
Parer, Warwick 54, 69, 73, 80n
Parkop, Powes 133, 147n
Partial Test-Ban Treaty 28
Peace Monitoring Group 92, 100
Pearman, Graeme 70
Permanent Court of International Justice 33
Peru 166

Philippines 141, 166
Pinochet, General A. 3
Pisani Plan 121
Pitcairn 199
pluralism approach 8-12, 14
PNG Defence Forces 92, 97
    and Bougainville 88, 91, 101, 104
    poor discipline 95, 102, 104
Pokawin, Stephen 108
Poland 62
Ponsonby, Arthur 13
Portugal 68, 116
    Caetano dictatorship 116
    and East Timor 125, 132
Powles, Sir Guy 32
precautionary principle 54, 56, 256
Prescott, John 68
public sector reform 183, 186, 187, 191-92, 195
    and aid donors 192, 195, 198, 203, 208,
    and international financial institutions 193-98, 211
    and Pacific Islands 183, 186, 189, 191-92, 194, 196-98, 254
Putnam, Robert D. 11

Queensland 66, 69, 99, 156

Rabuka, Sitiveni 160, 165
Rainbow Warrior 30
Rattray, K. O. 215n
Raustiala, K. 10
Reagan, Ronald 29
realist interpretations 5, 54
Reeves, Sir Paul 174
Renan, Ernest 151
Republic of Mekaamui 89
Republic of North Solomons 87
Reykjavik Summit 29
Rhodesia 118
Risse-Kappen, Thomas 11
Robinson, Mary 126
Roche, Douglas 45
Rogowski, Ronald 11
Rosenau, James 10
Rotblat, Joseph 25, 34

Rotuma 202, 215n
Rupesinghe, Kumar 90
Russia 77, 78
    organised crime in Pacific 189
Rwanda 1, 2, 25

sacred sites 167-68, 179n
Salmond, George 34
Samoa 140, 188, 189, 193, 194, 196, 199, 205, 209, 210-11, 225, 228, 236, 241
    assassination in 203
    auditor's suspension 207
    government delivery indicators 210-11
    location of 16
    public accounts 200, 207
    social system 202
'Sandline' episode 95-97, 102, 111
Saudi Arabia 62
Schroeder, G. 2
Science
    debate on climate change 52-54
    and politics 54
sea level rise 229, 244n
Self-determination 13, 110, 130, 137, 139, 150, 155, 163, 176, 178, 179, 257
Sereo, Perpetua 88
Shaw, Sir Patrick 127
Sikkink, K. 38
Sinato, Gerard 91, 108
Singapore 70
Singarok, Brigadier 96
Skate, William 96
Slade, Neroni 226
slavery 39, 49n
Slovenia 44
social change 7, 36-37, 48
'soft law' 76
Solomon Islands 93, 100, 102, 105, 111, 188, 189, 193, 194, 196, 199, 204, 205, 209, 210-11, 224, 225, 226, 228, 233, 238, 241
    community development 211
    corruption in 239
    forest depletion 232, 241
    government delivery indicators 210, 238
    Guadalcanal community 241
    inter-community strife 241

Index 273

location of 16
Malaita 241
Mamaloni government 241
public sector changes 197
Somalia 1
Somare, Sir Michael 106
South Africa 41, 62, 172
South Korea 62, 231
South Pacific
   cultural festival 1975 131
   map of 16
   non-governmental Forum 243
   nuclear testing 33, 41, 46
   representation of women 15, 212
South Pacific Applied Geoscience Commission 227
South Pacific Biodiversity Programme 226
South Pacific Committee for Mineral Resources Prospecting 223
South Pacific Community 199
South Pacific Forum 67, 68, 69, 129, 134, 140, 175, 193-94
   and Bougainville 93, 102, 104
   Declaration on Law Enforcement Cooperation 141, 245n
   Economic Action Plan 193, 237
   Economic Ministers 192, 203, 208
   Forum Fisheries Agency 224, 230
   and indigenous rights 165
   membership 134, 193, 194
   and New Caledonia 140-41
   renaming of 223
   Voluntary Code of Conduct on Logging 233, 240
South Pacific Nuclear Weapons Free Zone Treaty 46
South Pacific Organizations Coordinating Committee 223
South Pacific Regional Environmental Programme 222, 223, 234, 235, 241
   Action Plan 223
   Conventions 223, 241
sovereignty 7, 8, 110, 145, 151, 152, 157, 219, 220, 253, 257
Soviet Union 52, 131
Spain 62, 68
Stephen, Sir Ninian 70
St. John, Edward 32

Strange, Susan 4, 11
Strategic Arms Limitation 44
Suharto 4, 125, 128, 129, 138, 141, 142, 145, 256
Suntheralingham, Justice 92
Sununu, John 56
Survival International 129, 130
sustainable development 219, 242, 243, 244
sustainable human development 219
Sweden 44
   at the UN 42
Switzerland 71

Taiwan 224, 231
TAPOL 129
Tarrow, S. 37
telecommunications 207, 215n
Teosin, J. 87
terra nullius doctrine 155, 166
Texaco 63
Thatcher, Margaret 29, 68
Theorin, Maj-Britt 49n
Tjibaou, Jean Marie 122, 131
Tokelau 119
Tonga 96, 189, 193, 194, 196, 199, 204, 206, 225, 228
   location of 16
   public sector changes 197
Torres Islanders Protection Act 167
Trail Smelter case 28
Transparency International 189, 208
treaty compliance 220-22
Treaty of Waitangi 98, 157-59, 164, 168, 173, 178
Treaty of Waitangi Tribunal 158, 173, 178
Truce Monitory Group 92, 100
tuna resources 230
Tutsi people 1
Tuvalu 184, 193, 194, 196, 199, 204, 206, 225, 228, 236
   location of 16
   Prime Minister Paeniu 69

Ukraine 62, 78
United Kingdom 23, 29, 62, 117, 118, 178
United Nations 15, 47, 172, 175, 199
   Agenda 21 221, 227, 231-32, 241, 242,

254, 256
and Bougainville 87, 97, 101
Charter 5, 19n, 34, 35, 36, 117, 121, 143
Commission on Human Rights 91, 104, 130, 162, 163
Commission on Sustainable Development 56, 223, 226, 242
Conference on Environment and Development 56, 75, 77, 221, 223, 227
Declaration on Principles of International Law 136
Declonisation 117, 120, 121, 133, 135, 138, 141, 142, 143, 144, 146
Draft Declaration on Indigenous Rights 161, 162, 163, 164, 167, 170, 173, 177
and East Timor 125, 132, 146
Economic Social Commission for Asia Pacific (ESCAP) 197, 226
General Assembly 35, 42, 45
General Assembly Resolutions 23, 25, 117
Human Rights Commissioner 126
N'Diaye, Bacre Waly 104
Secretary General 8, 97
Security Council 8, 132, 146
Trusteeship Council 117
UNESCO 167, 168
UNICEF 107
and West Irian 127, 129, 133, 138, 142, 143
Working Group on Indigenous Populations 91
United Nations Development Programme (UNDP) 187, 197
UNDP Pacific Human Development Report 187, 201, 232
United Nations Environmental Programme 226, 236
United States 1, 2, 25, 29, 37, 42, 73, 75, 77, 80, 125, 165, 231, 255
Atomic Energy Commission 25
and climate change 74
Environmental Protection Agency 57
greenhouse gas emissions 53, 71
House of Representatives 130
and NPT 23
representation in Australia 67
Senate 2
South Pacific fisheries treaties 224, 230
and World Court Project 23
Unrepresented Nations and Peoples Organisation (UNPO) 94, 130

van Lierop, Robert 226
Vanuatu 96, 100, 131, 133, 145, 188, 189, 193, 194, 196, 199, 204, 209, 210-11, 225, 228, 233, 236, 238, 241
Ferrieux-Patterson, Marie-Noelle 206, 242
government delivery indicators 210
Korman, M. 206
location of 16
ombudsman 205, 206, 242
public sector changes 196
Vohor, S. 206
Victor, D. 79
Victoria, state of 65, 66
Vohor, S. 206
Vulnerability 184-85, 198, 202, 222
index of 185
and Pacific 184-85, 186, 198, 202, 222

Waigani Convention 223, 225
Walker, R. 7
Wallace, William 6
Ware, Alyn 26, 43
Weeramantry, Justice 36
Wensley, Penny 76
West Irian (Irian Jaya) 93, 126, 127-30, 143, 145, 253, 255, 256
'Act of Free Choice', 1969 127, 132, 137, 142, 252
independence demands 129, 133, 142
location of 16
map of 128
mining in 128
transmigrants 127
West Papua Peoples' Front 130
Western Australia 66
Westminster parliamentary system 154
Wilson, Sir Ronald 173
Wolfers, Edward 242

Index 275

Women, status of 105, 143, 212
World Bank 140, 191, 192, 197, 201, 239, 240
World Conservation Union 226
World Court Project 15, 24-27, 33, 37-43, 48, 249, 250, 257
   promotion of 38, 39, 41, 42, 46
   sponsoring organisations 26, 45
   at the UN 38
   at World Health Assembly 38

World Federalists 47
World Health Assembly 15, 33, 34, 42
World Health Organisation 33, 34
World Trade Organisation 62, 189, 198, 199
World War II 85, 130
World Wide Fund for Nature 238

Zammit-Cutajar, M. 72
Zimbabwe 34